Looking beyond the Structure

fb

Looking beyond the Structure

Critical Thinking for Designers and Architects

Dan Bucsescu
Pratt Institute

Michael Eng
John Carroll University

FAIRCHILD BOOKS

NEW YORK

Executive Editor: Olga T. Kontzias
Assistant Acquisitions Editor: Amanda Breccia
Editorial Development Director: Jennifer N. Crane
Development Editor: Sylvia L. Weber
Associate Art Director: Erin Fitzsimmons
Production Director: Ginger Hillman
Production Editor: Jessica Rozler
Cover Design: Erin Fitzsimmons
Cover Art: Guggenheim Museum in Bilbao, Spain. Image by © Guenter Rossenbach/
    Corbis.
Text Design: Erin Fitzsimmons
Page Composition: Barbara Barg Medley

Library of Congress Catalog Card Number: 2008940705
ISBN: 978-1-56367-719-9
GST R 133004424

Printed in the United States of America

TP09

CONTENTS

EXTENDED CONTENTS

PREFACE

Why did you choose to be a designer or architect?

After one of us posed this question to his first-year studio students, one young aspiring architect, Christine, thought long and hard before answering. She replied,

> I want to create a better environment where individuals can develop their utmost abilities, a self-sufficient setting that is not only lucrative but nature-friendly. It also feels as my duty to lessen the extent of unnecessary standards that society has imposed in this art, rules that restrain the architect's creativity.

The underlying utopian desire in Christine's answer has always been a central emotional and intellectual drive in the arts in general and in design and architecture in particular. As we can see from her response, socially responsible attitudes that informed utopian thinking in the past are still a powerful motivation in the present generation.

Along with this utopian impulse, however, another aspect Christine's response reveals is a profound lack of reflection on the concepts to which she is appealing. Many of the concepts she employs can be identified as inherited and are clearly ideas she believes she *should have* about design. When pressed, it becomes evident that Christine, and other students who take similar positions, do not have a surefooted sense of what *they themselves* understand by such terms as *nature, society,* or *creativity.* If you're an artist, then society must always be against you because the artist is a creative genius, and society is always too late in understanding you, right? As a first-year student, when has

Christine been able to test such a claim? What experience does she or any first year student have of the way society (whatever *that* is) imposes its standards on the designer's or architect's creativity?

In our experience, rather than develop a surefooted sense of what they mean when they employ such terms, students end up graduating without ever having had to rigorously interrogate their most basic assumptions about design and, more importantly, their place as actors in the world. Christine and all the other future designers like her need to be able to recognize when they are only repeating inherited beliefs (and, therefore, beliefs that are not really theirs) and developing their own paths in the desire to design idealistic, socially responsible, and norm-breaking structures.

PEDAGOGICAL STRATEGY

The goal of this book is to ask students to think critically about their most basic assumptions, to ask questions and to answer them for themselves at an early stage of their professional development. Our strategy, therefore, has been to offer models of critical thinking in the form of a dialogue between an architect and a philosopher that runs throughout the course of the book and in the form of critical reading passages, which we have identified as some of the key, guiding texts within both design and intellectual history.

In our experience, undergraduate design students are too often discouraged from thinking on their own because their teachers believe the students are not ready to answer complex philosophical questions. Most theoretical anthologies, unfortunately, only re-enforce this perception, though not because their readings are difficult, but because they take too much for granted in terms of the students' philosophical education and reference points.

In contrast, we are not interested in getting students ready for the complex theoretical debates; our aim is not to introduce them to the fields of design and architectural theory. What we desire is to instill in students a drive to think reflectively and relentlessly about the most important foundational questions of their chosen discipline in order that they become better prepared *for the practice of architecture and design.* As a result, we have chosen the readings we are including in the book with the requirement that they not be jargon-laden, even if they are complex. Where jargon does appear, in our dialogues or the readings, the new terms are highlighted in the text, as are familiar words and phrases that are the subject of critical analysis.

ORGANIZATION AND LEARNING FEATURES

Each chapter is devoted to exploring a basic concept often appealed to or presupposed by design students in their thinking and language.

There are, of course, many other questions one could pose, but we have identified these as fundamental. The mode of exploration we have constructed takes the form of a dialogue between an anonymous architect and an anonymous philosopher. In many cases, the dialogues we have written reflect actual conversations and debates we have had in the course of teaching together or in situations of collegial reflection. Our aim in using this form of exploration is to provide a model of critical thinking in practice for students and to emphasize the act of questioning itself rather than the determination of final answers.

The truth is that "critical thinking" is big business these days in higher education, and any educator will recognize the demand that accreditation agencies place on academic programs to "incorporate more critical thinking" in their curricula. However, critical thinking itself often remains undefined. Ironically, then, the first concept that needs critical reflection is critical thinking itself. It is for this reason that we begin our book with an elaboration of critical thinking's key characteristics and a reading excerpt from the American philosopher, John Dewey, who first inspired the contemporary critical thinking movement.

Each chapter closes with a series of activities, including questions for reflection about the selected reading and one or more critical thinking exercises that students may practice in the studio environment or as research projects.

WHO SHOULD USE THIS BOOK AND HOW

This book is targeted first at the beginning design student, but we also imagine it as a resource to which advanced students can return throughout their design training. The selected readings have been tested over a period of 20 years at both the beginning and advance level, in a first-year architectural theory course titled "Form and Culture" and as a fourth-year advanced theory seminar. Our belief is that at the beginning level, students will benefit most from the book when required to work through it collectively in a beginning or advanced seminar class associated with a design studio with the guidance and cooperation of the both instructors. This seminar could also be offered as an interdisciplinary liberal arts course required for all undergraduate or graduate design students.

Because the first chapter is dedicated to elaborating on a definition of critical thinking, we believe students would ideally begin there. However, though the dialogue follows a line of connections between concepts in order of chapter listing, students should be able to choose any chapter to read without having to read the chapters in the order of their presentation.

THE CULTURAL "BOX" WE ARE IN

The increasing pressure on architectural and design education to become responsive to the information revolution of the last 30 years introduces a special concern for the role of the designer or architect vis-à-vis practitioners in all other relevant areas of expertise.

The growing technical sophistication of fields like engineering; economics; computer science; and even political and social science, such as marketing, tends to induce a feeling of insecurity in designers and architects because of the scientific and quasi-scientific/statistical arguments coming from these fields. To these pressures there have been two standard responses: the first is to expand the role of the designer or architect by incorporating those other areas of expertise; thus, the role and responsibility of the designer or architect and those of the other professions are blurred. The second is to do the exact opposite, to narrow the role of the designer or architect by excluding everything but a concern for form and its manipulation. Both responses betray a lack of vision and an inability to cope with the challenges of an essentially interdisciplinary cultural climate.

In our opinion, this lack of vision can be attributed, at least in part, to the philosophical weakness of an architectural and design education. Traditionally, these were thought to play an intermediary role between science and art. Architects and designers were expected to be armed with the rational criteria and empirical data of science, and yet to operate deftly with the subjective and metaphorical tools of art. But the only way to do this competently was (and still is) by having a firm grasp of the relevant scientific *concepts* and by understanding, philosophically, how they can be expected to inform the subjective practices of design.

Thus, architectural and design education should provide a much stronger foundation in the philosophy of science and art. This could be accomplished by giving design students a better grounding in modern scientific concepts and in theories of knowledge as they relate to design, so that students will be able to evaluate *critically* the input of these other disciplines to their own design process.

This textbook is intended for a seminar that examines the relationship between built form and culture and serves as an introduction to architectural and design theory. Through a series of primary and secondary texts written by important architects, critics, and thinkers, students are introduced to paradigms or models for making and interpreting designed human artifacts.

The main goal of this book is to be an introduction to thinking philosophically about physical design. The readings can be interpreted and taught at different levels as appropriate for both beginning and advanced students.

ACKNOWLEDGMENTS

Several groups of people contributed at various times to the inspiration, development, and completion of this book. We wish to extend our sincere thanks to our friends and colleagues Dan Klein, Lex Braes, and Donald Cromley, who all commented on parts of the manuscript and added valuable insights along the way.

A good deal of thanks is due also to the many students at Pratt Institute who took part in the numerous iterations of our first-year architectural theory course *Form and Culture*, on which this book is based. The projects and in-class contributions of the following students from the spring 2006 semester course offerings proved invaluable in designing the initial plan for the book: Leah Boston, Rebecca Caillouet, Ha Lim Choi, Shirley Dolezal, Christine Durman, Zakiya Franklin, Nicolas Gomez, Paul Handford, Isobel Herbold, Paulina Kolodziejczyk, Kendrick Lam, Peechava Mekasuvanroj, Ryan Miccio, Rebecca Miller, Alan Rahman, Antoni Ricardo, Irving Safdieh, Chun Che Shen (Max), Katherine Spidel, Sun Yi, Alessandro Zanaboni.

We are also grateful to the following reviewers, selected by the publisher, for their recommendations: Cigdem T. Akkurt, Iowa State University; Brenda Johnson, IADT, Orlando; Bob Krikac, Washington State University; Roberto Rengel, University of Wisconsin, Madison; Roger Schluntz, University of New Mexico; JoEllen Weingart, Eastern Illinois University; and Linda Zimmer, University of Oregon.

Deep appreciation goes to the Fairchild editorial team, who first gave us the opportunity to realize the manuscript and persisted with us from beginning to end: Olga Kontzias, executive editor; Jennifer Crane, director of editorial development; Jessica Rozler, production editor; and Erin Fitzsimmons, associate art director. Very special thanks to Sylvia Weber, our development editor, who managed the project in all of its painstaking detail without the slightest hint of worry even in the most stressful of times, yet who also dutifully prodded us along and helped us overcome the many obstacles that presented themselves along the path. Her dedication to our project has been unmatched.

Lori Gibbs deserves singular thanks for her dedicated attention to producing the manuscript for delivery to Fairchild. Without her help, we would not have been able to complete the text.

Finally, Dan would like to thank his wife, Eva Johansson, for her support, and Michael would like to extend his appreciation to his wife, Kimberly Lamm, who took time away from her own research and teaching responsibilities to help in the writing of this book.

Dan Bucsescu and Michael Eng

Looking beyond the Structure

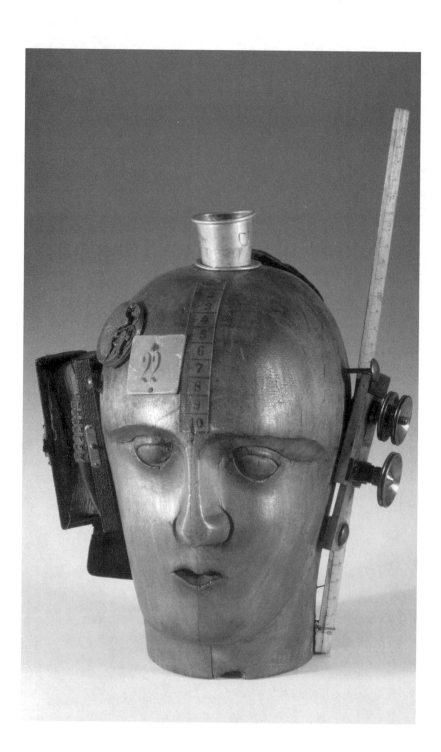

I

What Is Critical Thinking?

TOPICS

∽ Definition of critical thinking

∽ Critical thinking in design

∽ The paradoxes of design

∽ What is Design? What is Architecture?

FIGURE 1.1
Raoul Hausmann's sculpture, *The Spirit of Our Time*,
is a critical expression created to illustrate how he thought about
contemporary German society and the role of the individual in 1919.

ARCH: Dear Philo, our book is about critical thinking in design and architecture. But this area is typically reserved for such disciplines as philosophy and logic. So let's begin by answering a couple of questions that must be on everyone's mind. First, what do we mean by critical thinking, and second, why should critical thinking be part of the design disciplines?

Definition of Critical Thinking

PHILO: Well, let's start with **critical thinking** and how we define it. *Critical thinking* has one of its origins in the work of the nineteenth- to twentieth-century American philosopher John Dewey. Dewey described critical thinking—what he actually called *reflective thought*—as **consequential reasoning**. He defines it as "[a]ctive, persistent, and careful consideration of any belief or supposed form of knowledge in the light of the grounds that support it, and the further conclusions to which it tends."[1] In reflective thought, ideas build on one another; they don't just flow in some random order. Reflective or critical thought adheres to a method in which one idea follows rigorously from another. In the process, the basis of one thought—i.e., another, prior thought—gets tested as sound before being accepted and built upon.

ARCH: OK, but again, this sounds like it belongs to the province of logic. As you note, the idea is attributed originally to John Dewey, who was a philosopher.

PHILO: Let's be honest about things and note also that critical thinking is big business these days in higher education. It's been something of a buzzword for the last few years that no one takes the time to define. It's very fashionable, and everyone is supposed to be doing it. Notice two assumptions at work here: everyone is supposed to know what critical thinking means, but whatever it means, it's something that is supposed to be valued. Ironically, then, those who promote critical thinking are often not very critical in their use of the term.

ARCH: Still, critical thinking is worth valuing, don't you think? If we join those people who promote critical thinking, then we should distinguish ourselves from that group by defining what we mean by it.

PHILO: Agreed, agreed. Nonetheless, I felt it important to acknowledge the fact that education is not immune to fashion and trends.

ARCH: Of course. If anything, critical thinking needs to start at home, so to speak.

PHILO: Always. In any case, we are not just writing any book. We're writing a textbook, something targeted towards students. Dewey believed that you can't just insist on critical thinking. His book *How We Think* (1910) outlines the means by which we "train thought," as he describes it.

ARCH: So why should we train thought in the way you are describing in the design disciplines?

Critical Thinking in Design

PHILO: I'll give you an image of critical thought given by a guest critic in a design review I attended some years back. For this studio, students had to provide a short written description of their design, which I thought was a good requirement because it meant they had to reflect on how they would frame their project presentation.

ARCH: I agree. I often have similar requirements in my studios.

PHILO: I know, which is why I think this example will resonate with you. As anyone might expect, some descriptions were better written than others, but one is always going to find places where the reasoning falls a bit short. In response to one description that had some especially glaring problems, the critic, who was a professional writer, said that the student should learn how to edit his work (i.e., reflect on it in more than one draft), and that the editing process should be imagined as knocking on the walls of a structure to see which parts of the structure were sound and which were hollow.

ARCH: So you are suggesting this architectural metaphor the critic uses to assess writing could be employed in design as a way to test how designers conceptualize their projects.

PHILO: Exactly. It may sound a bit odd, putting it that way, but design is often quite abstract; it's seldom about actual built structures. This latter is mostly the area of construction management and engineering. Like writing, design preoccupies itself with ideas and concepts. Even physical models cannot be considered the architectural object in itself; they are projections of design concepts. Design works in the area of the conditional: This is how a building *should* look. This is how users of a space *would* move through it.

ARCH: This is where we might say thinking through writing and thinking through seeing—**visual thinking**—coincide.

PHILO: Yes, they're both forms of thinking that we can say are distinguished by differences in degree, not in kind.

ARCH: So, you're arguing that the common distinction one often finds in art and design schools between thinking and making doesn't hold here.

PHILO: That's right. It doesn't. I would say it never did. Writing is a form of making. It relies on **materials** — language, paper, ink, the computer monitor, even the electrons that run through my laptop as I am typing now.

ARCH: I don't believe writing and seeing are the same, though.

PHILO: Nor do I, but writing is often a form of seeing. It lets things appear. Seeing is a form of writing in that it discerns; it demarcates. Both can be employed critically.

ARCH: How so?

PHILO: What were we doing just now at the beginning of our discussion? What does Voltaire say in his chapter "Abuse of Words" from his *Philosophical Dictionary* (1764)? "We must repeat what [the seventeenth century English philosopher John] Locke has so strongly urged — *define your terms.*" In addition to defining our terms, we were:

1.   Questioning our presuppositions, and
2.   Being attentive to the context in which we were applying our terms

I would say our discussion is already a practice of critical thinking and is a form of knocking on the walls to see what is solid and what sounds empty regarding our ideas about critical thinking. Critical thinking about critical thinking.

ARCH: And based on this example, we can see the value, on the one hand, of writing as a tool in design to interrogate one's design concept. It is also interesting, on the other hand, to see model-making in this guise, as a tool that tests a concept rather than simply illustrates it.

PHILO: Isn't that a more accurate description of how models and drawings function in design? Don't designers take for granted the fact that one will have to go through many drawings and models, abandoning ones that don't work, not because they are bad models or drawings necessarily, but because they told the designer the concept needed reconsideration and therefore different models and drawings?

ARCH: That's an interesting way to describe the process. At a certain point, though, those drawings and models become the reference material that contractors use in constructing a building.

PHILO: Of course, but how does one arrive there? It's a long process, with many levels through which one has to pass.

ARCH: Well, what other examples come to mind? Can you tell me of a specific studio project where you thought critical thinking was an issue?

PHILO: I'll repeat an example you and I have discussed a number of times, especially when we were first conceiving this book, where I think those three aspects of critical thought would have been useful.

I remember being astonished during one architecture critique a few years back when a student spent 15 minutes (of the 20 he was allotted) explaining how he arrived at his project's final form. The program was a dormitory for athletes for the 2010 Olympic Games. Now, this was a final crit, and his entire project was pinned up, but he spent most of the time talking about how many times he folded an 8½" x 11" piece of paper (I think it was nine times altogether) as a method to generate the form his project would eventually take on. Clearly, he needed work on organizing his presentation properly, but because he spent so much time talking about this method, the first thing I asked him was what it had to do with the project's program. He couldn't say, and my continued puzzlement soon led to his own puzzlement as to why I would spend so much time asking him about this so-called method.

I soon realized "so-called" was the best way to describe the process he presented to us. For the student, it was a way to generate a form that would accommodate the program, which he expected all of us critics to understand. The point for him was that he employed a method, one that he could recount in detail. The actual decisions he made along the process were irrelevant as far as he was concerned. For the most part, I was the only critic who had a difficult time with this student's project. There was one other critic who agreed the student went on too long about his process, but most everyone else present simply lamented the fact that time had run out and we had no chance to get into the student's work.

ARCH: Your example is a good one because it not only describes a context in which critical thinking is lacking in a design project; it also describes a situation where critical thinking finds its limits.

PHILO: How do you mean?

ARCH: In the spirit of practicing critical thinking about critical thinking, I would say that, yes, in the example you describe, the student lacked critical thinking in the conceptual area of his project. I agree he was woefully unable to account for the reasons why he decided on the form-making methodology he employed, and I believe I would have been confused similarly by how he conceived the relationship between his project's form and its program.

PHILO: So how would you imagine a more critically reflective project?

ARCH: As incorporating the characteristics of critical thought you listed above: (1) Questioning presuppositions (i.e., the reasons why one decides to do this instead of that); (2) defining terms; (3) being attentive to the context in which terms are applied. I would add a fourth characteristic, which you remind us Dewey believed essential to critical thinking: Following through on the consequences of one's ideas.

PHILO: By **idea**, we don't just mean something floating around in our heads.

ARCH: That's right. That's why we said just a moment ago that models and drawings make ideas visual. A plan will show your decision to put a wall "here" and not "there." Why? What are the consequences of putting a wall "here" and not "there"? What if you put it "there" instead of "here"? One place you'll be able to see the consequences of your decisions is in the model, but then it might tell you to reconsider your decisions.

PHILO: So how do we encounter the limits of critical thinking, then?

ARCH: Now this is interesting. I believe critical thinking has its limits in the design process, but remarking on these limits allows us to reflect critically on architecture and the design disciplines in general.

PHILO: What are the limits of critical thinking in the design process?

ARCH: The design process contains several levels. There's a beginning phase where, after having read the project brief, you are simply in the mode of collecting data, pursuing any possibility or idea that will allow you to form a design concept in order to meet the project's demands. You're considering all kinds of factors at this stage: site, program, budget (although not necessarily in the school context), and the world of culture (ideas related to each particular project). Here, you're not really doing critical thinking because the idea is to not reject any ideas. You're practicing what Leibniz called modal logic. You're constantly asking, "What if?" What if I do this? What if I do that?

Each decision leads to a different possible world for Leibniz. The classic example to best illustrate what Leibniz meant is the following: Imagine that when you get dressed in the morning, you check the choices of colored shirts in your closet. Each color makes a possible world in which you will wear a certain colored shirt. You can choose only one. That becomes the actual world in which you, Philo, will wear a red shirt instead of black, which, as you know, is the color most academics and architects usually wear.

PHILO: Yes, very funny.

ARCH: At a certain point, however, you have to start whittling down ideas towards a solution. Design moves from many possibilities to one actually built form. Someone once described the design process as a gradual reduction of variety. As one designs, one must choose *this* and *not that.* Design is an act of closure. In contrast, philosophy in general, and critical thinking in particular, are open systems, moving from one question to many. You may be doing critical thinking to see which ideas actually hold water (or are sound and solid, to use your earlier image) and which do not. But then you can't keep this critical reflection up for long because you have to find an idea you believe will work and run with it. All ideas can be critically reflected upon and found lacking, so you've got to draw a limit somewhere.

The issue of critical thinking really does highlight a central **paradox** for us designers and architects.

PHILO: What do you mean by paradox?

The Paradoxes of Design

ARCH: I mean it the same way it is used in philosophy and logic: a dilemma between two acceptable alternatives that leads to an *unacceptable* contradiction. In philosophy, there is the paradox of omnipotence. Either God is omnipotent or He isn't. If He is, then He can create a stone that is too heavy for Him to lift. But then He's not omnipotent. If He can't create a stone too heavy for Him to lift, then He isn't omnipotent. Because God is defined as an omnipotent being, both alternatives lead to a contradiction. They make one conclude that God isn't God.

PHILO: That's a problem, at least for religion.

ARCH: In architecture and design, one also finds a paradox, a Gordian knot, if you will. On the one hand, by engaging in design, you are trying to solve a problem and are whittling down possibilities towards a solution. You are not engaged in critical thinking, which opens up possibilities by continually questioning assumptions and consequences of a given design and its concept. Critical thinking has to be cut off at some point because if you don't cut it off, you'll find you can always question something and will never be done with your design, which means you'll never find a solution, which means your design will fail.

On the other hand, if you don't engage in critical thinking while designing, then you will not have tested your concept as rigorously as is necessary. The result is that you will not be as attentive to the project's requirements as you need to be, and your design will fail.

PHILO: So how does one dissolve the paradox?

ARCH: I don't know whether you do. At least, I don't know whether you do during the design process. This is what I meant by the notion that the issue of critical thinking, while having limits in the design process, encourages thinking about the design disciplines in general. Critical thinking, when applied to the design disciplines as a question, provokes one to ask about what kinds of questions are allowed to be posed about design, and especially during design education.

PHILO: What kind of questions?

ARCH: While I consider architecture an art form, I also believe it is a **problem-solving** operation. We architects and designers are called upon by clients to come up with a solution to a particular problem: they need an apartment to be expanded in such and such a way; a law office needs to be insulated from sound; a museum needs to expand its space for its exhibitions, but it also needs residences, etc.

PHILO: As an architect, you don't decide all by yourself what to design; the project is determined beforehand by the needs and desires of the client.

ARCH: Right, but what form does design education often take? Design—at least in my experience, which spans more than 30 years—is typically taught as *puzzle*-solving, not *problem*-solving. It is the paradox of design: is it art or service.

PHILO: What distinguishes the two?

ARCH: I would say two things: Problem-solving is attentive to the fact that there's always a client and what always comes with the client—a budget. Puzzle-solving, in contrast, is an intellectual and artistic exercise. Art for art's sake. Although puzzle-solving may help develop skills needed in actual design situations, it itself is not realistic. No one is going to pay you to solve an intellectual puzzle. Your clients are paying you to resolve a very real problem for which they need what they describe as an "elegant"—and budget-conscious—solution.

PHILO: You've said in the past that the word "elegant" in this context is very vague. That this is how laymen speak about the role of the designer/architect. "Elegant" implies an aesthetic/artistic gesture that distracts one from the real problems design is supposed to grapple with.

ARCH: Yes, that is wrong!

PHILO: What's the saying by Louis Kahn you always like to take issue with?

ARCH: Kahn suggests asking materials what they want to be. He has this example where he says, "Brick, what do you want?"

PHILO: We should say this famous quotation comes from a lecture Kahn gave to students in the School of Fine Arts at the University of Pennsylvania in 1971. Kahn's son, Nathaniel Kahn, reproduces it in his film about his father, *My Architect* (2003). What Kahn says exactly is the following:[2]

> When you want to give something presence, you have to consult nature. And there is where design comes in. If you think of brick, for instance, you say to brick, "What do you want, brick?"
>
> And brick says to you, "I like an arch."
>
> And if you say to brick, "Look, arches are expensive. And I can use a concrete lintel over you. What do you think of that, brick?"
>
> Brick says, "I like an arch." [Laughs]
>
> And, it's important, you see, that you honor the material that you use. You don't bandy it around as though you said, "Well, we have a lot of material around. We can do it one way, we can do it another." It's not true. You can do it only if you honor the brick and glorify the brick instead of just short-changing it.

PHILO: What, exactly, do you find lacking in this characterization of design by Kahn?

ARCH: For one thing, Kahn perpetuates the myth of the architect as solitary, artistic genius. He also said once, "You can't write to Picasso and say, 'I want my portrait painted; I want two eyes in it, and one nose, and only one mouth, please.' In the same way, if you want an architect, you must let him [or her] deal with the spaces of the building, spaces which he [or she] will order and inspire."[3]

PHILO: What's wrong with that?

ARCH: Nothing, except that's not how things work in the real world of architecture, not even for Kahn. What is he saying? That there's only the material you build with and your inspired design? What's missing?

PHILO: The client.

ARCH: That's right! What does Kahn intentionally leave out in his description of design? The client. For him, all that matters in architecture is what the material (the brick) wants or what his inspiration dictates. Well, what about what the client wants? Without a client—and

FIGURE 1.2
Interior view of the circulation ramp in the Guggenheim Museum, New York City.

without *good* clients—Kahn would never have been able to build the buildings he did. The same goes for all of our architectural "heroes": Frank Lloyd Wright, Le Corbusier, etc. Wright's Guggenheim Museum is one of the most illogical ways to display art: a spiral in the form of a seashell that the museum visitor has to negotiate backwards by starting at the top and descending to the bottom. Yet, it became a brilliant and iconic building. This never would have happened had the museum trustees not entertained Wright's idiosyncratic design in the first place. No matter how much of a genius you are, you can't build a building all by yourself.

PHILO: But this raises other questions, though, about knowledge, expertise, and the role of society in general.

ARCH: Explain.

PHILO: I have to say I'm a little sympathetic to Kahn's position. Who else besides the engineer knows more about the material than the architect? And who else besides the architect knows more about the design? The fact is that most architects' clients aren't architects, so doesn't the architect have a duty to educate the client?

ARCH: Oh, I agree completely. I have always argued for that. I am surprised you are the one to say that.

PHILO: Well, we're having a debate, which means I can take whatever position I wish, whether I actually believe it or not. In this case, I may be taking the position of the *advocatus diaboli*—the devil's advocate.

ARCH: It's your Platonic bias coming out.

PHILO: Well, that's not fair—

ARCH: Isn't it? Isn't that the whole point of Plato's *Republic,* to have a philosopher-king who will educate and lead the masses?

PHILO: Even if it is, that doesn't mean the point is not valid. To whom does the architect really have a duty? To the client, who is just paying for what he or she thinks is a commodity, or to society in general, because buildings are collective objects? Buildings don't exist just for one person, even if the client is one person.

ARCH: Or is the architect's duty to "Architecture" with a capital A?

PHILO: Yes, or to Architecture.

ARCH: That was ultimately Kahn's position, I believe. But notice how quickly one falls into all kinds of mystifications that are anything but critical concepts. Kahn believed in the ability of material to express itself. Kahn wants us to ask the brick what it wants. Well, I've been an architect for some time now, and I would ask in response, "When was the last time a brick answered back?"

PHILO: The mystification you are attributing to Kahn's position, then, is a kind of animism, a belief that materials possess spirit.

ARCH: That's right. As someone who is a materialist in another sense, I think Kahn's conversation with the brick approaches the ridiculous. Again, it's a mystification. What's really at issue is what certain materials allow you to do in design and what they don't allow you to do. This is a point we'll return to in Chapter 3 on form and function—material as a cause of design.

PHILO: But we are circling the question rather than addressing it head on. To whom does the architect have a duty, if anybody at all? To the client, to society, or to Architecture?

ARCH: I don't think these are questions that get answered once and for all. Rather, it is important first to pose them and then to remember that they need to be posed repeatedly and held in tension to one another.

PHILO: Even in the design process?

ARCH: At least for a time. Then they have to recede into the background, as I've been saying, but you'd better be ready for these questions to return, because they will. Architecture lives on much longer than its design. But here, then, is the larger issue, the most fundamental of questions.

PHILO: Which is?

ARCH: The definition of what Architecture is. There's Voltaire again. You can't have a meaningful discussion without first defining the terms of your discussion. We can't decide whether the architect has a duty to Architecture without first defining what we mean by Architecture.

What Is Design? What Is Architecture?

PHILO: Let's conclude our discussion, then, by trying to say what Architecture is. Shouldn't the person among us who identifies as an architect be the one to say what Architecture is?

ARCH: That would be the logical assumption. Let's see how well I do. The problem, as we shall see in our book's other chapters, is that one question quickly leads to other questions. "What is architecture?" leads to "What is place?" "What is place?" leads to "What are form and meaning?" Etc., etc. These questions, I feel, are fundamental to the teaching of architecture and design. Yet as a philosopher, you know that such large questions can at times be hard to define and think about in a clear and short way. Such brevity and profoundness are sometimes found in the work of poets rather than architects, philosophers, and other theoreticians.

Would it surprise you to learn that the clearest expression of architecture can be found not in any specific building but in a poem by Wallace Stevens? To my mind, this poem is a complete theory of architecture and design in eight lines.

PHILO: Not necessarily, but it wouldn't be the first place I would look, either.

ARCH: Well, I believe Stevens offers us a wonderful definition of architecture. Not only that, it's in his poem, *Theory:* [4]

> I am what is around me.
> Women understand this.
> One is not duchess
> A hundred yards away from a carriage
> These, then are portraits:
> A black vestibule;
> A high bed sheltered by curtains.
> These are merely instances.

PHILO: Stevens is a wonderful poet, and I like this poem a lot. But how does it provide a definition of architecture?

ARCH: Perhaps *definition* is not the correct word. I would say the poem offers us a *map* of architecture. It is rather a condensed and precise map of architecture's territory. I chart it out like so, separating out the poem's lines:

I am what is around me.	Place, the "I"—discourse
Women understand this.	Discourse of "the other"
One is not duchess	Code
A hundred yards away from a carriage	Measure, proxemics
These, then are portraits:	Particular/universal
A black vestibule;	Syntax, geometry, type
A high bed sheltered by curtains.	
These are merely instances.	Time, chance, and necessity

PHILO: I'm afraid you'll have to explain some more.

ARCH: I'll elaborate slightly, without going into too much explanation, because I see these lines as projecting different areas—*topoi,* as the Greeks would say, and in keeping with the mapping metaphor—which our book's subsequent chapters address.

Architecture and design have to do with transforming our environment, either on the macro scale, such as with cities or neighborhoods, or on the micro scale, such as in industrial and fashion design. Though we may focus often on the objects of designs—buildings, furniture, clothing, etc.—we shouldn't forget design is really about transforming our lived experience.

PHILO: Design addresses directly what it means to live in the world, what it means to have a world at all.

ARCH: Yes. We'll get more into this in Chapter 4, "What Is Place?" for instance. But the fundamental question, I believe, the one that orients my reading of Stevens's poem and opens other basic questions in architecture and design, is this: what does it mean to be human?

PHILO: That's philosophy's fundamental concern as well, I would say.

ARCH: Of course. How could it not be? Even physics, which studies the universe, must ultimately arrive at the question of the place of human beings in the universe.

PHILO: Ahem. So the poem . . .

ARCH: Ah yes, I'm getting distracted. For me, the poem begins with the problem of where "I" begin and where the environment begins.

I am what is around me.

This is a claim of identity. Yet it also says that "I" cannot be separated from my environment. "I am what is around me" answers the question of 'where' I am, but it also places this 'where' in question.

Let's continue:

Women understand this.

Suddenly, the discourse of the "I," which has been complicated by 'where,' is complicated further with the introduction of the other person. Where does the other person fit into the relationship between the "I" and what is around the "I?" The other person can't be part of the environment because he or she ("they," in this case, "women") are human beings. They are not the same as trees and park benches. Yet they can't be the "I," can they? The other person represents, I think, the presence of the client, as we were saying above, or of society in general.

> One is not duchess
> A hundred yards away from a carriage

These two lines connote to my mind the combination of social code and measurement. I know "who" I am by the place where I live or the land I control.

> These, then are portraits:

Now a portrait is a very interesting "genre," artistically speaking. A portrait could be described as a common form whose content is very particular. A portrait isn't supposed to capture just the likeness of the individual, but also the individual's personality. But again, the particular personality expressed in a portrait is supposed to be something that can be communicated, so that means it is part of some universal structure as well. Can architecture and design in general be seen as constructing portraits of places and the people who use them?

> A black vestibule;
> A high bed sheltered by curtains.

These two lines are very interesting. They combine the language of type (vestibule, bed), as well as structure and sign, or form and meaning. By describing a bed as "sheltered by curtains," the poem brings out the implication that a bed is a refuge. By describing the vestibule as black, a very specific meaning is implied. How would the meaning change if the vestibule were white?

> These are merely instances.

This is the most philosophically profound line of the poem, I feel. It is a reminder not only that architecture and design are finite and ephemeral, that they won't last forever; this fact also emphasizes that we are finite and ephemeral as well. At times, I think architecture and design try to hide this fact, to make us forget that we are here by chance ultimately. The most powerful kinds of design, though, should remind us of our mortality and of time's passing.

CRITICAL READING PASSAGE

Chapter 1, "What Is Thought?"
from *How We Think*
John Dewey
1910

ABOUT THE AUTHOR

John Dewey (1859–1952) was an American philosopher and educational reformer whose work focused on the theory of knowledge. Dewey founded, along with the philosophers Charles Sanders Pierce and William James, the American school of philosophy known as pragmatism. Influenced a great deal by Charles Darwin's theory of evolution, pragmatism considered knowledge inseparable from a human being's everyday engagement with his or her life. Knowledge, pragmatism held, is therefore always dependent on the specific, pragmatic circumstances in which it was employed. Dewey's work *How We Think,* whose first chapter we present here, applies his theory of knowledge to education and is considered by many in the philosophy of education to offer one of the first definitions of "critical thinking."

§ I. VARIED SENSES OF THE TERM

No words are oftener on our lips than *thinking* and *thought*. So profuse and varied, indeed, is our use of these words that it is not easy to define just what we mean by them. The aim of this chapter is to find a single consistent meaning. Assistance may be had by considering some typical ways in which the terms are employed. In the first place *thought* is used broadly, not to say loosely. Everything that comes to mind, that "goes through our heads," is called a thought. To think of a thing is just to be conscious of it in any way whatsoever. Second, the term is restricted by excluding whatever is directly presented; we think (or think of) only such things as we do not directly see, hear, smell, or taste. Then, third, the meaning is further limited to beliefs that rest upon some kind of evidence or testimony. Of this third type, two kinds—or, rather, two degrees—must be discriminated. In some cases, a belief is accepted with slight or almost no attempt to state the grounds that support it. In other cases, the ground or basis for a belief is deliberately sought and its adequacy to support the belief examined. This process is called reflective thought; it alone is truly educative in value, and it forms, accordingly, the principal subject of this volume. We shall now briefly describe each of the four senses.

I. In its loosest sense, thinking signifies everything that, as we say, is "in our heads" or that "goes through our minds." He who offers "a penny for your thoughts" does not expect to drive any great bargain. In calling the objects of his demand *thoughts,* he does not intend to ascribe to them dignity, consecutiveness, or truth. Any idle fancy, trivial recollection, or flitting impression will satisfy his demand. Daydreaming, building of castles in the air, that loose flux of casual and disconnected material that floats through our minds in relaxed moments are, in this random sense, *thinking.* More of our waking life than we should care to admit, even to ourselves, is likely to be whiled away in this inconsequential trifling with idle fancy and unsubstantial hope.

In this sense, silly folk and dullards *think.* The story is told of a man in slight repute for intelligence, who, desiring to be chosen selectman in his New England town, addressed a knot of neighbors in this wise: "I hear you don't believe I know enough to hold office. I wish you to understand that I am thinking about something or other most of the time." Now reflective thought is like this random coursing of things through the mind in that it consists of a succession of things thought of; but it is unlike, in that the mere chance occurrence of any chance "something or other" in an irregular sequence does not suffice. Reflection involves not simply a sequence of ideas, but a *con*-sequence—a consecutive ordering in such a way that each determines the next as its proper outcome, while each in turn leans back on its predecessors. The successive portions of the reflective thought grow out of one another and support one another; they do not come and go in a medley. Each phase is a step from something to something—technically speaking, it is a term of thought. Each term leaves a deposit which is utilized in the next term. The stream or flow becomes a train, chain, or thread.

II. Even when thinking is used in a broad sense, it is usually restricted to matters not directly perceived: to what we do not see, smell, hear, or touch. We ask the man telling a story if he saw a certain incident happen, and his reply may be, "No, I only thought of it." A note of invention, as distinct from faithful record of observation, is present. Most important in this class are successions of imaginative incidents and episodes which, having a certain coherence, hanging together on a continuous thread, lie between kaleidoscopic flights of fancy and considerations deliberately employed to establish a conclusion. The imaginative stories poured forth by children possess all degrees of internal congruity; some are disjointed, some are articulated. When connected, they simulate reflective thought; indeed, they usually occur in minds of logical capacity. These imaginative enterprises often precede thinking of the close-knit type and prepare the way for it. But *they do not aim at knowledge, at belief about facts or in truths;* and thereby they are marked off from reflective thought even when they most resemble it. Those who express such thoughts do not expect credence, but rather credit for a well-constructed plot or a well-arranged climax. They produce good stories, not—unless by chance—knowledge. Such thoughts are an efflorescence of feeling; the enhancement of a mood or sentiment is their aim; congruity of emotion, their binding tie.

III. In its next sense, thought denotes belief resting upon some basis, that is, real or supposed knowledge going beyond what is directly present. It is marked by *acceptance or rejection of something as reasonably probable or improbable.* This phase of thought, however, includes two such distinct types of belief that, even though their difference is strictly one of degree, not of kind, it becomes practically important to consider them separately. Some beliefs are accepted when their grounds have not themselves been considered, others are accepted because their grounds have been examined.

When we say, "Men used to think the world was flat," or, "I thought you went by the house," we express belief: something is accepted, held to, acquiesced in, or affirmed. But such thoughts may mean a supposition accepted without reference to its real grounds. These may be adequate, they may not; but their value with reference to the support they afford the belief has not been considered.

Such thoughts grow up unconsciously and without reference to the attainment of correct belief. They are picked up—we know not how. From obscure sources and by unnoticed channels they insinuate themselves into acceptance and become unconsciously a part of our mental furniture. Tradition, instruction, imitation—all of which depend upon authority in some form, or appeal to our own advantage, or fall in with a strong passion—are responsible for them. Such thoughts are prejudices, that is, prejudgments, not judgments proper that rest upon a survey of evidence.[1]

---

[1] This mode of thinking in its contrast with thoughtful inquiry receives special notice in the next chapter.

IV. Thoughts that result in belief have an importance attached to them which leads to reflective thought, to conscious inquiry into the nature, conditions, and bearings of the belief. To *think* of whales and camels in the clouds is to entertain ourselves with fancies, terminable at our pleasure, which do not lead to any belief in particular. But to think of the world as flat is to ascribe a quality to a real thing as its real property. This conclusion denotes a connection among things and hence is not, like imaginative thought, plastic to our mood. Belief in the world's flatness commits him who holds it to thinking in certain specific ways of other objects, such as the heavenly bodies, antipodes, the possibility of navigation. It prescribes to him actions in accordance with his conception of these objects.

The consequences of a belief upon other beliefs and upon behavior may be so important, then, that men are forced to consider the grounds or reasons of their belief and its logical consequences. This means reflective thought— thought in its eulogistic and emphatic sense.

Men *thought* the world was flat until Columbus *thought* it to be round. The earlier thought was a belief held because men had not the energy or the courage to question what those about them accepted and taught, especially as it was suggested and seemingly confirmed by obvious sensible facts. The thought of Columbus was a *reasoned conclusion.* It marked the close of study into facts, of scrutiny and revision of evidence, of working out the implications of various hypotheses, and of comparing these theoretical results with one another and with known facts. Because Columbus did not accept unhesitatingly the current traditional theory, because he doubted and inquired, he arrived at his thought. Skeptical of what, from long habit, seemed most certain, and credulous of what seemed impossible, he went on thinking until he could produce evidence for both his confidence and his disbelief. Even if his conclusion had finally turned out wrong, it would have been a different sort of belief from those it antagonized, because it was reached by a different method. *Active, persistent, and careful consideration of any belief or supposed form of knowledge in the light of the grounds that support it, and the further conclusions to which it tends,* constitutes reflective thought. Any one of the first three kinds of thought may elicit this type; but once begun, it is a conscious and voluntary effort to establish belief upon a firm basis of reasons.

§ 2. THE CENTRAL FACTOR IN THINKING

There are, however, no sharp lines of demarcation between the various operations just outlined. The problem of attaining correct habits of reflection would be much easier than it is, did not the different modes of thinking blend insensibly into one another. So far, we have considered rather extreme instances of each kind in order to get the field clearly before us. Let us now reverse this operation; let us consider a rudimentary case of thinking, lying between careful examination of evidence and a mere irresponsible stream of fancies. A man is walking on a warm day. The sky was clear the last time he observed it; but presently he notes, while occupied primarily with other things, that the air is cooler. It occurs to him that it is probably going to rain; looking up, he sees a dark cloud between him and the sun, and he then quickens his steps. What, if anything, in such a situation can be called thought? Neither the act of walking nor the noting of the cold is a thought. Walking is one direction of activity; looking and noting are other modes of activity. The likelihood that it will rain is, however, something *suggested*. The pedestrian *feels* the cold; he *thinks of* clouds and a coming shower.

So far there is the same sort of situation as when one looking at a cloud is reminded of a human figure and face. Thinking in both of these cases (the cases of belief and of fancy) involves a noted or perceived fact, followed by something else which is not observed but which is brought to mind, suggested by the thing seen. One reminds us, as we say, of the other. Side by side, however, with this factor of agreement in the two cases of suggestion is a factor of marked disagreement. We do not *believe* in the face suggested by the cloud; we do not consider at all the probability of its being a fact. There is no *reflective* thought. The danger of rain, on the contrary, presents itself to us as a genuine possibility—as a possible fact of the same nature as the observed coolness. Put differently, we do not regard the cloud as meaning or indicating a face, but merely as suggesting it, while we do consider that the coolness may mean rain. In the first case, seeing an object, we just happen, as we say, to think of something else; in the second, we consider the *possibility and nature of the connection between the object seen and the object suggested*. The seen thing is regarded as in some way *the ground or basis of belief* in the suggested thing; it possesses the quality of *evidence*.

This function by which one thing signifies or indicates another, and thereby leads us to consider how far one may be regarded as warrant for belief in the other, is, then, the central factor in all reflective or distinctively intellectual thinking. By calling up various situations to which such terms as *signifies* and *indicates* apply, the student will best realize for himself the actual facts denoted by the words *reflective thought*. Synonyms for these terms are: points to, tells of, betokens, prognosticates, represents, stands for, implies.[2] We also say one thing portends another; is ominous of another, or a symptom of it, or a key to it, or (if the connection is quite obscure) that it gives a hint, clue, or intimation.

Reflection thus implies that something is believed in (or disbelieved in), not on its own direct account, but through something else which stands as witness, evidence, proof, voucher, warrant; that is, *as ground of belief*. At one time, rain is actually felt or directly experienced; at another time, we infer that it has rained from the looks of the grass and trees, or that it is going to rain because of the condition of the air or the state of the barometer. At one time,

---

[2] *Implies* is more often used when a principle or general truth brings about belief in some other truth; the other phrases are more frequently used to denote the cases in which one fact or event leads us to believe in something else.

we see a man (or suppose we do) without any intermediary fact; at another time, we are not quite sure what we see, and hunt for accompanying facts that will serve as signs, indications, tokens of what is to be believed.

Thinking, for the purposes of this inquiry, is defined accordingly as *that operation in which present facts suggest other facts (or truths) in such a way as to induce belief in the latter upon the ground or warrant of the former.* We do not put beliefs that rest simply on inference on the surest level of assurance. To say "I think so" implies that I do not as yet *know* so. The inferential belief may later be confirmed and come to stand as sure, but in itself it always has a certain element of supposition.

§ 3. ELEMENTS IN REFLECTIVE THINKING

So much for the description of the more external and obvious aspects of the fact called *thinking.* Further consideration at once reveals certain subprocesses which are involved in every reflective operation. These are: (*a*) a state of perplexity, hesitation, doubt; and (*b*) an act of search or investigation directed toward bringing to light further facts which serve to corroborate or to nullify the suggested belief.

(*a*) In our illustration, the shock of coolness generated confusion and suspended belief, at least momentarily. Because it was unexpected, it was a shock or an interruption needing to be accounted for, identified, or placed. To say that the abrupt occurrence of the change of temperature constitutes a problem may sound forced and artificial; but if we are willing to extend the meaning of the word *problem* to whatever—no matter how slight and commonplace in character—perplexes and challenges the mind so that it makes belief at all uncertain, there is a genuine problem or question involved in this experience of sudden change.

(*b*) The turning of the head, the lifting of the eyes, the scanning of the heavens, are activities adapted to bring to recognition facts that will answer the question presented by the sudden coolness. The facts as they first presented themselves were perplexing; they suggested, however, clouds. The act of looking was an act to discover if this suggested explanation held good. It may again seem forced to speak of this looking, almost automatic, as an act of research or inquiry. But once more, if we are willing to generalize our conceptions of our mental operations to include the trivial and ordinary as well as the technical and recondite, there is no good reason for refusing to give such a title to the act of looking. The purport of this act of inquiry is to confirm or to refute the suggested belief. New facts are brought to perception, which either corroborate the idea that a change of weather is imminent, or negate it.

Another instance, commonplace also, yet not quite so trivial, may enforce this lesson. A man traveling in an unfamiliar region comes to a branching of the roads. Having no sure knowledge to fall back upon, he is brought to a standstill of hesitation and suspense. Which road is right? And how shall perplexity be resolved? There are but two alternatives: he must either blindly and arbitrarily take his course, trusting to luck for the outcome, or he must discover grounds for the conclusion that a given road is right. Any attempt to decide the matter by thinking will involve inquiry into other facts, whether brought out by memory or by further observation, or by both. The perplexed wayfarer must carefully scrutinize what is before him and he must cudgel his memory. He looks for evidence that will support belief in favor of either of the roads—for evidence that will weight down one suggestion. He may climb a tree; he may go first in this direction, then in that, looking, in either case, for signs, clues, indications. He wants something in the nature of a signboard or a map, and *his reflection is aimed at the discovery of facts that will serve this purpose.*

The above illustration may be generalized. Thinking begins in what may fairly enough be called a *forked-road* situation, a situation which is ambiguous, which presents a dilemma, which proposes alternatives. As long as our activity glides smoothly along from one thing to another, or as long as we permit our imagination to entertain fancies at pleasure, there is no call for reflection. Difficulty or obstruction in the way of reaching a belief brings us, however, to a pause. In the suspense of uncertainty, we metaphorically climb a tree; we try to find some standpoint from which we may survey additional facts and, getting a more commanding view of the situation, may decide how the facts stand related to one another.

Demand for the solution of a perplexity is the steadying and guiding factor in the entire process of reflection. Where there is no question of a problem to be solved or a difficulty to be surmounted, the course of suggestions flows on at random; we have the first type of thought described. If the stream of suggestions is controlled simply by their emotional congruity, their fitting agreeably into a single picture or story, we have the second type. But a question to be answered, an ambiguity to be resolved, sets up an end and holds the current of ideas to a definite channel. Every suggested conclusion is tested by its reference to this regulating end, by its pertinence to the problem in hand. This need of straightening out a perplexity also controls the kind of inquiry undertaken. A traveler whose end is the most beautiful path will look for other considerations and will test suggestions occurring to him on another principle than if he wishes to discover the way to a given city. *The problem fixes the end of thought and the end controls the process of thinking.*

§ 4. SUMMARY

We may recapitulate by saying that the origin of thinking is some perplexity, confusion, or doubt. Thinking is not a case of spontaneous combustion; it does not occur just on "general principles." There is something specific which occasions and evokes it. General appeals to a child (or to a grown-up) to think, irrespective of the existence in his own experience of some difficulty that troubles him and disturbs his equilibrium, are as futile as advice to lift himself by his boot-straps.

Given a difficulty, the next step is suggestion of some way out—the formation of some tentative plan or project, the entertaining of some theory which will account for the peculiarities in question, the consideration of some solution for the problem. The data at hand cannot supply the solution; they can only suggest it. What, then, are the sources of the suggestion? Clearly past experience and prior knowledge. If the person has had some acquaintance with similar situations, if he has dealt with material of the same sort before, suggestions more or less apt and helpful are likely to arise. But unless there has been experience in some degree analogous, which may now be represented in imagination, confusion remains mere confusion. There is nothing upon which to draw in order to clarify it. Even when a child (or a grown-up) has a problem, to urge him to think when he has no prior experiences involving some of the same conditions, is wholly futile.

If the suggestion that occurs is at once accepted, we have uncritical thinking, the minimum of reflection. To turn the thing is at once accepted, we have uncritical thinking, the minimum of reflection. To turn the thing over in mind, to reflect, means to hunt for additional evidence, for new data, that will develop the suggestion, and will either, as we say, bear it out or else make obvious its absurdity and irrelevance. Given a genuine difficulty and a reasonable amount of analogous experience to draw upon the difference, *par excellence,* between good and bad thinking is found at this point. The easiest way is to accept any suggestion that seems plausible and thereby bring to an end the condition of mental uneasiness. Reflective thinking is always more or less troublesome because it involves overcoming the inertia that inclines one to accept suggestions at their face value; it involves willingness to endure a condition of mental unrest and disturbance. Reflective thinking, in short, means judgment suspended during further inquiry; and suspense is likely to be somewhat painful. As we shall see later, the most important factor in the training of good mental habits consists in acquiring the attitude of suspended conclusion, and in mastering the various methods of searching for new materials to corroborate or to refute the first suggestions that occur. To maintain the state of doubt and to carry on systematic and protracted inquiry—these are the essentials of thinking.

QUESTIONS FOR REFLECTION

1. How does Dewey distinguish between thinking in a general, everyday sense and "reflective thought"?

2. What is the difference between knowledge and belief?

3. How does Dewey tie all thinking to actual experience?

CRITICAL THINKING EXERCISES

1. Define your terms. The sentence "Architecture is . . ." has been completed reductively by such one-liners as "Architecture is (1) a machine, (2) an organism, and (3) a language." Consider the meaning of each metaphor as a definition of architecture, and as a definition of design. Does choosing one or more of these definitions make a difference in how you would proceed in design? If "critical thinking" means redefining and questioning the basic terms and concepts on which your design is based, then considering these three paradigms is important.

2. Theory or History Paradox: Permanence versus Change: It has often been said that there is no such thing as architectural theory. What exists is only a history of ideas about architecture, no timeless principles or archetypal forms.

Think about that and define the following terms for yourself: architectural theory, principles, archetypal forms.

3. Reread Stevens's poem, "Theory." If pragmatism considers all knowledge as situational (as emerging from the specific situations in which human beings find themselves), to what extent can we interpret "Theory" as a form of pragmatic thinking? Locate evidence in the poem to support your interpretation.

 FOR FURTHER READING

Austin, J. L. 1975. *How to Do Things with Words.* Cambridge, MA: Harvard University Press.

2

What Are Appearance and Reality?

FIGURE 2.1 The Parthenon

ARCH: Let's begin our discussion of appearance and reality with an anecdote about one of my friends who is also an architect. She took her child to visit the Acropolis in Athens, Greece. They came to the Parthenon, and the tour guide pointed out the best spot from which to see the temple in all its majesty. However, this is at the end of the day and the child, being only seven years old, was bored by a whole day of visiting ruins. You know how children can be. The child wandered off to touch and hug the cool stone column. It was a hot day, and the column offered a bit of relief. Looking up, happy, the child said, "The column isn't straight!"

PHILO: Was the child right or wrong?

ARCH: I think the answer will depend on whether the person who answers is an architect or a philosopher, and what point of view that person brings to the situation.

PHILO: I agree. As a philosopher, I can imagine some possible questions I would ask the child if I were the parent: "What do you mean by straight?" "How do you know it isn't straight?" And so on.

ARCH: But as an architect, my colleague said something different. Her conversation with her child was more like the following:

> "My dear child, from where you are, the column *appears* as if it isn't straight. But come over here and sit next to me. It appears straight and majestic, tall and strong, doesn't it?"
>
> The child was confused. "How can it be both?"
>
> "It's like that because of entasis."
>
> "What's that?" the seven-year-old asked.
>
> The architect explained, "Whenever you find a column wider in the middle than it is on its ends, it is called **entasis**, which literally means 'to strain' in Greek. You can see this technique in a lot of Greek and Roman architecture. Not everyone agrees why the Athenians did this. Many say they designed columns to be this way to make them look tall, strong, and majestic, to overcome the illusion they are too thin."
>
> "But isn't it strong enough even if you don't use entasis?" asked the child.

"Sure it is, but it's important to make it look strong, too."

"Why do you have to do that?"

"Because people believe what they see, but this is not always how things are. See for yourself. Look at the column with your left eye closed and your right eye open. Then do it again with the right eye closed and the left eye open. What do you see?"

"The column moves from left to right, but then it's in the middle when I'm looking at it with both eyes," answered the kid.

"So where's the column?"

"In the middle."

"Why?"

"Because I'm always looking at it with both eyes open."

"What if you were blind in one eye? Where would the column be then?"

Our young friend was unsure, as I bet a good many adults would be as well. The parent said, "Go around the temple again. Stand in different places, and look at it from all different angles. Is the temple the same from each place you see it? It shouldn't be. It should change. That's called **perspective**."

Entasis and Perspective

ARCH: On the first day of almost all architectural history introduction courses, beginning students of design and architecture learn—or I believe should learn—about this constructive fact: that the columns of a Greek temple are tapered and that this tapering—or entasis— was done to compensate for the optical illusion due to perspective.

Students learn this by analyzing works such as the Parthenon as well as by reading the treaties of Vitriuvius and Palladio. You know, of course, that perspective is a constant factor in design. One of the first questions for a designer or an architect is how to represent and portray a room or a building in a perspective or a model. The designer must always decide from what point of view to do this. The basic fact the historical example of entasis teaches us is that *perspective distorts*. Thus, all the means a designer uses to represent a project—plans and sections, orthogonal projections—change how the object will be

FIGURE 2.2

"The column in each order was formed in such a manner that the diameter of the column may be smaller at the upper part than at the bottom, with a kind of swelling in the middle. It is to be observed in the diminutions, that the higher the columns are, the less they must diminish, because the height, by reason of the distance, has that effect." Andrea Palladio, *The Four Books of Architecture,* First Book, Chapter XII.

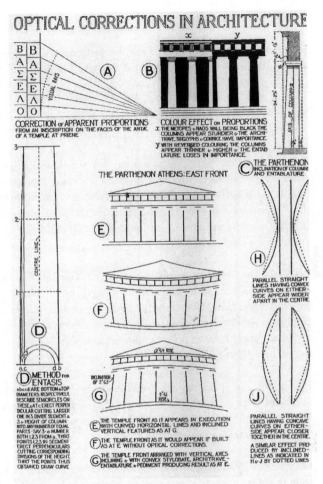

FIGURE 2.3

"Of the swelling and diminution of columns, and of the intercoumniatios and pilasters." Andrea Palladio, *The Four Books of Architecture*, First Book, Chapter XII.

seen and, therefore, understood. Representations capture only partial aspects of reality, like shadows on the cave wall in Plato's *Republic*.

PHILO: There you go Arch, we're back to philosophy again, and it's architecture that led us there.

Representation and Reality

PHILO: So, Arch, is this how you argue the distinction between **appearance** and **reality** as a central concern of design—whether the designer realizes it or not?

ARCH: Yes, *especially* when designers are unaware they are at work in the design process.

PHILO: But could you say more precisely how they are at work? In class the other day you brought up Bertrand Russell's essay "Appearance and Reality" from his book *The Problems of Philosophy* and made the claim that "appearance and reality" is a fundamental problem for design. I can see how the appearance of an object is an important consideration for the designer.

ARCH: Yes Philo, the architect needs to decide how the design will look to the client. In architecture and interior design, the success of a project depends upon how effectively the designer communicates how the client will experience its spaces. In my experience, however, appearance and reality have to do with more philosophical issues regarding the problem of knowledge.

PHILO: Philosophically speaking, it's possible to doubt the appearance of an object, which then leads to uncertainty about the object's existence. Isn't that the sense in which Russell discusses the relationship between appearance and reality?

ARCH: Yes, of course, you're right. Russell discusses "appearance and reality" from the standpoint of **epistemology**, philosophy's name for the theory of knowledge. As someone trained in philosophy, Philo, you came to know Russell the so-called traditional way. You must remember, though, that I came to Russell through my practice in architecture.

PHILO: How did reading Russell from the perspective of a designer help you?

ARCH: In reading Russell, I discovered he was describing a problem designers deal with every day in their work.

To say again, whether they realize it or not, there is a great deal of uncertainty in the design process. As an architect, I need to describe to my clients how they will experience the spaces I design for them.

PHILO: How do you do it?

ARCH: With drawings, mock-ups, renderings, etc. This is what architecture means when it refers to **representation**, which does not mean the same thing to philosophers when they hear this word.

PHILO: Nonetheless, both architects and philosophers can understand that if an object depends upon its representation—and more specifically, the *tools* one uses to construct representations of an object—then it becomes a fundamental problem how one is to adequately communicate how someone *will* experience a space.

ARCH: Well, it still remains a problem after a space is built, let me tell you! But that is something we'll save for our discussion of Chapter 7, What Is Time?

PHILO: Let's stay with Russell for the moment. The example he uses is a table. He argues that because we can't be sure a table has a single, uniform color, or a single, uniform texture, we can't say a table has either a color or texture inherent to it. Russell basically shows us that because we can't say a table *has* those characteristics belonging to it, we also can't say we experience anything other than those sensations, which he calls **sense-data**.

ARCH: What is the table, then, if it is not this particular experience we have of it? Furthermore, if the experience of an object depends on the person who experiences it, then how can we guarantee our clients will see, smell, feel, and hear our design in the ways we suggest they will? Again, this is one of the first problems design deals with, and it's also a philosophical one.

PHILO: Yes, its one important place where architecture and philosophy intersect.

ARCH: Right, and as a colleague of ours likes to say, much of design is "faith-based." There is no guarantee a client or someone who uses a designed space will experience it the way the designer intends it to be experienced. The process is surrounded by uncertainty.

PHILO: OK. Because each spectator experiences an object differently, how can we be sure everyone's experiences coincide in such a way that we know we are all talking about the same object? I doubt your clients are as troubled by this question as philosophers are, though.

ARCH: Oh, you'd be surprised, believe me. Sometimes, that's all they are troubled by. Isn't that the lesson entasis reveals?

PHILO: I would agree. To explore this theme in more detail, don't you think it would be worth looking a bit closer at Russell's essay? Because you mention Plato, reading the chapter you mention, commonly called "The Allegory of the Cave," could be useful as well for farther reading.

ARCH: Yes, let's do it. We can continue our discussion after looking at those more closely.

Appearance, Reality, and Critical Thinking

PHILO: It seems to me, Arch, that we can begin to think of design as a kind of critical thinking.

ARCH: Yes, fundamentally so. Recall from our reading of Russell his contention that philosophy deepens our interest in the world by asking basic questions about the conditions of experience, such as the appearance and reality of the objects we see, hear, touch, and feel.

PHILO: Or rather, I should say, the objects we *believe* we see, hear, touch, and feel. Philosophy provokes us to reflect on the ordinary and see it in a new way by questioning our basic assumptions in everyday experience. It gives us a valuable tool: skepticism. Not the radical skepticism that can doubt the world away, like the form Descartes performs for us, but a skepticism that takes nothing for granted. A skepticism like the one performed by Socrates that allows us to ask larger questions and see more than what we may be expected to see.

ARCH: Isn't this what design does as well? As an architect, I take a previous condition—a site, a plan—and transform it into a new condition. In order to do that, though, I must be attentive to what constitutes the previous condition, to all the factors that make up the site, for instance, not only physical and material factors but social, political, and historical factors that determine in many ways a site's material conditions.

PHILO: The trouble is when the critical thinking you are describing as fundamental to the design process becomes confused with problem-solving.

Problem-solving involves the creation of solutions to given problems; there is no questioning why we have been given such a set of problems to solve and from whom, just the fact that we are supposed to solve them. Critical thinking, though, asks about the conditions of a given problem. Why is this a problem to begin with? Relative to what or whom? Who is posing this as a problem? What means is this person using to represent the problem as such? Etc. We spoke about this in Chapter 1, but now I think we can list some more specific aspects of critical thinking based upon the work we've done in this chapter. I think we can now say critical thinking involves reflection on

- The tools of perception and representation
- Language, so far as this can be considered fundamental to how things are represented and then communicated to others
- The distinction between real problems and apparent problems

Russell intimates with his example of the microscope that even the tools we use to perceive things can offer only a position from a certain perspective. It is always possible to experience the object from a different perspective, which changes our experience and sometimes challenges our experience. The opposition between **objectivity** and **subjectivity** becomes irrelevant, or at least falls away temporarily, because objective representations of things still rely on **material conditions** situated in the world and in history.

ARCH: Philo, the language is becoming abstract. Let me say this in another way: the drawing in front of the design student, be it a physical drawing or a computer model, is for many nights and months a representation of something that does not yet exist. (In fact, in design school, it usually never comes into any further existence than the drawings and models the student produces.) The future reality of the project *appears* on paper or in pixels, so to speak. The drawing or model is the *appearance* of that "future reality," one that is necessarily imperfect because it is partial and incomplete. It *must* be so because it is impossible to represent all the possible perspectives from which to experience the object. This does not change if the project becomes built. Though the project "becomes real" in the use of actual building materials, one still has to experience the building from a certain perspective, at a certain time of day, during a specific season and climate, in time and space. Even tools for exact measurement give us only a narrow aspect of the total reality of a thing.

I'll give you an example from my own days as a student. When I attended my first design studio, we were given the rules for making plans and sections the first or second day. The example we were given was a Greek temple, like the Parthenon in the example we discussed at the beginning of this chapter. These days, I take this rule for granted, which I find is a big mistake.

PHILO: Why?

ARCH: Because I find students are being taught about it less and less, and it is affecting their ability to think in the design process.

In any case, the rule is this: one never cuts a section through a column when attempting to represent the nature of space in an interior section of a building.

PHILO: Why is that? Isn't a column a part of the space, just as any other element?

ARCH: Let me explain. When a student makes the mistake of cutting through a column in a section drawing, that column, represented as a thick black line, reads as a wall. The result is that it breaks up the space into two separate rooms that are not there when you look at the open plan.

PHILO: I see. Your example emphasizes the fact that drawings and renderings are representations of an object intended to communicate characteristics of the object. You even say cutting a section through a column results in a misreading of the column as a wall. Drawing as a form of language in design, then, is subject to correct and incorrect interpretations and readings.

ARCH: Yes, and matters become more complex when we consider the student or designer in general must also present their project in oral and written form to an audience that is often composed of non-experts.

PHILO: I see. So then there becomes an additional problem of translation?

ARCH: Yes, and questions how one translates architectural representations, (which are ways designers communicate with one another) into a language the lay person can understand. Believe me, this is not a trivial problem because the non-expert we are talking about is most often the client, who is sponsoring the project.

In philosophy, you don't face this particular problem, Philo. In design, however, the client is the one who is going to decide whether your project ever becomes that "future reality" represented in your design, so you better find a way to communicate your design clearly to him or her. So not only must you think about how you intend to present your design to those that speak your "language" (fellow experts), but also to your client.

PHILO: Well, I would try to. For the design audience, I would feel I could expand on issues involving perception and perspective. For my client, though, I might present the designs as part of an architectural history dating back to the Greeks. Some clients might even find it interesting to think their commission could be part of a long tradition while still departing from it.

ARCH: Sold!

PHILO: Not so fast. I think I need a bit more experience and training before I can open up my own office. In any case, I haven't given up doing philosophy, at least not yet. I want to add one more comment before we continue to some critical thinking activities students can perform to help them work through these questions.

ARCH: Well, as an architect what I find compelling in the questions we are raising in this chapter is just how fundamental appearance and reality are to critical thinking in general. If we are right in saying critical thinking differs from problem-solving, in that with the former the designer questions the problems he or she is given to solve, then what designers do is differentiate between real problems and apparent problems. What is a real problem? A real problem attends to what is really at stake in a certain situation, whereas an apparent problem distracts us from asking the relevant questions. The Parthenon's columns, for instance, can be discussed in conventional aesthetic terms. The Greeks designed the column to be wider in the middle to compensate for an illusion due to perspective. If we find ourselves satisfied with such an answer, though, we are missing a critical opportunity to ask why correcting for perspective was a problem for the Greeks in the first place.

PHILO: Doesn't this cause us to wonder about the status of architecture in general?

ARCH: Yes, many believe architecture is fully practical in the sense that all it is concerned with is creating space for a certain set of activities and uses and making sure this space reflects a structural integrity (I admit this second aspect is less and less a concern these days). Entasis shows us architecture, at least with the Greeks, is more than a practical science. It entails a reflection on the human spectator and a reflection on the limits of human perception. If entasis "corrects" for an illusion due to human perspective, then one could argue architecture concerns itself also with a shaping of perception. The spectator, then, changes with the encounter with architecture. His or her perception changes. This is an insight contemporary theorists of architecture have explored. I won't elaborate because it threatens to become more abstract, but these questions do allow us to think about issues we might not have entertained if we approached the problem of entasis in the conventional, expected ways.

CRITICAL READING PASSAGE

"Appearance and Reality,"
from *The Problems of Philosophy*
Bertrand Russell
1912

ABOUT THE AUTHOR

Bertand Russell (1872–1970) is regarded as one of the most influential philosophers of the twentieth century. Described as the "father of analytic philosophy" (philosophy originating in the Anglo-American context devoted to logic
and epistemology), Russell was also, and perhaps more importantly, one of the
twentieth century's foremost public intellectuals and a mathematician. He was
an avowed pacifist, protesting World Wars I and II and the war in Vietnam, and
he was awarded the Nobel Prize in Literature in 1950. Russell published *The
Problems of Philosophy* in 1912, based on lectures he gave while a Fellow of
Trinity College in Cambridge, a post from which he was dismissed in 1916 as the
result of having been convicted and fined in connection with anti-war protests.

I s there any knowledge in the world which is so certain that no reasonable man could doubt it? This question, which at first sight might not seem difficult, is really one of the most difficult that can be asked. When we have realized the obstacles in the way of a straightforward and confident answer, we shall be well launched on the study of philosophy—for philosophy is merely the attempt to answer such ultimate questions, not carelessly and dogmatically, as we do in ordinary life and even in the sciences, but critically after exploring all that makes such questions puzzling, and after realizing all the vagueness and confusion that underlie our ordinary ideas.

In daily life, we assume as certain many things which, on a closer scrutiny, are found to be so full of apparent contradictions that only a great amount of thought enables us to know what it is that we really may believe. In the search for certainty, it is natural to begin with our present experiences, and in some sense, no doubt, knowledge is to be derived from them. But any statement as to what it is that our immediate experiences make us know is very likely to be wrong. It seems to me that I am now sitting in a chair, at a table of a certain shape, on which I see sheets of paper with writing or print. By turning my head I see out of the window buildings and clouds and the sun. I believe that the sun is about ninety-three million miles from the earth; that it is a hot globe many times bigger than the earth; that, owing to the earth's rotation, it rises every morning, and will continue to do so for an indefinite time in the future. I believe that, if any other normal person comes into my room, he will see the same chairs and tables and books and papers as I see, and that the table which I see is the same as the table which I feel pressing against my arm. All this seems to be so evident as to be hardly worth stating, except in answer to a man who doubts whether I know anything. Yet all this may be reasonably doubted, and all of it requires much careful discussion before we can be sure that we have stated it in a form that is wholly true.

To make our difficulties plain, let us concentrate attention on the table. To the eye it is oblong, brown and shiny, to the touch it is smooth and cool and hard; when I tap it, it gives out a wooden sound. Any one else who sees and feels and hears the table will agree with this description, so that it might seem as if no difficulty would arise; but as soon as we try to be more precise our troubles begin. Although I believe that the table is "really" of the same colour all over, the parts that reflect the light look much brighter than the other parts, and some parts look white because of reflected light. I know that, if I move, the parts that reflect the light will be different, so that the apparent distribution of colours on the table will change. It follows that if several people are looking at the table at the same moment, no two of them will see exactly the same distribution of colours, because no two can see it from exactly the same point of view, and any change in the point of view makes some change in the way the light is reflected.

For most practical purposes these differences are unimportant, but to the painter they are all-important: the painter has to unlearn the habit of thinking that things seem to have the colour which common sense says they "really" have, and to learn the habit of seeing things as they appear. Here we have already the beginning of one of the distinctions that cause most trouble in philosophy—the distinction between "appearance" and "reality", between what things seem to be and what they are. The painter wants to know what things seem to be, the practical man and the philosopher want to know what they are; but the philosopher's wish to know this is stronger than the practical man's, and is more troubled by knowledge as to the difficulties of answering the question.

To return to the table. It is evident from what we have found, that there is no colour which preeminently appears to be *the* colour of the table, or even of any one particular part of the table—it appears to be of different colours from different points of view, and there is no reason for regarding some of these as more really its colour than others. And we know that even from a given point of view the colour will seem different by artificial light, or to a colour-blind man, or to a man wearing blue spectacles, while in the dark there will be no colour at all, though to touch and hearing the table will be unchanged. This colour is not something which is inherent in the table, but something depending upon the table and the spectator and the way the light falls on the table. When, in ordinary life, we speak of *the* colour of the table, we only mean the sort of colour which it will seem to have to a normal spectator from an ordinary point of view under usual conditions of light. But the other colours which appear under other conditions have just as good a right to be considered real; and therefore, to avoid favouritism, we are compelled to deny that, in itself, the table has any one particular colour.

The same thing applies to the texture. With the naked eye one can see the gram, but otherwise the table looks smooth and even. If we looked at it through a microscope, we should see roughnesses and hills and valleys, and all sorts of differences that are imperceptible to the naked eye. Which of these is the "real" table? We are naturally tempted to say that what we see through the microscope is more real, but that in turn would be changed by a still more powerful microscope. If, then, we cannot trust what we see with the naked eye, why should we trust what we see through a microscope? Thus, again, the confidence in our senses with which we began deserts us.

The *shape* of the table is no better. We are all in the habit of judging as to the "real" shapes of things, and we do this so unreflectingly that we come to think we actually see the real shapes. But, in fact, as we all have to learn if we try to draw, a given thing looks different in shape from every different point of view. If our table is "really" rectangular, it will look, from almost all points of view, as if it had two acute angles and two obtuse angles. If opposite sides are parallel, they will look as if they converged to a point away from the spectator; if they are of equal length, they will look as if the nearer side were longer. All these things are not commonly noticed in looking at a table, because experience has taught us to construct the 'real' shape from the apparent shape, and the "real" shape is what interests us as practical men. But the "real" shape is not what we see; it is something inferred from what we see. And what we see is constantly changing in shape as we move about the room; so that here again the senses seem not to give us the truth about the table itself, but only about the appearance of the table.

Similar difficulties arise when we consider the sense of touch. It is true that the table always gives us a sensation of hardness, and we feel that it resists pressure. But the sensation we obtain depends upon how hard we press the table and also upon what part of the body we press with; thus the various sensations due to various pressures or various parts of the body cannot be supposed to reveal *directly* any definite property of the table, but at most to be signs of some property which perhaps *causes* all the sensations, but is not actually apparent in any of them. And the same applies still more obviously to the sounds which can be elicited by rapping the table.

Thus it becomes evident that the real table, if there is one, is not the same as what we immediately experience by sight or touch or hearing. The real table, if there is one, is not *immediately* known to us at all, but must be an inference from what is immediately known. Hence, two very difficult questions at once arise; namely, (1) Is there a real table at all? (2) If so, what sort of object can it be?

It will help us in considering these questions to have a few simple terms of which the meaning is definite and clear. Let us give the name of "sense-data" to the things that are immediately known in sensation: such things as colours, sounds, smells, hardnesses, roughnesses, and so on. We shall give the name "sensation" to the experience of being immediately aware of these things. Thus, whenever we see a colour, we have a sensation *of* the colour, but the colour itself is a sense-datum, not a sensation. The colour is that *of* which we are immediately aware, and the awareness itself is the sensation. It is plain that if we are to know anything about the table, it must be by means of the sense-data—brown colour, oblong shape, smoothness, etc.—which we associate with the table; but, for the reasons which have been given, we cannot say that the table is the sense-data, or even that the sense-data are directly properties of the table. Thus a problem arises as to the relation of the sense-data to the real table, supposing there is such a thing.

The real table, if it exists, we will call a "physical object." Thus we have to consider the relation of sense-data to physical objects. The collection of all physical objects is called "matter." Thus our two questions may be re-stated as follows: (1) Is there any such thing as matter? (2) If so, what is its nature?

The philosopher who first brought prominently forward the reasons for regarding the immediate objects of our senses as not existing independently of us was Bishop Berkeley (1685–1753). His *Three Dialogues between Hylas and Philonous, in Opposition to Sceptics and Atheists,* undertake to prove that there is no such thing as matter at all, and that the world consists of nothing but minds and their ideas. Hylas has hitherto believed in matter, but he is no match for Philonous, who mercilessly drives him into contradictions and paradoxes, and makes his own denial of matter seem, in the end, as if it were almost common sense. The arguments employed are of very different value: some are important and sound, others are confused or quibbling. But Berkeley retains the merit of having shown that the existence of matter is capable of being denied without absurdity, and that if there are any things that exist independently of us they cannot be the immediate objects of our sensations.

There are two different questions involved when we ask whether matter exists, and it is important to keep them clear. We commonly mean by "matter" something which is opposed to "mind," something which we think of as occupying space and as radically incapable of any sort of thought or consciousness. It is chiefly in this sense that Berkeley denies matter; that is to say, he does not deny that the sense-data which we commonly take as signs of the existence of the table are really signs of the existence of *something* independent of us, but he does deny that this something is nonmental, that it is neither mind nor ideas entertained by some mind. He admits that there must be something which continues to exist when we go out of the room or shut our eyes, and that what we call seeing the table does really give us reason for believing in something which persists even when we are not seeing it. But he thinks that this something cannot be radically different in nature from what we see, and cannot be independent of seeing altogether, though it must be independent of *our* seeing. He is thus led to regard the "real" table as an idea in the mind of God. Such an idea has the required permanence and independence of ourselves, without being—as matter would otherwise be—something quite unknowable, in the sense that we can only infer it, and can never be directly and immediately aware of it.

Other philosophers since Berkeley have also held that, although the table does not depend for its existence upon being seen by me, it does depend upon being seen (or otherwise apprehended in sensation) by *some* mind—not necessarily the mind of God, but more often the whole collective mind of the universe. This they hold, as Berkeley does, chiefly because they think there can be nothing real—or at any rate nothing known to be real except minds and their thoughts and feelings. We might state the argument by which they support their view in some such way as this: "Whatever can be thought of is an idea in the mind of the person thinking of it; therefore nothing can be thought of except ideas in minds; therefore anything else is inconceivable, and what is inconceivable cannot exist."

Such an argument, in my opinion, is fallacious; and of course those who advance it do not put it so shortly or so crudely. But whether valid or not, the argument has been very widely advanced in one form or another; and very many philosophers, perhaps a majority, have held that there is nothing real except minds and their ideas. Such philosophers are called "idealists." When they come to explaining matter, they either say, like Berkeley, that matter is really nothing but a collection of ideas, or they say, like Leibniz (1646–1716), that what appears as matter is really a collection of more or less rudimentary minds.

But these philosophers, though they deny matter as opposed to mind, nevertheless, in another sense, admit matter. It will be remembered that we asked two questions; namely, (1) Is there a real table at all? (2) If so, what sort of object can it be? Now both Berkeley and Leibniz admit that there is a real table, but Berkeley says it is certain ideas in the mind of God, and Leibniz says it is a colony of souls. Thus both of them answer our first question in the affirmative, and only diverge from the views of ordinary mortals in their answer to our second question. In fact, almost all philosophers seem to be agreed that there is a real table. They almost all agree that, however much our sense-data—colour, shape, smoothness, etc.—may depend upon us, yet their occurrence is a sign of something existing independently of us, something differing, perhaps, completely from our sense-data whenever we are in a suitable relation to the real table.

Now obviously this point in which the philosophers are agreed—the view that there is a real table, whatever its nature may be is vitally important, and it will be worth while to consider what reasons there are for accepting this view before we go on to the further question as to the nature of the real table. Our next chapter, therefore, will be concerned with the reasons for supposing that there is a real table at all.

Before we go farther it will be well to consider for a moment what it is that we have discovered so far. It has appeared that, if we take any common object of the sort that is supposed to be known by the senses, what the senses *immediately* tell us is not the truth about the object as it is apart from us, but only the truth about certain sense-data which, so far as we can see, depend upon the relations between us and the object. Thus what we directly see and feel is merely "appearance", which we believe to be a sign of some "reality" behind. But if the reality is not what appears, have we any means of knowing whether there is any reality at all? And if so, have we any means of finding out what it is like?

Such questions are bewildering, and it is difficult to know that even the strangest hypotheses may not be true. Thus our familiar table, which has roused but the slightest thoughts in us hitherto, has become a problem full of surprising possibilities. The one thing we know about it is that it is not what it seems. Beyond this modest result, so far, we have the most complete liberty of conjecture. Leibniz tells us it is a community of souls: Berkeley tells us it is an idea in the mind of God; sober science, scarcely less wonderful, tells us it is a vast collection of electric charges in violent motion.

Among these surprising possibilities, doubt suggests that perhaps there is no table at all. Philosophy, if it cannot answer so many questions as we could wish, has at least the power of asking questions which increase the interest of the world, and show the strangeness and wonder lying just below the surface even in the commonest things of daily life.

QUESTIONS FOR REFLECTION

1. In his concluding paragraphs, Russell compares the accounts different philosophers likely would give concerning the reality of the table he discusses in his examples. Russell describes "sober science" as "scarcely less wonderful" than the explanations afforded by Leibniz and Berkeley. What does he mean by "sober science" in this context? On what grounds do you think Russell arrives at this characterization of "sober science?" Provide an argument supporting his claim; then compose an argument denying it.

2. Russell claims none of the characteristics we would associate with the table—color, texture, form—inherent to it. Reconstruct his argument. What does he mean by "are inherent to it?" Challenge yourself by constructing a counter-argument disproving Russell's conclusion.

3. Russell marks a distinction between the ways a "practical" person, a painter, and a philosopher might approach the problem of appearance and reality. Critically assess this distinction by constructing and answering questions that test its definitions. For example: Is the painter closer to a "practical" person or to a philosopher? How is the philosopher not practical? How is the practical person not a philosopher?

4. Russell suggests we may be tempted to believe objects observed with the aid of a microscope are "more real" than objects seen with the "naked eye." Why do you think we would believe that? What is Russell saying about so-called "tools of perception"?

5. Russell coins the term "sense-data" in order to distinguish between the characteristics we experience of the table and the table itself. According to Russell, we do not know the table "immediately;" our knowledge of the table is mediated by our perception of certain sense-data: color, form, texture, etc. What we have an immediate relationship to is our perception of the table, not the table itself. We thus infer the existence of the table, Russell argues, from our perception of these sense-data. What do you think Russell's concept of sense-data says about the space of experience? Where do we experience the table? Is our experience of the table outside of us or within our own perceptions? Is it public or private?

FIGURE 2.4A
Giorgio de Chirico's *Gare Montparnasse (The Melancholy of Departure)* (1914).

FIGURE 2.4B
Giorgio de Chirico's
Enigma of a Day (1914).

VISUAL CRITICAL THINKING EXERCISE

In Chapter 1, we discussed the relationship between critical thinking and critical visual analysis. Conduct critical visual analyses of Giorgio de Chirico's *Gare Montparnasse (The Melancholy of Departure)* and his *Enigma of a Day* and answer the following questions:

1. What decisions did de Chirico make to represent architecture? Is it closer to appearance or to reality?

2. In what ways does de Chirico's painting support Bertrand Russell's description of the painter in "Appearance and Reality"?

3. How does a "painterly representation" of architecture differ from architectural representation in the form of plans, section drawings, and orthogonal projections? Which is "more real?"

CRITICAL THINKING RESEARCH EXERCISE

Research Frank Lloyd Wright's Robie House (1916) by locating photographic images, section drawings, and plans of the house and reading accounts of its design and construction. Reverse engineer the design of the house based on the archival photographs, and reproduce the plans and section drawings by hand. Determine who Frank Lloyd Wright's client was for the house, then put yourself in the place of the architect and present the design proposal to your client. How does the identity of the client influence the language you would use in your presentation? How do representations of the design, as well as the built structure, influence how the house appears? What are the limits of the forms of representation you used to present your proposal?

FOR FURTHER READING

Plato. 1991. Book VII (514a–520a). In *The Republic of Plato*. Trans. Allan Bloom. New York: Basic Books.

3

What Is Form?
What Is Function?

FIGURE 3.1
Design for a flying machine operated by a man standing
upright; Leonardo da Vinci, 1488.

ARCH: Philo, in Chapter 1, "What is Critical Thinking?" you describe your exasperation while listening to a student's presentation during a studio crit. Along with the question of method that emerged from your story, another interesting problem seems to present itself in that experience, and that is the **relationship between form and function.**

PHILO: After emerging from the haze that can sometimes accompany a day-long critique, I reflected some more on that particular student and his project. I realized the reason why I was the only one who seemed to be stuck on the issue of the student's method was that the critics held the same assumptions the student did: it matters little how the architect arrives at the form that will house the project's program; the point is to arrive at something—anything (hopefully something interesting)—and then make the program fit the form.

ARCH: What name would you give to the assumption you are describing with this story?

PHILO: I would say what the student and the other critics seemed invested in was a kind of **formalism**, which disengaged form from any one-to-one relationship to program or function. The danger of this is that it treats architecture almost like sculpture, less about the people who might occupy it and more about how it appears in the landscape.

ARCH: Well, yes, that has certainly been one criticism of formalism, although I wouldn't say thinking of architecture as sculpture is necessarily a bad thing. What formalism assumes is that architecture should be aesthetically pleasing to the eye. Are you saying we shouldn't be concerned with aesthetics when we design?

PHILO: Of course not. But it works the same way for what might be opposed to formalism, that is to say, functionalism. **Functionalism** is the idea that form and function should strictly be derived from each other. The form and appearance of a building would be developed out of how the building is intended to be used and function.

ARCH: Yes, Louis Sullivan's famous slogan, "Form follows function."

PHILO: There are a plenty of buildings that have been characterized historically as functionalist that are at the same time aesthetically pleasing, so I think that's a false dilemma. Think of Alder & Sullivan's Auditorium Building (1885–1890), for example. Or Adolf Loos's House on Michaelerplatz in Vienna (1911–1912), also called the Loos Haus.

ARCH: Fine, but let's first delve further into the relationship between form and function that is presupposed in Sullivan's slogan. I want us to focus on the conceptual issues involved with defining form, function, and how these concepts are supposed to follow from the former to the latter.

PHILO: Yes, examining and understanding the root of the ideas, rather than just the personalities associated with movements in thought, is an important part of critical thinking.

ARCH: For me, this is the core question. Too often, discussions of architectural functionalism fail to depart from historical debates—which architect or building was functionalist, which was formalist—and thereby fail to ask about what motivates one to adopt one standpoint versus the other. Notice I say "motivates" in the present tense.

PHILO: Yes, Arch, though functionalism and formalism tend to be considered historical styles in architecture and design, they continue to appear as attitudes in contemporary design, as I learned in the critique I participated in.

ARCH: Even so-called "computationalism" is very fashionable these days in architecture. This movement makes claims to overcome the form-function opposition; however, it is lacking in the kind of questioning we're trying to undertake here. In any case, I would like to come back to the examples of the Auditorium Building and the Loos House after discussing, what I am calling, these conceptual issues.

Here is my question: What do you mean by function?

PHILO: Well, it's less a matter of what I mean by function than what function has meant in architecture and maybe even philosophy. So I don't think we can, or should, exclude history from our discussion. That seems like a bit of fantasy, in my judgment.

Understanding Aristotle's Four Causes

ARCH: Fine, of course that's right. Let's begin then with philosophical mean-
        ings of function. One I can think of immediately is Aristotle's.

PHILO: Absolutely. The idea that form follows function can be understood
        from the standpoint of Aristotle's theory of causation, of what brings
        something into existence. According to Aristotle, there are four kinds
        of cause that explain why something exists or how a certain state of
        affairs came to be. The *Stanford Encyclopedia of Philosophy* offers a
        good summary, using a bronze statue as an example.

        Let's take a look at Cao Chongen's bronze statue of Bruce Lee on the
        Avenue of Stars in Hong Kong.

FIGURE 3.2
Cao Chongen's statue of Bruce Lee on the Avenue of Stars in Hong Kong
illustrates Aristotle's theory of causation.

ARCH: So what are the four causes?

PHILO: According to Aristotle, there are four causes (he uses the term *aitia*) that answer "why" the bronze Bruce Lee came to be. I'm quoting from Book II of Aristotle's *Physics:*

1. A **material cause** "that out of which a thing comes to be and which persists"
2. A **formal cause** "the form or archetype" of a thing
3. An **efficient** or **primary cause** "the primary source of the change or coming to rest"
4. A **final cause** the "end or 'that for the sake of which' a thing is done"

ARCH: What is the material cause of Cao Chongen's *Bruce Lee?*

PHILO: Bronze. The statue's formal cause is the statue's shape. The organization of its parts, its position in a fighting stance, etc., *cause* it to be a statue *of* Bruce Lee. The statue's primary cause is what we typically think of as a causal relationship. It is the sculptor who shaped the material into a statue of Bruce Lee. The wish to commemorate Bruce Lee as one of Hong Kong's greatest stars serves as the final cause of the statue, the reason why the sculptor embarked on making the statue in the first place.

ARCH: An understanding of Aristotle's four causes shows us that functionalism unites the second and fourth notions of cause. In functionalism, the final cause of a building (what the building is to be used for) determines the building's form, and how its parts—or, in architectural terms, its plan—will be organized. Thus one thing that is presupposed in the phrase "form follows function" is the idea of cause, as well as several different types of causes at work; as long as we follow Aristotle's schema. There is a formal cause, a final cause, and the idea that the final cause—use, intention—of a building will serve as a cause to bring about a certain form.

Understanding the Notion That Form Follows Function

PHILO: Exactly. You can see the idea is at least as old as Aristotle. Even though it may make sense to us to unite those two notions of cause, we should be wary of thinking "form follows function" as self-evident or commonsensical. It is not the case that "everybody knows" form follows function; rather, the notion appears as common sense only after many people have taken it up and repeated it in their thinking and practices.

ARCH: Historically, the exact phrase "form follows function" appeared first in Sullivan's *Kindergarten Chats* (1901–02). Whether he was intentionally repeating themes that could originally be found in Aristotle is not the point; Sullivan's "chats" between an architectural master and an apprentice emphasize how Sullivan believed architecture *should* be designed. Moreover, as you just demonstrated, Sullivan can be seen to be elaborating Aristotle's original schema by linking formal and final causes together, recasting Aristotle's theory even as he is repeating aspects of it.

PHILO: Well, this helps to clarify one presupposition at work in functionalism, that function as an end or goal can cause a form to come about. But uncovering this presupposition raises more questions.

ARCH: Yes, especially as we work our way towards a discussion of the Auditorium Building and the Loos Haus, which we mentioned a moment ago.

PHILO: What other questions does this raise for you?

ARCH: I'm thinking of some of the issues Stanford Anderson outlines in his essay "The Fiction of Function." From my understanding, he poses two main points: (1) functionalism is a poor way to characterize all of modern architecture, and (2) it is not clear how exactly function *translates* into form.

PHILO: What is the reasoning behind Anderson's points?

ARCH: In terms of the first point, Anderson shows how no modern architect adhered exclusively to a functionalist design strategy, and those who have been labeled or even identified themselves as functionalist often differed radically from one another in their individual practices. This first point leads into Anderson's second point because it shows that every architect still has to *interpret* the meaning of this or that function in a certain way in order to come up with a form that would suit it.

PHILO: But there is a problem: How can you tell whether a building's form really suits a particular function? By just looking at it? By "experiencing" it? By "using" it? How does someone use a building?

ARCH: This is why Anderson calls "function"—again, what we would call nowadays "program"—a "fiction." It is first a *story* the architect tells about how his or her building is supposed to be used and how the form he or she has designed serves as a means for realizing that use.

PHILO: The problem you are describing is one of what philosophers since Plato have called *mimēsis,* imitation. What is assumed in "form follows function" is that a building's form should offer a mirror image of how the building functions.

ARCH: Exactly.

PHILO: The other way function is a fiction is in terms of how functionalism is used by architects and architectural historians as a stylistic label to characterize the whole of modern architecture when the "evidence," as you just summarized, is that the story was a lot messier, as history always is.

ARCH: Yes. In fact, as Anderson recounts, it was Henry-Russell Hitchcock and Philip Johnson's *The International Style* book and 1932 exhibition for the Museum of Modern Art in New York that greatly influenced modern architecture's identification with functionalism.

PHILO: Let's explore the messiness of history just a bit more though by turning as we promised earlier to Adler & Sullivan's Auditorium Building and Adolf Loos's House on Michaelerplatz. Why did you bring up these two examples Arch?

ARCH: I mentioned these two buildings earlier because they are both of the modern era in architecture, and both Sullivan and Loos expressed some manner of a functionalist attitude towards designing. Yet these two buildings are quite different in how they realize the relationship between form and function. I would say they contradict the whole idea that form follows function in some seamless and transparent way. As a result, they also present questions concerning not only how function should be interpreted, but how form should be understood.

PHILO: How so?

The Loos Haus

ARCH: You recall that the Loos Haus was originally a commission for the then well-known men's fashion atelier, Goldman and Salatsch. The project is sometimes referred to as being originally a department store, but that is misleading because it never resembled what we commonly associate with a department store. A department store typically has a relatively open plan, lots of glass, etc. Loos interpreted the program as having to do with tailoring, and as the architectural historian Leslie Topp details in her book *Architecture and Truth in Fin-de-Siècle Vienna*. Loos interpreted tailored clothing as a play between appearance and reality. Tailored clothing is designed to display certain parts of the body while keeping other parts hidden. Remember that this is at the end of the nineteenth century and the beginning of the twentieth. Men's business suits took on a certain "architecture" at the time that concealed the fact that, with the increased industrial production of commodities, men were becoming less active and less fit.

PHILO: How else did Loos design the space to function as an atelier?

ARCH: Well, Loos not only designed the rooms of the building to be appropriate to the kind of work performed in each room. Loos gave each workshop space a specific ceiling height appropriate to the kind of work being performed inside. For example, a seamstresses had a room with a 6-foot, 10-inch ceiling height, 17 feet was allocated for the ironing room to offer proper ventilation.[1] He also designed the display areas with twists and turns to conceal the connection of the interior spaces. The entering customers could not see the whole of the shop as in a conventional department store; instead, they had to discover it.

PHILO: I see. So he also used form to hide function in some ways? Isn't this contradictory to the "form follows function" logic?

ARCH: For the author of the famous essay "Ornament and Crime" (1908), in which he argues for an "honest" architecture free of ornament, the Loos Haus' interior certainly seems contradictory. It can be said to express the building's function as a tailoring shop as long as you accept Loos's view of tailoring as a play between appearance and reality.

PHILO: But then, is it being honest or not by concealing parts of the building from the spectator's view?

ARCH: The building's façade, especially, intensifies this kind of question, I would think. Though it was originally controversial because of the lack of ornamentation in its upper flights, it also displays non-load-bearing columns on the ground level, which serve no architectural function, at least in terms of an engineering or tectonic sense.

PHILO: So are they ornamental? Or is the ornament a kind of honesty about tailoring and clothing?

ARCH: Well, we now see how difficult it can be to keep a clear idea about how form and function translate into one another.

PHILO: Indeed. How far do we extend form? Where does the form of a building end and where does it begin? When does a building perform its intended function and when does it cease to perform this function? Who decides a building's function? And for how long? Don't the very same questions arise regarding the Auditorium Building?

FIGURE 3.3
Adolf Loos, Haus am Michaelerplatz, (1911–1912), Vienna, Austria

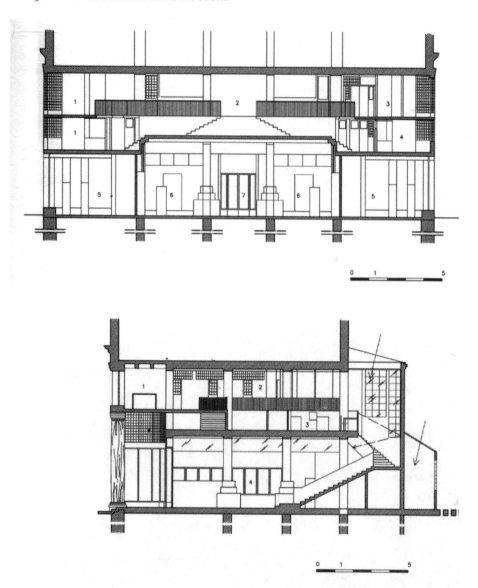

FIGURE 3.4
Section of Haus am Michaelerplatz.

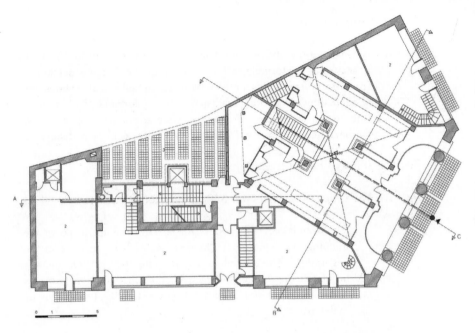

FIGURE 3.5
Plan sections of Haus am Michaelerplatz.

The Auditorium Building

ARCH: I would say the very same questions arise regarding *any* building or design, but yes, certainly. Although the Auditorium Building's history is very different. The Auditorium building was always intended to house a mixed-use program, and there was no controversy around its construction in the manner witnessed around the Loos Haus. Also, Sullivan never eschewed ornament the way Loos did. The Auditorium Building opens itself to contradiction, but only if we insist on interpreting Sullivan's design theory in strict, mechanical terms.

PHILO: How do you mean?

Questioning Formalism

ARCH: Here is where careful reading of Sullivan's writings is crucial. Although he may offer the formula of "form follows function" in one instance in the *Kindergarten Chats,* in the next instance Sullivan also states one shouldn't design with blind allegiance to any formula. "Form follows function" is not a plug-and-chug operation, as one says in physics and mathematics. It is what you philosophers call a **regulative ideal**.

PHILO: It is a goal towards which you direct your actions.

ARCH: Yes. Listen to Sullivan's words. Regarding formulas, he says:

> . . . formulas are dangerous things. They are apt to prove the undoing of a genuine art, however helpful they may be in the beginning to the individual. The formula of an art remains and becomes more rigid with time, while the spirit of that art escapes and vanishes forever. It cannot live in text-books, in formulas, or in definitions.[2]

As for form and function, he writes:

> We may talk for years on the inter-relationship of function and form, and get only an average and a fairly good start. But it will be a right start, I believe. We may, perhaps, see where the end lies, but it will be, like a star in the sky, unreachable and of unknown distance; or it will be like life itself, elusive to the last, even in death. Or it will be like a phantom beacon on a phantom stormy sea; or as a voice calling afar in the woods; or, like the shadow of a cloud upon a cloud, it will remain diaphanous and imponderable, floating in the still air of the spirit.[3]

PHILO: When we think of these statements in terms of the Auditorium Building's history, we can understand why both Adler and Sullivan were frustrated by the Auditorium Association's Board of Directors' desire to minimize the amount of ornamentation on the building's façade.

ARCH: Yes, the façade's ornamentation, displayed in Adler & Sullivan's early designs, was intended to match the ornamentation of the building's interior, which remained consistent throughout the phases of the building's design and construction. The façade's ornamentation was intended as a sign for the onlooker to read the function of the building as one of housing the various arts.

PHILO: So once again we arrive at the question of form and its limit. But we also arrive at the question of the life of function. Like the Loos Haus, which is now a bank, the Auditorium Building is no longer an arts center and hotel. Roosevelt University now occupies the building. Is this an unintended use of the building, or can we say, with Sullivan's remark concerning the life of function, that Adler & Sullivan's design somehow anticipated this future use of the building, or at least kept the question of function open for future lives of the building?

ARCH: "Life" here is the key term, especially for Sullivan, but I think also for Loos. If form is to express a function, which could be *read* by the onlooker or occupant of architecture, then function is really a substitution for "life," the fact that people use architecture and designed

FIGURE 3.6

"Form follows Function" in the Auditorium Building, designed by Louis Sullivan and Dankmar Adler, Chicago, 1886-1889; exterior street view.

space in order to carry out what the twentieth century Austrian philosopher Ludwig Wittgenstein called "forms of life."

PHILO: But architecture is not just a container that allows for use. It can also
display possible forms of life; it can have a projective quality, not just
a representative quality to it.

FIGURE 3.7
Interior view of the Auditorium Building, which was designed to combine
an opera house, offices, and hotel within a single structure.

ARCH: Oh, yes. Absolutely, which is why Le Corbusier's famous definition
of the house as a *machine à habiter*—a **machine for living**—is, in my
opinion, too mechanistic, too task-oriented. Living is not the same
thing as life, is it? Architecture projects possibilities of forms of life;
it does not, or at least should not, distribute prescriptions for living.
In fact, this reminds me of a text I wanted to discuss since we began
this conversation, Horatio Greenough's "American Architecture"
(1843).

PHILO: I'm not familiar with it.

ARCH: That's because Greenough is often left out of discussions of functionalism, even though his work predates that of Sullivan and Loos
and certainly Le Corbusier. In his work, we find all the themes we
discussed earlier—communication, expression, the limits of form and
function, life—and we can see his writings taking place at a crucial
point in American history. Did you know he placed himself in debate
with none other than Thomas Jefferson?

PHILO: Regarding what?

ARCH: Regarding the proper forms *American* architecture should adopt.
This is the beginning of the United States, so at the time, there was
no American architecture to really speak of. The really interesting
question here is: how does one invent what is called an architectural
vernacular, a way of speaking in architectural terms that expresses a
cultural sentiment? How do you design an architecture for a country
which, in the American case, was not only just born but whose birth
is predicated on making a break from all the old regimes of Europe?

PHILO: Yes, these are major questions of form expressing not only function
but cultural identity. Let's read the text and come together again to
discuss it.

CRITICAL READING PASSAGE

"American Architecture,"
from *Form and Function*
Horatio Greenough
1843

ABOUT THE AUTHOR

Horatio Greenough (1805–1852) was an American sculptor and landscape architect. Born in Boston, he graduated from Harvard in 1825 and then trained in Rome, Italy, eventually establishing a permanent studio in Florence. He is famous for a controversial statue of George Washington he completed in 1841, which was commissioned by the United States Congress and installed originally in the Rotunda of the Capitol. Modeled after Zeus from Ancient Greek mythology, the statue depicted Washington partially clothed, which many found offensive.

Interestingly enough, Greenough's 1843 essay, "American Architecture," advocates breaking-away from Classical forms in favor of founding an architecture that would convey a unique American identity, rather than simply imitate Classical architectural forms. Though the American architect Louis Sullivan is credited with coining the phrase "form follows function," it is actually Greenough who first emphasized the connection between form and function in the American architectural context, thereby anticipating American functionalism by half a century.

We have heard the learned in matters relating to art express the opinion that these United States are destined to form a new style of architecture. Remembering that a vast population, rich in material and guided by the experience, the precepts, and the models of the Old World, was about to erect durable structures for every function of civilized life, we also cherished the hope that such a combination would speedily be formed.

We forgot that, though the country was young, yet the people were old; that as Americans we have no childhood, no half-fabulous, legendary wealth, no misty, cloud-enveloped background. We forgot that we had not unity of religious belief, nor unity of origin; that our territory, extending from the white bear to the alligator, made our occupations dissimilar, our character and tastes various. We forgot that the Republic had leaped full-grown and armed to the teeth from the brain of her parent, and that a hammer had been the instrument of delivery. We forgot that reason had been the dry nurse of the giant offspring, and had fed her from the beginning with the strong bread and meat of fact; that every wry face the bantling ever made had been daguerreotyped, and all her words and deeds printed and labeled away in the pigeonholes of official bureaus.

Reason can dissect, but cannot originate; she can adopt, but cannot create; she can modify, but cannot find. Give her but a cockboat, and she will elaborate a line-of-battle ship; give her but a beam with its wooden tooth, and she turns out the patent plow. She is not young; and when her friends insist upon the phenomena of youth, then is she least attractive. She can imitate the flush of the young cheek, but where is the flash of the young eye? She buys the teeth—alas! she cannot buy the breath of childhood. The puny cathedral of Broadway,[1] like an elephant dwindled to the size of a dog, measures her yearning for Gothic sublimity, while the roar of the Astor House, and the mammoth vase of the great reservoir, shows how she works when she feels at home and is in earnest.

The mind of this country has never been seriously applied to the subject of building. Intently engaged in matters of more pressing importance, we have been content to receive our notions of architecture as we have received the fashion of our garments and the form of our entertainments, from Europe. In our eagerness to appropriate, we have neglected to adapt, to distinguish,—nay, to understand. We have built small Gothic temples of wood and have omitted all ornaments for economy, unmindful that size, material, and ornament are the elements of effect in that style of building. Captivated by the classic symmetry of the Athenian models, we have sought to bring the Parthenon into

---

* In *English Traits* (1856), Emerson said of this essay that it "announced in advance the leading thoughts of Mr. Ruskin on the *morality* in architecture, notwithstanding the antagonism of their views of the history of art." Greenough's "American Architecture" was first published in 1843, in the *United States Magazine and Democratic Review*. Ruskin's *Seven Lamps of Architecture*, in which he indicated his idea that the buildings and art of a people express their morality, first appeared in 1849.

[1] The reference is apparently to Trinity Church, which was completed in 1846. Trinity is a sizable church, but puny if compared with the great European cathedrals.

our streets, to make the temple of Theseus work in our towns.[2] We have shorn them of their lateral colonnades, let them down from their dignified platform, pierced their walls for light, and, instead of the storied relief and the eloquent statue which enriched the frieze and graced the pediment, we have made our chimneytops to peer over the broken profile and tell, by their rising smoke, of the traffic and desecration of the interior. Still the model may be recognized, some of the architectural features are entire; like the captive king, stripped alike of arms and purple and drudging amid the Helots of a capital, the Greek temple, as seen among us, claims pity for its degraded majesty, and attests the barbarian force which has abused its nature and been blind to its qualities.

If we trace architecture from its perfection in the days of Pericles to its manifest decay in the reign of Constantine, we shall find that one of the surest symptoms of decline was the adoption of admired forms and models for purposes not contemplated in their invention. The forum became a temple; the tribunal became a temple; the theater was turned into a church; nay, the column, that organized member, that subordinate part, set up for itself, usurped unity, and was a monument! The great principles of architecture being once abandoned, correctness gave way to novelty, economy and vainglory associated produced meanness and pretension. Sculpture, too, had waned. The degenerate workmen could no longer match the fragments they sought to mingle, nor copy the originals they only hoped to repeat. The moldering remains of better days frowned contempt upon such impotent efforts, till, in the gradual coming of darkness, ignorance became contempt, and insensibility ceased to compare.

We say that the mind of this country has never been seriously applied to architecture. True it is that the commonwealth, with that desire of public magnificence which has ever been a leading feature of democracy, has called from the vasty deep of the past the spirits of the Greek, the Roman, and the Gothic styles; but they would not come when she did call to them! The vast cathedral, with its ever-open portals, towering high above the courts of kings, inviting all men to its cool and fragrant twilight, where the voice of the organ stirs the blood, and the dim-seen visions of saints and martyrs bleed and die upon the canvas amid the echoes of hymning voices and the clouds of frankincense — this architectural embodying of the divine and blessed words, "Come to me, ye who labor and are heavy laden, and I will give you rest!" demands a sacrifice of what we hold dearest. Its cornerstone must be laid upon the right to judge the claims of the church. The style of Greek architecture, as seen in the Greek temple, demands the aid of sculpture, insists upon every feature of its original organization, loses its harmony if a note be dropped in the execution, and when so modified as to serve for a customhouse or bank, departs from its original beauty and propriety as widely as the crippled gelding of a hackney coach differs from the bounding and neighing wild horse of the desert. Even where, in the fervor of our faith in shapes, we have sternly adhered to the dictum of

---

[2] "The public sentiment just now runs almost exclusively and popularly into the Grecian school. We build little besides temples for our churches, our banks, our court-houses, and our dwellings. A friend of mine has just built a brewery on the Temple of the Winds."—Aristabulus Bragg, in Cooper's novel, *Home As Found* (1838).

another age, and have actually succeeded in securing the entire exterior which echoes the forms of Athens, the pile stands a stranger among us, and receives a respect akin to what we should feel for a fellow citizen in the garb of Greece. It is a make-believe. It is not the real thing. We see the marble capitals; we trace the acanthus leaves of a celebrated model—incredulous;[3] it is not a temple.

The number and variety of our experiments in building show the dissatisfaction of the public taste with what has been hitherto achieved; the expense at which they have been made proves how strong is the yearning after excellence; the talents and acquirements of the artists whose services have been engaged in them are such as to convince us that the fault lies in the system, not in the men. Is it possible that out of this chaos order can arise?—that of these conflicting dialects and jargons a language can be born? When shall we have done with experiments? What refuge is there from the absurdities that have successively usurped the name and functions of architecture? Is it not better to go on with consistency and uniformity, in imitation of an admired model, than incur the disgrace of other failures? In answering these questions let us remember with humility that all salutary changes are the work of many and of time; but let us encourage experiment at the risk of license, rather than submit to an iron rule that begins by sacrificing reason, dignity, and comfort. Let us consult nature, and in the assurance that she will disclose a mine richer than was ever dreamed of by the Greeks, in art as well as in philosophy. Let us regard as ingratitude to the author of nature the despondent idleness that sits down while one want is unprovided for, one worthy object unattained.

If, as the first step in our search after the great principles of construction, we but observe the skeletons and skins of animals, through all the varieties of beast and bird, of fish and insect, are we not as forcibly struck by their variety as by their beauty? There is no arbitrary law of proportion, no unbending model of form. There is scarce a part of the animal organization which we do not find elongated or shortened, increased, diminished, or suppressed, as the wants of the genus or species dictate, as their exposure or their work may require. The neck of the swan and that of the eagle, however different in character and proportion, equally charm the eye and satisfy the reason. We approve the length of the same member in grazing animals, its shortness in beasts of prey. The horse's shanks are thin, and we admire them; the greyhound's chest is deep, and we cry, beautiful! It is neither the presence nor the absence of this or that part, or shape, or color, that wins our eye in natural objects; it is the consistency and harmony of the parts juxtaposed, the subordination of details to masses, and of masses to the whole.

The law of adaptation is the fundamental law of nature in all structure. So unflinchingly does she modify a type in accordance with a new position, that some philosophers have declared a variety of appearance to be the object aimed at; so entirely does she limit the modification to the demands of necessity,

---

[3] In Greenough's pseudonymous *Travels* this is "incredulous odi" for *incredulus odi* in Horace's line, "Quodcunque ostendis mihi sic incredulus odi" ("Scenes put before me in this way move only my incredulity and disgust").

that adherence to one original plan seems, to limited intelligence, to be carried to the very verge of caprice. The domination of arbitrary rules of taste has produced the very counterpart of the wisdom thus displayed in every object around us; we tie up the camelopard to the rack; we shave the lion, and call him a dog; we strive to bind the unicorn with his band in the furrow, and make him harrow the valleys after us!

When the savage of the South Sea islands shapes his war club, his first thought is of its use. His first efforts pare the long shaft, and mold the convenient handle; then the heavier end takes gradually the edge that cuts, while it retains the weight that stuns. His idler hour divides its surface by lines and curves, or embosses it with figures that have pleased his eye or are linked with his superstition. We admire its effective shape, its Etruscan-like quaintness, its graceful form and subtle outline, yet we neglect the lesson it might teach. If we compare the form of a newly invented machine with the perfected type of the same instrument, we observe, as we trace it through the phases of improvement, how weight is shaken off where strength is less needed, how functions are made to approach without impeding each other, how straight becomes curved, and the curve is straightened, till the straggling and cumbersome machine becomes the compact, effective, and beautiful engine.

So instinctive is the perception of organic beauty in the human eye, that we cannot withhold our admiration even from the organs of destruction. There is majesty in the royal paw of the lion, music in the motion of the brindled tiger; we accord our praise to the sword and the dagger, and shudder our approval of the frightful aptitude of the ghastly guillotine.

Conceiving destruction to be a normal element of the system of nature equally with production, we have used the word beauty in connection with it. We have no objection to exchange it for the word character, as indicating the mere adaptation of forms to functions, and would gladly substitute the actual pretensions of our architecture to the former, could we hope to secure the latter.

Let us now turn to a structure of our own, one which, from its nature and uses, commands us to reject authority, and we shall find the result of the manly use of plain good sense, so like that of taste, and genius too, as scarce to require a distinctive title. Observe a ship at sea! Mark the majestic form of her hull as she rushes through the water, observe the graceful bend of her body, the gentle transition from round to flat, the grasp of her keel, the leap of her bows, the symmetry and rich tracery of her spars and rigging, and those grand wind muscles, her sails. Behold an organization second only to that of an animal, obedient as the horse, swift as the stag, and bearing the burden of a thousand camels from pole to pole! What academy of design, what research of connoisseurship, what imitation of the Greeks produced this marvel of construction? Here is the result of the study of man upon the great deep, where Nature spake of the laws of building, not in the feather and in the flower, but in winds and waves, and he bent all his mind to hear and to obey.[4] Could we carry into our civil architecture the responsibilities that weigh upon our shipbuilding, we should ere long have edifices as superior to the Parthenon, for the purposes that we require, as the *Constitution* or the *Pennsylvania* is to the galley of the Argonauts. Could our blunders on terra firma be put to the same dread test that those of shipbuilders are, little would be now left to say on this subject.

Instead of forcing the functions of every sort of building into one general form, adopting an outward shape for the sake of the eye or of association, without reference to the inner distribution, let us begin from the heart as the nucleus, and work outward. The most convenient size and arrangement of the rooms that are to constitute the building being fixed, the access of the light that may, of the air that must be wanted, being provided for, we have the skeleton of our building. Nay, we have all excepting the dress. The connection and order of parts, juxtaposed for convenience, cannot fail to speak of their relation and uses. As a group of idlers on the quay, if they grasp a rope to haul a vessel to the pier, are united in harmonious action by the cord they seize, as the slowly yielding mass forms a thorough-bass to their livelier movement, so the unflinching adaptation of a building to its position and use gives, as a sure product of that adaptation, character and expression.

What a field of study would be opened by the adoption in civil architecture of those laws of apportionment, distribution, and connection which we have thus hinted at? No longer could the mere tyro huddle together a crowd of ill-arranged, ill-lighted, and stifled rooms and, masking the chaos with the sneaking copy of a Greek façade, usurp the name of architect. If this anatomic connection and proportion has been attained in ships, in machines, and, in spite of false principles, in such buildings as made a departure from it fatal, as in bridges and in scaffolding, why should we fear its immediate use in all construction? As its first result, the bank would have the physiognomy of a bank, the church would be recognized as such, nor would the billiard room and the chapel wear the same uniform of columns and pediment. The African king, standing in mock majesty with his legs and feet bare, and his body clothed in a cast coat of the Prince Regent, is an object whose ridiculous effect defies all power of face. Is not the Greek temple jammed in between the brick shops of Wall Street or Cornhill, covered with lettered signs, and occupied by groups of money-changers and applewomen, a parallel even for his African majesty?

We have before us a letter in which Mr. Jefferson recommends the model of the Maison Carrée for the State House at Richmond. Was he aware that the Maison Carrée is but a fragment, and that, too, of a Roman temple? He was; it is beautiful—is the answer. An English society erected in Hyde Park a cast in bronze of the colossal Achilles of the Quirinal, and, changing the head,

---

[4] Greenough would not allow a figurehead, certainly not a carved wooden statue painted in imitation of marble, as an embellishment to a ship. Having remarked one that had lost both arms and a leg, he wrote: "I was delighted with another proof that I had found of the perfect organization of ships, viz., that the only part of the hull where function will allow a statue to stand without being in Jack's way is one where the plunge bath so soon demolishes it!"—*Travels*, p. 179.

transformed it into a monument to Wellington. But where is the distinction between the personal prowess, the invulnerable body, the heaven-shielded safety of the hero of the Iliad and the complex of qualities which makes the modern general? The statue is beautiful—is the answer. If such reasoning is to hold, why not translate one of Pindar's odes in memory of Washington, or set up in Carolina a colossal Osiris in honor of General Greene?

The monuments of Egypt and of Greece are sublime as expressions of their power and their feeling. The modern nation that appropriates them displays only wealth in so doing. The possession of means, not accompanied by the sense of propriety or feeling for the true, can do no more for a nation than it can do for an individual. The want of an illustrious ancestry may be compensated, fully compensated; but the purloining of the coat-of-arms of a defunct family is intolerable. That such a monument as we have described should have been erected in London while Chantrey flourished, when Flaxman's fame was cherished by the few, and Baily and Behnes were already known, is an instructive fact. That the illustrator of the Greek poets and of the Lord's Prayer should in the meanwhile have been preparing designs for George the Fourth's silversmiths, is not less so.

The edifices in whose construction the principles of architecture are developed may be classed as organic, formed to meet the wants of their occupants, or monumental, addressed to the sympathies, the faith, or the taste of a people. These two great classes of buildings, embracing almost every variety of structure, though occasionally joined and mixed in the same edifice, have their separate rules, as they have a distinct abstract nature. In the former class the laws of structure and apportionment, depending on definite wants, obey a demonstrable rule. They may be called machines each individual of which must be formed with reference to the abstract type of its species. The individuals of the latter class, bound by no other laws than those of the sentiment which inspires them, and the sympathies to which they are addressed, occupy the positions and assume the forms best calculated to render their parent feeling. No limits can be put to their variety; their size and richness have always been proportioned to the means of the people who have erected them.

If, from what has been thus far said, it shall have appeared that we regard the Greek masters as aught less than the true apostles of correct taste in building, we have been misunderstood. We believe firmly and fully that they can teach us; but let us learn principles, not copy shapes; let us imitate them like men, and not ape them like monkeys. Remembering what a school of art it was that perfected their system of ornament, let us rather adhere to that system in enriching what we invent than substitute novelty for propriety. After observing the innovations of the ancient Romans, and of the modern Italian masters in this department, we cannot but recur to the Horatian precept—

"exemplaria Graeca Nocturna versate manu, versate diurna!"

To conclude: The fundamental laws of building found at the basis of every style of architecture must be the basis of ours. The adaptation of the forms and magnitude of structures to the climate they are exposed to, and the offices for which they are intended, teaches us to study our own varied wants in these respects.[5] The harmony of their ornaments with the nature that they embellished, and the institutions from which they sprang, calls on us to do the like justice to our country, our government, and our faith. As a Christian preacher may give weight to truth, and add persuasion to proof, by studying the models of pagan writers, so the American builder by a truly philosophic investigation of ancient art will learn of the Greeks to be American.

The system of building we have hinted at cannot be formed in a day. It requires all the science of any country to ascertain and fix the proportions and arrangements of the members of a great building, to plant it safely on the soil, to defend it from the elements, to add the grace and poetry of ornament to its frame. Each of these requisites to a good building requires a special study and a lifetime. Whether we are destined soon to see so noble a fruit may be doubtful; but we can, at least, break the ground and throw in the seed.

We are fully aware that many regard all matters of taste as matters of pure caprice and fashion. We are aware that many think our architecture already perfect; but we have chosen, during this sultry weather, to exercise a truly American right—the right of talking. This privilege, thank God, is unquestioned—from Miller,[6] who, robbing Béranger, translates into fanatical prose, "Finissons-en! le monde est assez vieux!" to Brisbane,[7] who declares that the same world has yet to begin, and waits a subscription of two hundred thousand dollars in order to start. Each man is free to present his notions on any subject. We have also talked, firm in the belief that the development of a nation's taste in art depends on a thousand deep-seated influences beyond the ken of the ignorant present; firm in the belief that freedom and knowledge will bear the fruit of refinement and beauty, we have yet dared to utter a few words of discontent, a few crude thoughts of what might be, and we feel the better for it. We promised ourselves nothing more than that satisfaction which Major Downing[8] attributes to every man "who has had his say, and then cleared out," and we already have a pleasant consciousness of what he meant by it.

---

[5] "The fault just now is perhaps to consult the books too rigidly, and to trust too little to invention; for no architecture, and especially no domestic architecture, can ever be above reproach, until climate, the uses of the edifice, and the situation, are respected as leading considerations. Nothing can be uglier, *per se*, than a Swiss cottage, or anything more beautiful under its precise circumstances. As regards these mushroom temples which are the offspring of Mammon, let them be dedicated to whom they may, I should exactly reverse the opinion and say, that while nothing can be much more beautiful, *per se*, nothing can be in worse taste than to put them where they are"—*Cooper's Home As Found* (1838).

[6] William Miller, founder of the sect of Millerites, who prophesied that the world would be destroyed in 1843.

[7] Albert Brisbane, the father of American Fourierism. Proposals for one of his communal "Associations" called for public subscription to $400,000 of capital stock, half of which must be paid in cash.

[8] Major Downing was the pseudonym of Seba Smith, in his letters in Yankee dialect.

QUESTIONS FOR REFLECTION

1. In his essay, Greenough argues that Americans should "learn principles" from the Greeks, "not copy shapes" from them. What examples of Greek principles does Greenough offer?

2. How does copying just the shapes of Greek architecture show, in Greenough's judgment, a disregard for history and particular forms of life?

3. How does Greenough's description of the temple's formalism inform his criticism of Thomas Jefferson?

CRITICAL THINKING RESEARCH EXERCISE

Research Robert Mills's original 1836 proposal for the Washington Monument. Using Greenough's argument from "American Architecture," formulate a critique of Mills's proposal. (Alternately, students may construct a dialogue between Mills and Greenough discussing the merits and flaws of Mills's proposal.) Then read Greenough's actual critique of Mills from his 1851 essay "Aesthetics at Washington." Where were you right in imagining how Greenough would criticize Mill? Where were you wrong?

VISUAL CRITICAL THINKING EXERCISE

Select two objects in the same category, e.g., restaurant interiors, residential facades, athletic shoes, chairs, laptops, but that are very different in appearance. Provide images of both. Compare and contrast their function. Who defines their function? The client? The designer or architect? Someone else or other group? How does the form of each support its function? Describe any ways in which the form of each anticipates or generates new functions.

❦ FOR FURTHER READING ❦

Falcon, Andrea. "Aristotle on Causality." http://plato.stanford.
edu/entries/aristotle-causality/

Aristotle, *Physics* II, Ch 3.

Anderson, Stanford. 1987. "The Fiction of Function." *Assemblage* 2:19–31.

Greenough, Horatio. 1843. "Aesthetics at Washington," "American
Architecture." In *Form and Function: Remarks on Art, Design, and
Architecture.* Ed. Harold A. Small. 1947. Berkeley, Los Angeles, London:
University of California Press.

Loos, Adolf. 1908. "Ornament and Crime." In *Ornament and Crime.* Trans.
Michael Mitchell. 1997. Riverside, CA: Ariadne Books.

Topp, Leslie. 2004. *Architecture and Truth in Fin-de-Siècle Vienna.* Cambridge:
Cambridge University Press.

Wittgenstein, Ludwig. 1953. *Philosophical Investigations.* Trans. G.E.M.
Anscombe. 3rd ed. New York: Macmillan.

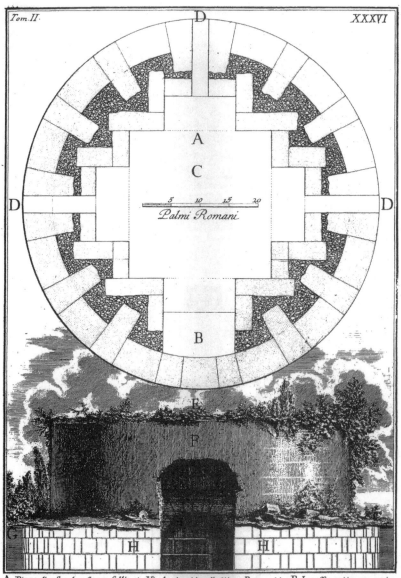

A. Pianta d'un Sepolcro situato sull'antica Via Appia vicino alla Vigna Buonamici. B Ingresso oggi in parte rovina-
to. C Stanza quadrata con Nicchioni nei lati. D Finestre in parte interrate dalle Rovine. E Elevazione.
F Masso fabbricato a Corsi di scaglie di Selce con Calce, e Puzzolana. G Piano presente della Campagna. H Traver-
tini, i quali vestivano tutto l'esterno del Sepolcro, ora coperti dal terreno: poichè quelli, che restavano sopra terra, sono
stati staccati dal Masso, ed asportati altrove.

4

What Is Place?

FIGURE 4.1
Giovanni Battista Piranesi's use of an architectural plan coupled with a rendered elevation gives the viewer a sense of articulated space and how it is experienced as a unique place.

ARCH: Allow me to start the discussion of "place" with the first line in Wallace Steven's poem *Theory*, which we introduced in Chapter 1 on critical thinking:

> I am what is around me

This line provokes many associations in all areas of design. It goes to the core of many beginning questions of design education.

PHILO: In which ways?

ARCH: I would like to break, for a moment, with the customary professional jargon and speak of the word **place** in a more general way. In everyday language one may say, "I found my place!" or ask, "Is this the right place for me? "We put them in their place!" These are all familiar sayings. So again, what does it mean for someone to say, "I found my place"? It generally means that one is pleased with where one is "in life." It is a declaration that a person has staked out a personal comfort zone, a space where he or she is "at home." This, we might say, is a somewhat difficult state of mind to achieve within an increasingly globalized, mobile, and culturally interconnected world of today. Such questions, although not strictly design related, are nevertheless pertinent if a design student is to think critically beyond the narrow problem-solving task of a designer or architect.

The image of the tenant's home beside the Mississippi perfectly illustrates this quotation: "To settle in the landscape means to delimit an area, a place. We stop our wandering and say: *Here!* Then we create an 'inside' within an encompassing 'outside.' The settlement is therefore a point of arrival."[1]

PHILO: Can you talk more specifically about design education and the concept of place?

ARCH: Again, the poem's first line provides a perfect starting point to begin thinking about the concept of place. All beginning design studios, from fashion design to industrial design, interior design, and architecture, start with the question of the body in space, be it clothing, a chair, a room, a house. This includes the large scale of urban and landscape design commonly called the **city**. At all **scales**, the question of the body and its place is part of any design studio. Whenever we ask, "Where am I?" or "Where does *here* end and *there* begin?" we are identifying the body and its place in **space**.

FIGURE 4.2
Tenant's home beside the Mississippi River
(near Lake Providence, Louisiana).

These questions apply at all design scales from the dress you wear
and how you move in it, to the spot your bed occupies in your house,
to your favorite place at the dinner table, as well as to your neighborhood, your city, and a geographic region and its landscape.

The ultimate goal of design is to create unique memorable places,
site-specific and time-appropriate, as well as functional places that
are comprehensible and legible. We will return to the subject of
design, architecture, and "memory" in Chapter 9. For the moment, I
think it would be worthwhile discussing just what we mean by *place*,
especially in distinction to space. The body, which I also mentioned,
deserves its own chapter as well (Chapter 8). But Philo, undoubtedly
you have recognized the philosophical references I've made. You must
have something to say.

PHILO: Interestingly enough, **space** and place have been distinguished from
one another throughout the history of philosophy and architecture,
though not always in the same ways.

ARCH: In architecture, one typically says that an architect designs spaces,
which then are hoped to take on unique characteristics as places.

PHILO: Yes, that's how I see the distinction in architecture. *Space* is an objective, quantitative term. It can be measured. *Place* is a qualitative, subjective term. One gets a sense of a place from the way one has a feeling regarding a thing, whether it is a feeling of sentimentality or horror or something in between. Architects, and designers in general, can say all they want about evoking a sense of place, but I think most of that depends on conditions outside their control. They can't legislate over a feeling of place.

ARCH: What about the philosophical distinction between space and place?

Classical Meanings of Space and Place

PHILO: Space and place were popular themes in early Greek philosophy. The Presocratics, like Anaximander, Anaxagoras, and Anaximenes, constructed competing theories of space and place. One term they often employed in their discussions what that of *peras,* **boundary**. Aristotle would use *peras* as a way to define his concept of place, which he designated with the word *topos* (from where we get the words topology and topography), as a way to distinguish place from the Platonic notion of space or *khôra*.

ARCH: Plato uses the term *khôra* for space in his dialogue, the *Timaeus*.

PHILO: Yes, it's often translated as "the receptacle" because Plato's understanding of space was that it was like a vacuum. It wasn't a thing itself, but a container that received things. I'm simplifying things drastically here; it's much, much more complicated than that, but the basic gist is correct. Philosophers and classicists continue to debate the meaning of Plato's *khôra* to this day.

ARCH: Yes, as well as Aristotle's concept of place.

PHILO: Indeed. For Aristotle, a thing's place is its boundary (*peras*), and its boundary is that which immediately surrounds it (*periekhein*). One notable scholar has described Aristotle's conception of place as the "*space* [a thing] *fits into*."[2]

ARCH: *To perikhein*—that which surrounds. "I am what is around me!"

PHILO: Yes, in a way, you can read Stevens's first line from an Aristotelian standpoint, sure. However, let's not go so fast.

ARCH: Why not?

PHILO: Well, when I say, "I am what is around me," what do I mean exactly? The air, this table at which we are seated, you, with whom I am speaking?

ARCH: Of course, that's what is meant by that which surrounds, no?

PHILO: No. Aristotle contends that a thing's place is determined by that which limits it or surrounds it in a "maximal" sense.[3] So "my" place is determined not by you, this table, or the air, but rather by that which contains all these things and limits "me."

ARCH: That does complicate things.

PHILO: Our question need not be an epistemological one. It shouldn't be how we know what actually surrounds us and how. That's philosophy, even science, perhaps. In terms of design, I would think the problem of place has a different resonance.

The Modern Designer's Concept of Space and Place

ARCH: Yes, of course. The question of "What is around me?" belongs to what we described in Chapter 1 on critical thinking as the "I discourse." It belongs to the issue of where "I" begin in relationship to my surroundings, which I take to mean my environment, my living space, my friends, my neighborhood, my city, etc., etc. How do we measure such things design-wise? Where does a site begin and end? Doesn't the problem of place reveal how design can actually intervene in determining limits, and, therefore, places? Should these limits be determined solely in relation to me and my body? What about other people and their bodies? Don't they have a claim on space as far as their places are concerned? You see what I mean when I suggest that these philosophical questions have close links to design question at all scales?

Now we have arrived to the central design question at any scale: What is a boundary? What does it mean to design a private space for one person or a group? What is an area rug? What is a room? What is a wall that separates one place from another? What is a vestibule in a house or a lobby in a large building as an entry space? What is the edge of a neighborhood? What is the boundary of a city center? And so on. You see what I mean?

PHILO: Yes, I see. That raises another interesting question regarding "where" a boundary is located, doesn't it? If a place is a qualitative concept, then how do we know where a place begins and ends? What does this say about identity? If I am what is around me, then am I ever the same person? Because my surroundings change, doesn't my identity— don't "I"—change? What about group identities, then? This recalls Heraclitus's famous fragment regarding change: that we never step into the same river twice. If both Heraclitus and Stevens are right, then I am never the same "I" twice.

ARCH: In a way, I think many designers believe this, or at least count on this. Think about it. If place and identity *weren't* malleable, then there would be no reason to design in the first place, right? That's the hidden presumption at work in design, isn't it? That we *can* change our surroundings, and as a result bring about a change in our identity.

PHILO: Indeed, coming back to philosophical history about this point remember that Plato defined place as a "container at rest." Aristotle stressed change of place as movement. That was consistent with the Greek view of a finite unchanging universe. Of course there were others (pre-Socratic Heraclitus, for example) who envisioned a universe in perpetual change as reflected in the famous saying: "You never step twice in the same river." The river, as a known place, that may appear the same yet the river bottom continuously changes as molecules of water flow by. This environment appears the same, it is still identified and experienced as a river, but the actual elements that create the river are constantly changing. Thinking about man-made interventions and designs, rather than ecological models such as rivers, brings forth the question of expression of identity for the designer.

ARCH: Yes so, if we modify our surroundings, do we then modify our own identities?

PHILO: Well, that's a very *American* presumption. Recall Chapter 3 on form and function. Greenough's starting thesis was that this young country, the United States of America, needed to create a new architectural vernacular, a new formal vocabulary, for itself in order to forge an identity separate from British colonial power.

ARCH: That's very true; point taken. However, we'll soon consider an example where we'll see this is not just an American prejudice. In our globalized world, who's to say what is American and not American any longer?

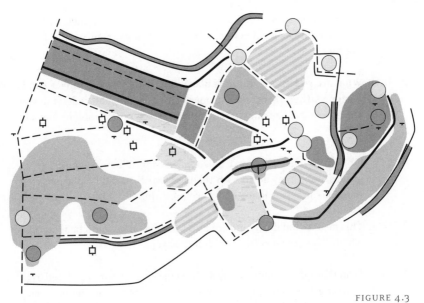

FIGURE 4.3
The visual form of Boston as seen in the field
from *The City and Its Element* by Kevin Lynch.

In any case, one of the first figures to thematize the importance of
place is the British architectural theorist Kenneth Frampton. His
well-known essay, "Towards a Critical Regionalism: Six Points for an
Architecture of Resistance," emphasized site-specificity—the specific qualities contained in a site, such as ambient light and climate,
as well as availability and tactile qualities of local materials—as a way
to revisit what Frampton then characterized as the increasing globalization of architectural form.

PHILO: The "globalization of architectural form"?

ARCH: Yes, the proliferation of the same building types around the globe,
which are designed and erected without any regard for local culture
or materials.

PHILO: So once again, the presumption is that the specificity of what surrounds a thing—in this case, a site—composes a thing's identity.

ARCH: Yes, and designers, I think, are justified in believing that a certain
identity of a place can be evoked, if not manipulated, through the

organization of space. Place, then, is as much an **image** as it is a material thing or collection of physical things in proximity to one another.

PHILO: What are you saying, then? If place is an image, and if a place can be designed, then this means images belong to the materials of design. Designers are as much image-makers as organizers of physical spaces.

ARCH: Of course. That shouldn't be so surprising. When designers create spaces, don't they do so with the idea that they can be places we can imagine ourselves living and working within?

PHILO: This means that designers are also working on people's imaginations, which is a very powerful position to occupy.

ARCH: I can't disagree, which is why architects especially are attracted, right or wrong, to elucidating the power design has to shape people's imaginations, lifestyles, and relationships to both their environment and other people.

The Work of Kevin Lynch

PHILO: This can no doubt be seen in Kevin Lynch's *The Image of the City* (1960), from which we are drawing our critical reading passage for this chapter.

ARCH: At this point, I believe we should introduce our critical reading passage for this topic: the opening of Chapter III. "The City and its Elements" in *The Image of the City*. This has been a classic reading for first or second-year architecture students. Someone may ask, how that would be relevant to all design students at any scale? Well, as I said before, the question of boundary (one of Lynch's elements) exists at all scales from a piece of furniture to a room to a city. All of the elements that Lynch identifies in a "legible" or "imaginable" city apply at all scales of design. We will return to this notion in Chapter 6, where Bachelard writes about the house and the universe.

Lynch investigates the city resident's mental image of the city and the sense of identity by comparing several American cities.

Let's return to the Wallace Stevens poem that we started with. The line "I am what is around me" relates to what several philosophers called "The 'I' discourse". Although these questions deal with many aspects of human existence, we must focus here specifically on how a physical surrounding, natural or manmade, contributes to the construction of an individual's and/or a group's sense of identity. Our identity is strongly the result of a specific place and geography. Variations on this kind of geographic determinism can be found everywhere in popular culture. How often we ascribe opposing personal characteristics to people who were born and grew up in the mountains, by the sea, or on the desert, or strongly distinguish between urban and rural types of temperaments. Romanian writer Mihail Sebastian wrote, "You are what the land makes you." Although this strikes me as a strongly causal and naively deterministic statement; we constantly use such assertions to explain human behavior; the question of how much remains valid.

Other Modern Interpretations of Place

PHILO: Yes such arguments, along with biology, language, religion, economics, and politics, and more generally "a world view," are pointed to as the conditions under which our sense of "who we are" is formed. Many have pointed out that existence is spatial. Without contradicting this idea, we can say that it is a debatable proposition since nomadic peoples can live in time equally.

> In our everyday experience, a place is a definite here and there, where we ourselves and things are at a certain distance and in definable direction from each other.[4]

In the homogeneous cultural context of the past, where people experienced a slower pace of change in archetypal meanings, the act of communication and signification was successful enough for a coherent projection of intended and recognized symbols. On the other hand, in the rapidly changing cultural situation and largely heterogeneous world we live in, established meanings and symbols weaken fast.

ARCH: Another central theme that flows from the question of "I am what is around me" and the question of the meaning of place is symbolism, or more precisely semiology, the language of objects (see the reading by Roland Barthes in Chapter 6, "What Is Meaning"). We can't discuss this subject without an understanding of how human perception and cognition function. In other words, how humans form and retain (memory) mental representations of their physical environment, natural and artificial (human made).

Architectural theoreticians such as Christian Norberg-Schultz, Josep Muntañola, and Kenneth Frampton, to name a few, continued to use the term *place*. Although the concepts of place differ for philosophers and architects, they are all concerned with the meaning and representations of place. Architects generally emphasize spatial relationships, whereas for the others—philosophers and social scientists—the emphasis is on experience (perception) of place and placeness. Frampton's "critical regionalism" was born in a criticism of modernism and the lack of "placeness" produced by a bland internationalism. The question of place is closely linked to a discussion of time and space, and the identity ascribed to a particular place in time and space. Definitions of the concept in philosophy and architectural theory differ. What is geographic determinism? What is a good place to live in? We attempt to link the word *place* with *episode* (Harre), *event* (Deleuze), and with mental events and actual human spatial experience. Existence is defined as spatial. Perception, cognition, semiology and memory design are understood as "place making activity."

Norberg-Schultz and Muntañola trace their definitions of "place" to the phenomenological tradition of Merleau-Ponty, Bachelard, and Heidegger, as well as notion of cognition of space in Piaget. Norberg-Schultz (1972) defined architectural space as a "concretization of existential space." He uses the term *existential space* to mean "cognitive space," and defines it as a relatively stable system of perceptual schemata, or an image humans develop by interacting with the environment. He considers "place" (or in his vocabulary), *center,* as one type of structural component of the mental schema that humans posses about the experience of space and time.

PHILO: Addressing itself to this very point, the theory of place conceptualizes architectural experience as emergent through being and acting in a physical world. (Ponti, body) *Place*, as used by recent writers, serves to derive conclusions about environmental cognitions from what people actually see and do in an architectural space, rather than evaluating it by speculating about its assumed meanings built into architectural form.

ARCH: Let's return to the issue of design and place. You have asked on several occasions to define my view of what is design. Now, at the start of a discussion on the concept of place is a very good time to do it. Architecture and interior design are place-making activities. In other words, the goal of design is the creation of well-defined memorable spatial experiences. These are locations in space and time that become part of our mental representations of the physical environment. I inherit this notion from Mutañola (1975), professor of architectural theory at Barcelona Architecture School. His use of the term *place* is more general, and it becomes the basic structural component of a spatial schema. He particularly attempts to establish; place as a concept, linking several research areas concerned with relating space and society, anthropology, psychology, linguistics, and architecture, as well as planning. Central to his approach is the idea that architectural design is a place-making activity.

Dear Philo, this is a good point at which to end our dialogue. In the Visual Critical Thinking Exercise about "Our Town," the students can map the play for identifiable "places" in the town.

CRITICAL READING PASSAGE

Excerpts from Chapter 3,
"The City Image and Its Elements,"
from *The Image of the City*
Kevin Lynch
1960

ABOUT THE AUTHOR

Kevin Lynch (1918–1984) was an American urban planner. After receiving his degree in city planning from MIT in 1947, Lynch worked briefly as an urban planner in Greensboro, North Carolina, but then returned to MIT in 1949 to take a post as a professor of urban planning. *The Image of the City* (1960), from which this chapter's critical reading passage is excerpted, is one of Lynch's most famous works. Based in part on interviews conducted with a small sample of city inhabitants from Boston, Massachusetts; Los Angeles, California; and Jersey City, New Jersey, the book was a groundbreaking study in the then-emerging field of environmental psychology. The city, Lynch argues, is not simply the organization of its physical elements; it is instead both the image the organization of its physical elements as a whole and how this image appears to the individual city inhabitant. Each individual inhabitant of the city, Lynch holds, takes this image of the city in and adds to this image his or her own experiences and memories. The "city," as a result, is never a fixed, physical object, but a particular image specific to each individual city inhabitant. By attending to what he names the city's "imageability," Lynch contends urban planners can affect directly how the city appears to its inhabitants.

There seems to be a public image of any given city which is the overlap of many individual images. Or perhaps there is a series of public images, each held by some significant number of citizens. Such group images are necessary if an individual is to operate successfully within his environment and to cooperate with his fellows. Each individual picture is unique, with some content that is rarely or never communicated, yet it approximates the public image, which, in different environments, is more or less compelling, more or less embracing.

This analysis limits itself to the effects of physical, perceptible objects. There are other influences on imageability, such as the social meaning of an area, its function, it history, or even its name. These will be glossed over, since the objective here is to uncover the role of form itself. It is taken for granted that in actual design form should be used to reinforce meaning, and not to negate it.

The contents of the city images so far studied, which are referable to physical forms, can conveniently be classified into five types of elements: paths, edges, districts, nodes, and landmarks. Indeed, there elements may be of more general application, since they seem to reappear in many types of environmental images, as may be seen by reference to Appendix A. These elements may be defined as follows:

1. *Paths.* Paths are the channels along which the observer customarily, occasionally, or potentially moves. They may be streets, walkways, transit lines, canals, railroads. For many people, these are the predominant elements in their image. People observe the city while moving through it, and along these paths the other environmental elements are arranged and related.

2. *Edges.* Edges are the linear elements not used or considered as paths by the observer. They are the boundaries between two phases, linear breaks in continuity: shores, railroad cuts, edges of development, walls. They are lateral references rather than coordinate axes. Such edges may be barriers, more or less penetrable, which close one region off from another; or they maybe seams, lines along which two regions are related and joined together. These edge elements, although probably not as dominant as paths, are for many people important organizing features, particularly in the role of holding together generalized areas, as in the outline of a city by water or wall.

3. *Districts.* Districts are the medium-to-large sections of the city, conceived of as having two-dimensional extent, which the observer mentally enters "inside of," and which are recognizable as having some

common, identifying character. Always identifiable from the inside, they are also used for exterior reference if visible from the outside. Most people structure their city to some extent in this way, with individual differences as to whether paths or districts are the dominant elements. It seems to depend not only upon the individual but also upon the given city.

4. *Nodes.* Nodes are points, the strategic spots in a city into which an observer can enter, and which are the intensive foci to and from which he is traveling. They may be primarily junctions, places of a break in transportation, a crossing or convergence of paths, moments of shift from once structure to another. Or the nodes may be simply concentrations, which gain their importance from being the condensation of some use or physical character, as a street-corner hangout or an enclosed square. Some of these concentration nodes are the focus and epitome of a district, over which their influence radiates and of which they stand as a symbol. They may be called cores. Many nodes, of course, partake of the nature of both junctions and concentrations. The concept of node is related to the concept of path, since junctions are typically the convergence of paths, events on the journey. It is similarly related to the concept of district, since cores are typically the intensive foci of districts, their polarizing center. In any event, some nodal points are to be found in almost every image, and in certain cases they may be the dominant feature.

5. *Landmarks.* Landmarks are another type of point-reference, but in this case the observer does not enter within them, they are external. They are usually a rather simply defined physical object: building, sign, store, or mountain. Their use involves the singling out of one element from a host of possibilities. Some landmarks are distant ones, typically seen from many angles and distances, over the tops of smaller elements, and used as radial references. They may be within the city or at such a distance that for all practical purposes they symbolize a constant direction. Such are isolated towers, golden domes, great hills. Even a mobile point, like the sun, whose motion is sufficiently slow and regular, may be employed. Other landmarks are primarily local, being visible only in restricted localities and from certain approaches. These are the innumerable signs, store fronts, trees, doorknobs, and other urban detail, which fill in the image of most observers. They are frequently used clues of identity and even of structure, and seem to be increasingly relied upon as a journey becomes more and more familiar.

The image of a given physical reality may occasionally shift its type with different circumstances of viewing. Thus an expressway may be a path for the driver, and edge for the pedestrian. Or a central area may be a district when a city is organized on a medium scale, and a node when the entire metropolitan area is considered. But the categories seem to have stability for a given observer when he is operating at a given level.

None of the element types isolated above exist in isolation in the real case. Districts are structure with nodes, defined by edges, penetrated by paths, and sprinkled with landmarks. Elements regularly overlap and pierce one another. If this analysis begins with the differentiation of the data into categories, it must end with their reintegration into the whole image. Our studies have furnished much information about the visual character of the element types. This will be discussed below. Only to a lesser extent, unfortunately, did the work make revelations about the interrelations between elements, or about image levels, image qualities, or the development of the image. These latter topics will be treated at the end of this chapter.

ACTIVITY FOR REFLECTION

Using Lynch's five elements of the city (paths, edges, districts, nodes, and landmarks), map the city or town in which you now live. How may the image of your city or town change depending on your movement through space, e.g., whether you are driving in a car, riding a bicycle, or walking?

VISUAL CRITICAL THINKING EXERCISE

Read *Our Town* by Thornton Wilder and then develop a schematic town plan at several scales based on the stage directions.

As we have seen, Norberg-Schultz bases much of his work on what Lynch did in *The Image of the City*. In this exercise we will look at Thornton Wilder's image of a New England town as portrayed in the play *Our Town*. Taking the play as your data, reconstruct the town's plan, using Lynch's concepts from clues in the play. Carefully analyze the play and find those parts of the text that give clues about the physicality of the town. This is similar to the task of a designer of sets and props, but here you're asked to go beyond what the theater-goer may see on stage and go into those areas that also exist off-stage. If Thornton Wilder had a clear image in his mind of the social and political aspects of a New England town, one would expect that he also had a strong and clear mental representation of the landscape and architecture of it. Find it.

Bring back to class a (plan) map of the town constructed in terms of Lynch's (and Norberg-Schultz's) five elements (center/place/center, path/axis, domain, boundary, and gate) on a single sheet of 11" × 17" paper.

Stage directions from the beginning of the play:

ACT 1

No curtain. No scenery.

The audience, arriving, sees an empty stage in half-light.

Presently the stage MANAGER, hat and pipe in mouth, enters and begins placing a table and three chairs downstage left, and a table and three chairs downstage right. He also places a low bench at the corner of what will be the Webb house, left. "Left" and "right" are from the point of view of the actor facing the audience. "Up" is towards the back wall. As the house lights go down he has finished setting the stage and leading against the right proscenium pillar watches the late arrivals in the audience.

When the auditorium is in complete darkness, he speaks. *(He proceeds to describe the town.)*

Stage Manager: This play is called "Our Town." It was written by Thornton Wilder, produced and directed by A . . . The name of the Town is Grover's Corner, New Hampshire—just across the Massachusetts line: latitude 42 degrees 40 minutes, longitudes 70 degrees 37 minutes. The First Act shows a day in our town. The day is May 7, 1901.The time is just before dawn.

A rooster crows. The day is beginning to show some streaks of light in the East there, behind our mount'in. The morning star always gets wonderful bright the minute it has to go, doesn't it?

He stares for a moment, then goes upstage. Well, I'd better show you how our town lies. Up there . . . That's in parallel with the back wall . . . is Main street. . . .

FOR FURTHER READING

Cache, Bernard. 1995. *Earth Moves: The Furnishing of Territories.* Trans. Anne Boyman. Cambridge, MA: MIT Press.

Kwon, Miwon. 2004. *One Place after Another: Site-Specific Art and Locational Identity.* Cambridge, MA: MIT Press.

5

What Is Natural?
What Is Artificial?

FIGURE 5.1
A roof structure being moved by men in Vietnam.

PHILO: After our discussion of place, an interesting paradox occurred to me: in order to gain a sense of a place's natural elements—ambient light, temperature, geological characteristics of the site—something artificial has to be constructed.

The Difference between the Artificial and the Natural

ARCH: It's great that you bring that up. One theme I've been preoccupied with for some years now is the distinction between the natural and artificial. It's an interesting problem from a design perspective because we typically assume that what we designers do is artificial, perhaps even an improvement upon nature, and that the material we manipulate is natural. What if that was not the case?

PHILO: I've also been interested in this theme, but less from an epistemological standpoint than a pedagogical one. I already know what the difference is between the natural and the artificial.

ARCH: Oh, you do?

PHILO: I do. There is no difference.

ARCH: How can you say there isn't a difference? When a natural disaster strikes a developed area and levels it, do you believe it is an event brought about by human beings? Isn't it what we typically call "an act of God"?

PHILO: See, that's exactly what I mean. Even if we are confronted with so-called natural disasters, we tend to assign it some human characteristic, or we conceptualize it as some kind of impersonal, objective force. We call it either "God" or "Nature," with a capital N. As for whether human beings can be the cause of nature striking or not, you don't have to look any further than what happened with Hurricane Katrina when it struck the U.S. Gulf Region in 2005.

ARCH: In what ways was that brought about by human beings? There's no hurricane machine yet, is there?

PHILO: Well, clearly the effects of the hurricane cannot be separated from the way we've transformed the planet with industry and technology. Many of the disastrous events surrounding Hurricane Katrina were facilitated by our manipulation of the so-called "natural landscape." New Orleans is a city that was built below sea-level and is maintained, at least ideally, through artificial means, such as the levee system.

ARCH: So, how does this translate into a pedagogical concern for you?

PHILO: It is very common to hear designers refer to nature as if it is this pure, untouched object independent of human beings. Think back to our discussion of place. One of Kenneth Frampton's criteria for a critical regionalism was the incorporation of a site's natural elements—ambient light, little to no air conditioning, local materials. Our experience of "place" that is supposed to emanate from the incorporation of these elements is supposed to be somehow a pure one. This unreflective appeal to nature occurs all too often, in my judgment, when it is clear there is no such object that fits that description. It's a cultural fantasy.

ARCH: It's true that if you look at the history of such places as Central Park in New York City or even the creation of the National Parks System by Theodore Roosevelt, one would see that most everything we refer to as "natural" has been shaped by human beings.

PHILO: In fact, the National Parks System required the removal of a great many Native Americans who already occupied the lands designated for development into parks. Yet, we think of Yosemite as natural, even wilderness.

ARCH: I want to come back to this after we consider some of the reasons I have been moved to reconsider the distinction between the natural and the artificial. For you, it seems that what is at stake in the distinction is cultural and maybe even social-political. The distinction between the natural and artificial is really a distinction between nature and culture, and any attempt to delineate strong boundaries between the two can be seen to have social and political motivations, such as the displacement of Native Americans in terms of the National Park System and the plight of those in New Orleans resulting from Hurricane Katrina.

PHILO: That's right. I think we often appeal to nature when we don't want to take responsibility for something. In the case of the National Park System, preservation of nature is used as an excuse to relocate— mostly kill—other human beings and take their land. In the case of

Katrina, the "act of God" that was the hurricane was used as an excuse to say we couldn't do anything to prevent it, which I take to be a false claim. To be sure, we could have prevented much of the hurricane's damage if the levee system had been built better. Then the nature of the hurricane would have appeared very different to us.

ARCH: I understand what you're saying, but for me, the issue is largely epistemological. I'm using a philosophical term, I know, but it's due to my interest in viewing design as a human practice that comes out of nature and then transforms nature. To what extent can we consider design a natural activity of human beings? This means critiquing radically the distinction between the natural and the artificial, but with a different intention from the ones you expressed just now. I think they are connected, your concerns and mine, but to show how they are, I first have to go through the basis of my concerns. A very influential text for me is the French biologist Jacques Monod's *Chance and Necessity: An Essay on the Natural Philosophy of Modern Biology*, which we feature as the reading for the current chapter.

PHILO: Please, lead us through it a bit.

ARCH: Well, I begin by joining Monod in asking a puzzling question: what are the more general properties that characterize living beings and distinguish them from the rest of the material world?[1] Monod imagines the task of a Martian arriving on earth and attempting to tell the difference between artificial and natural objects. At the end of his essay, Monod identifies three criteria that the Martian could employ in order to distinguish between natural and artificial things: (1) autonomous morphogenesis (internal autonomous determinism); (2) reproductive invariance (the ability to transmit information corresponding to their own structure); and (3) teleonomy (purpose). It is teleonomy, that is, the notion of purpose or intention that distinguishes nature from human artifacts.

Here is an example between a concrete block house and a natural cave.

PHILO: OK. We can all wonder about something that seems obvious to us: "a rock, a mountain, a river, or a cloud: these are natural objects; a house, a car, a knife: so many artificial objects, artifacts." As Monod writes, "[A]nalyze these judgments, however, and it will be seen that they are neither immediate nor strictly objective."[2]

FIGURE 5.2

On the left, a structure built by human beings (Pratt House, Great Barrington, 1993), and on the right, a natural cave in Utah, create space that evolved naturally over time. (Photo on left by Dan Bucsescu and photo on right by Travis Craw.)

ARCH: Well, I found his essay extremely useful in discussing the topic of this chapter: What is nature? And, more importantly, what flows from this is how designed objects, artificial objects made by humans, are similar to and/or different from things made by nature. Can one tell them apart and if so, in what way? Does the emergence of intelligent life prove that nature is creative and purposeful in the same way human activity is spoken of? That is a crucial question if we are to understand the nature of human design. Monod, after identifying three general properties that characterize living beings, finds both similarities and crucial differences. He points to some paradoxes in our scientific understanding of nature. The notion that human-designed objects exhibit the clear intention or purpose that gave rise to their production is paradoxical to Monod because no intention or purpose can be attributed to nature. Nature, according to the scientific model, is objective and purposeless. Philo, that should trouble us about the entire philosophical question of human intentionality we have talked a lot about.

FIGURE 5.3
This image illustrates
an exploration of the
relationship between
the form of the human
body and mechanical and
robotic components. Pierre
Jaquet-Droz, Switzerland,
1721–1790; *Young Writer*,
c. 1770.

PHILO: Yes. I recognize the question. Monod thinks it's strange that we assume that natural objects don't exhibit any intention. However, the paradox relies on the idea that we can't really distinguish between objects created by human beings and natural objects. If we can't tell the difference between natural objects and objects made by human beings, then why do we assume nature expresses no intention while assuming at the same time that objects made by humans necessarily exhibit an intention?

ARCH: That's right.

PHILO: We should note, though, that this is only recently the case. The medieval period in Europe, for example, reflected a belief that the world displayed the intention of God. Knowledge of the world was then defined in terms of discerning God's intention.

ARCH: Yes, I am aware of that history. Although some of us have moved away from attributing nature and all natural events to God's design, we still commonly hold humans (such as artists, designers, architects, engineers, lawyers, or politicians) responsible for their intentional actions as "manifested" in the artifacts they produce. We spoke about that at the start of our dialogue in reference to the New Orleans hurricane disaster.

PHILO: Yes, we have. And I have argued that there is no difference, as you quote Monod.

ARCH: Not so fast. That is the case if we compare things at a sub-molecular level, where we find regularity and repetition. Looking at the world at that level, all things are crystals. But Monod also finds that, at a higher scale of analysis, the macro, the third criterion, teleonomy (or purpose), becomes critical in order to distinguish between natural and artificial things in the world. It is here that I become interested in Monod's argument. Of course I have a bias because, as a designer/ architect, I look for a worldview, a paradigm that supports as wide a degree of freedom as possible for the maker of human artifacts. Such freedom of choice exposes the maker's intentions in the act of design. Does that make any sense to you?

PHILO: Yes. On the other hand, as a philosopher approaching this question, I do not seek to justify my actions in that way. I only search for the best possible answer for the question at hand. Because we come from and are part of nature, it is not clear to me how we can make the distinction implied by the notion of teleonomy, that is, of human purpose, while denying same to nature. I don't want to live with Monod's paradox if I can help it.

ARCH: Fair enough. And still I would argue, if I may, for human exceptionalism, however unfashionable. That is, for me, a necessary prerequisite assumption for the idea of creativity. That is, the use of language (symbolic representation) on the basis of which any cultural production of artifacts (both ideas and things) and then the memory of them is made possible. Karl Popper allows for this distinction in his three-world model of existence.

PHILO: To the best of my knowledge Popper argues for an interactionist, dualist model on the issue of the mind body problem.

ARCH: Yes. That is my understanding as well. The products of the mind (human culture), as recorded, matter to natural evolution.

PHILO: I agree with that as well. How could I do otherwise as a philosopher?

ARCH: Popper refers to Monod.[3] This would be a critical thought for Chapter 9 on creativity.

> The existence of great and unquestionable creative works of art and of science shows the creativity of man, and with it of the universe that has created man.
>
> What I here describe by the word creative is described by Jaques Monod [1970], [1975] when he speaks of the unpredictability of the emergence of life on earth, the unpredictability of the various species and especially of our own human species we were unpredictable before we appeared, he says. ([1975], p. 23.)

PHILO: Yes. This is useful and requires further exploration.

ARCH: Given what he considers "the admittedly vague idea of creative evolution or emergent evolution"[4] Popper goes on to identify the role of such products of the human mind as explanatory myths, scientific theories, and works of art. He develops a table of "Some Cosmic Evolutionary Stages." Here it is:[5]

> World 3
> (6) Works of Art and of Science—the products of the human mind (including technology)
> (5) Human Language. Theories of Self and Death
>
> World 2
> (4) Consciousness of Self and Death (the world of subjective experiences)
> (3) Sentience (animal consciousness)
>
> World 1
> (2) Living Organisms (the world of physical objects)
> (1) The Heavier elements: Liquids and Crystals

PHILO: Now tell me why you go to such lengths in quoting Popper. How does this add to our question about the role of design of artifacts and natural evolution?

ARCH: Well, in the first place, his definition of "World Three" helps a lot. That is the world of recorded thought, of cultural products or artifacts that live longer than humans. That is to say, the world of shared cultural memory that is passed on by being manifested in the things we make, build, or write down. It is this stuff that we call the information transmitted from one generation to the next. It is here where design and architecture are to be understood as cultural production that are an addition to nature, and not as some form of imitation of nature as some fashionable notions in the academia are proposing these days.

PHILO: OK. I follow you so far. Go on.

ARCH: I took the liberty of redefining Monod's notion of "reproductive invariant" in cultural terms rather than biological. That is to suggest that the term "reproductive invariant" becomes similar to the idea of a "meme."

PHILO: What do you mean?

ARCH: It is here, at this moment in our dialogue, that Richard Dawkins's argument in the chapter titled, "Memes: the New Replicators," in his book *The Selfish Gene* is very helpful.

PHILO: Yes, I see your concern. On the other hand, Dawkins also writes, "Most of what is unusual about man can be summed up in one word 'culture': Cultural transmission is analogous to genetic transmission in that, although basically conservative, it can give rise to a form of evolution."[6]

ARCH: Yes but he also points out that "Language seems to 'evolve' by non-genetic means, and at a rate which is orders of magnitude faster than genetic evolution.

Examples of memes are tunes, ideas, catch-phrases, clothes, clothes fashions, ways of making pots or of building arches."[7] When Dawkins proposes the notion of an *idea-meme* as an entity that is capable of being "transmitted from one brain to another" and "could regard an organized church, with its architecture, rituals, laws, music, art, and written tradition,"[8] are we not revisiting the original mnemonic (memory) function of architecture and all design?

PHILO: Yes, memory is part of the discussion in Chapter 6 on meaning.

ARCH: Well, isn't this in tune with Dawkins's suggestion that "the survival value of a good meme in the meme pool results from its great psychological appeal. It provides a superficially plausible answer to deep and troubling questions about existence. ... It looks as though meme transmission is subject to continuous mutation and also blending."[9] In other words, ability to transmit information over time (individual and group memory). Wasn't architecture regarded as timeless until recently, when the notion of time and event has gained philo-sophical dominance?

PHILO: There is a lot to say here.

The Metaphorical and the Literal: Three Metaphors Defining Design and Architecture

ARCH: I would like to return here to the three metaphors used in the twen-tieth century in defining what the activities of design and architec-ture are like. If you recall from Chapter 1, they are *machine, organism,* and *language.* These distinct terms, I think, can summarize the major theoretical approaches to design.

PHILO: Yes, we talked about that in our discussion of critical thinking. How do they throw light on the discussion of what is nature?

ARCH: By considering the similarities and the differences between these three ways of defining design/architecture, we develop critical think-ing about the question at hand and clearly distinguish between the natural and the artificial (the human made). Machines and languages are artifacts of human culture while organisms are a product of nature. I may be pointing to the obvious, but it must be said here.

PHILO: But remember what we just talked about. If we really can't distinguish between the natural and the artificial, then any attempt to determine their differences must be questioned. I think the real problem is the fact that we somehow need to provide models—images—of design production.

ARCH: Of course. Models of design production are all we are talking about in this book. Allow me to continue. Another important point about these three models for design or architecture is that machines and organisms have something in common. They obey universal laws of nature, unlike language, which is arbitrary and conventional. In other words, a human social contract. That makes these notions very, very different. Whether we say design/architecture is machine, organism, or language makes a huge difference in approach.

PHILO: That may be a bit too academic. Could you clarify?

ARCH: Each term, when used to define the activity of design, carries with it a set of values and assumptions about the nature of human beings and their behavior. Such paradigmatic underlying assumptions have direct practical affects on the task of design. Design is never automatic or free from our way of defining the terms. Isn't that what critical thinking aims at?

PHILO: Yes. What does that have to do with the question of nature?

ARCH: I will tell you.

PHILO: OK. Go on.

ARCH: The notion that the human body and mind are machines has been around for a long time. The dream of a "perpetuum mobile" (a never ending machine), that is, a machine that defies friction and can function for ever, has not disappeared from today's culture. This techno-utopia is very much present in schools of design. This idea now, in its latest form, suggests that the mind and the body are computers. In other words, the machine and organism metaphors are the dominant paradigms for design of any kind, at all scales. The linguistic model was thrown out with the decline of "post-modernism." That is, of course, a mistake. What is the saying, "throwing the baby out with the bath water"? The notion that design and architecture are not, in the end, engineering problems, but semiological conventions is the topic of the Chapter 6 on meaning.

PHILO: So, I still don't quite grasp the source of your anxiety about this paradigm shift. I, as you know, am closer to your inclination towards language as the best term in defining design and architecture. What is the source of your concern?

ARCH: Dear Philo, I must share with you my concerns about my future as an architect. These days some people argue that in not so distant future, designers and architects will be extinct. Intelligently designed objects and buildings, capable to transform themselves with the aid of nano-technology, will respond to any of a client's desires. In an article titled "Why the Future of Architecture Does Not Need Us" by Labce Hosey, the author argues that "buildings will become more like us, but we may become more like them, as well ... new types of bodies will be considered ... our future bodies may look and act nothing like our current bodies."[10]

The other dominant notion is that architecture *grows* like a crystal, like a flower, or like a genetic generative code, imitating a natural process. These metaphors defining design have gained great popularity in the academia in recent years. The common thread in all of this is that "form is not something we invent, but something that appears."[11]

PHILO: Well, I am not totally unsympathetic to these developments. They have their place in recent technological developments. We must not reject them without evaluating them for the value they bring to human life. They might be helpful.

ARCH: Of course, I also am not against technological progress. Nevertheless, allow me to complete my cautionary argument.

PHILO: Go on.

ARCH: At least for a hundred years, this notion has been known as *organicism*. This has been stimulated to a great extent by the advent of computer software that attempts to mimic that process. This has recently been known as *computationalism,* and the main goal of this techno-utopia is a kind of technological salvation from human folly and the subjectivity involved in any product of human design. The ideal, its supporters say, is to imitate nature's methods of production.

PHILO: What is wrong with that? Considering the sorry state of the world, a certain skepticism that we humans can suppress our subjective desires for the common good is in order. If that is applicable today to the business and political and social worlds, why wouldn't it apply to architecture and design?

ARCH: Of course. I don't dispute such concerns. They were part of the early modernist thinking be they by scientists, politicians, philosophers, or artists. They all tried to clear our thinking of "preconceptions" of one kind or another and move our views toward a more objective grasp of the natural world. Among designers and architects of the early twentieth century, the dream of modeling engineers was central. The question, "Are we poets or engineers?" where poets are thought to give expression to human subjectivity whereas engineers are humble facilitators of nature's material conditions to be expressed in design, has always seemed to me to be a confused false dichotomy.

PHILO: I share your concerns. This seems to me as a good question. Let's ask our students to consider this question.

CRITICAL READING PASSAGE

Chapter 1, "Of Strange Objeᴄ̄ts,"
from *Chance and Necessity: An Essay on the*
Natural Philosophy of Modern Biology
Jacques Monod
1971

ABOUT THE AUTHOR

French biologist and philosopher of science, Jacques Monod (1910–1976) was awarded the Nobel Prize in Physiology or Medicine in 1965. Monod's work in biology focused on genes and DNA, and he also contributed to the field of enzymology, the study of enzyme behavior. "Of Strange Objects" is the first chapter of Monod's *Chance and Necessity,* which attends to what Monod describes as a contradiction at the heart of the study of life. According to Monod, science assumes nature is objective: it does not express a purpose; it just *is.* At the same time, however, science views human beings, who are of course "products" of nature, so to speak, as expressing an intention in what they create. Science thus assumes that human beings are "projective," but does not account for how something projective can arise out of something objective. How, Monod asks, should biology resolve this contradiction?

The difference between artificial and natural objects seems immediately and unambiguously apparent to all of us. A rock, a mountain, a river, or a cloud—these are natural objects; a knife, a handkerchief, a car—so many artificial objects, artifacts.* Analyze these judgments, however, and it will be seen that they are neither immediate nor strictly objective. We know that the knife was man-made for a use its maker visualized beforehand. The object renders in material form the preexistent intention that gave birth to it, and its form is accounted for by the performance expected of it even before it takes shape. It is another story altogether with the river or the rock which we know, or believe, to have been molded by the free play of physical forces to which we cannot attribute any design, any "project" or purpose. Not, that is, if we accept the basic premise of the scientific method, to wit, that nature is *objective* and not *projective.*

Hence it is through reference to our own activity, conscious and projective, intentional and purposive—it is as makers of artifacts—that we judge of a given object's "naturalness" or "artificialness." Might there be objective and general standards for defining the characteristics of artificial objects, products of a conscious purposive activity, as against natural objects, resulting from the gratuitous play of physical forces? To make sure of the complete objectivity of the criteria chosen, it would doubtless be best to ask oneself whether, in putting them to use, a program could be drawn up enabling a computer to distinguish an artifact from a natural object.

Such a program could be applied in the most interesting connections. Let us suppose that a spacecraft is soon to be landed upon Venus or Mars; what more fascinating question than to find out whether our neighboring planets are, or at some earlier period have been, inhabited by intelligent beings capable of projective activity? In order to detect such present or past activity we would have to search for and be able to recognize its *products,* however radically unlike the fruit of human industry they might be. Wholly ignorant of the nature of such beings and of the projects they might have conceived, our program would have to utilize only very general criteria, solely based upon the examined objects' structure and form and without any reference to their eventual function.

The suitable criteria, we see, would be two in number: (a) regularity, and (b) repetition. By means of the first one would seek to make use of the fact that natural objects, wrought by the play of physical forces, almost never present geometrically simple and straightforward structures: flat surfaces, for instance, or rectilinear edges, right angles, exact symmetries; whereas artifacts will ordinarily show such features, if only in an approximate or rudimentary manner.

Of the two criteria, repetition would probably be the more decisive. Materializing a reiterated intent, homologous artifacts meant for the same use

---

* In the literal sense: products of human art or workmanship.

reflect, faithfully in the main, the constant purpose of their creator. In that respect the discovery of numerous specimens of closely similar objects would be of high significance.

These, briefly defined, are the general criteria that might serve. The objects selected for examination, it must be added, would be of *macroscopic* dimensions, but not *microscopic*. By macroscopic is meant dimensions measurable, say, in centimeters; by microscopic, dimensions normally expressed in angstroms (a hundred million of which equal one centimeter). This proviso is crucial, for on the microscopic scale one would be dealing with atomic and molecular structures whose simple and repetitive geometries, obviously, would attest not to a conscious and rational intention but to the laws of chemistry.

Now let us suppose the program drawn up and the machine built. To check its performance, the best possible test would be to put it to work upon terrestrial objects. Let us invert our hypotheses and imagine that the machine has been put together by the experts of a Martian NASA aiming at detecting evidence of organized, artifact-producing activity on Earth. And let us suppose that the first Martian craft comes down in the Forest of Fontainebleau, not far, let's say, from the village of Barbizon. The machine looks at and compares the two series of objects most prominent in the area: on the one hand the houses in Barbizon, on the other hand the rock formations of Apremont. Utilizing the criteria of regularity, of geometric simplicity, and of repetition, it will have no trouble deciding that the rocks are natural objects and the houses artifacts.

Focusing now upon lesser objects, the machine examines some pebbles, near which it discovers some crystals-quartz crystals, let us say. According to the same criteria it should of course decide that while the pebbles are natural, the quartz crystals are artificial objects. A decision which appears to point to some "error" in the writing of the program. An "error" which, moreover, proceeds from an interesting source: if the crystals present perfectly defined geometrical shapes, that is because their macroscopic structure directly reflects the simple and repetitive microscopic structure of the atoms or molecules constituting them. A crystal, in other words, is the macroscopic expression of a microscopic structure. An "error" which, by the by, should be easy enough to eliminate, since all *possible* crystalline structures are known to us.

But let us suppose that the machine is now studying another kind of object: a hive built by wild bees, for example. There it would obviously find all the signs indicating artificial origin: the simple and repeated geometrical structures of the honeycombs and the cells composing them, thanks to which the hive would earn classification in the same category of objects as the Barbizon dwellings. What are we to make of this conclusion? We know the hive is "artificial" insofar as it represents the product of the activity of bees. But we have good reasons for thinking that this activity is strictly automatic—immediate, but not consciously projective. At the same time, as good naturalists we view bees as "natural" beings. Is there not a flagrant contradiction in considering "artificial" the product of a "natural" being's automatic activity?

Carrying the investigation a little further, it would soon be seen that if there is contradiction, it results not from faulty programming but from the ambiguity of our judgments. For if the machine now inspects, not the hive, but the bees themselves, it cannot take them for anything but artificial, highly elaborated objects. The most superficial examination will reveal in the bee elements of simple symmetry: bilateral and translational. Moreover and above all, examining bee after bee the computer will note that the extreme complexity of their structure (the number and position of abdominal hairs, for example, or the ribbing of the wings) is reproduced with extraordinary fidelity from one individual bee to the next. Powerful evidence, is it not, that these creatures are the products of a deliberate, constructive, and highly sophisticated order of activity? Upon the basis of such conclusive documentation, the machine would be bound to signal to the officials of the Martian NASA its discovery, upon Earth, of an industry compared with which their own would probably seem primitive.

In this little excursion into the not-so-very-farfetched, our aim was only to illustrate the difficulty of defining the distinction—elusive, for all its obviousness to our intuitions—between "natural" and "artificial" objects. In fact, on the basis of structural criteria, macroscopic ones, it is probably impossible to arrive at a definition of the artificial which, while including all "veritable" artifacts, such as the products of human workmanship, would exclude objects so clearly natural as crystalline structures, and indeed, the living beings themselves which we would also like to classify among natural systems.

Looking for the cause of the confusion—or in any case, seeming confusion—the program is leading to, we may perhaps wonder whether it does not arise from our having wished to limit it to considerations only of form, of structure, of geometry, and so divesting our notion of an artificial object of its essential content. This being that any such object is defined or explained primarily by the function it is intended to fulfill, the performance its inventor expects of it. However, we shall soon find that by programming the machine so that henceforth it studies not only the structure but the eventual performance of the examined objects, we end up with still more disappointing results.

For let us suppose that this new program does enable the machine to analyze correctly the structure and the performance of two series of objects—horses running in a field and automobiles moving on a highway, for example. The analysis would tend to the conclusion that these objects are closely comparable, those making up each series having a built-in capacity for swift movement, although over different surfaces, which accounts for their differences of structure. And if, to take another example, we were to ask the machine to compare the structure and performance of the eye of a vertebrate with that of a camera, the program would have to acknowledge their profound similarities: lenses, diaphragm, shutter, light-sensitive pigments: surely, the same components could not have been introduced into both objects except with a view to getting similar performances from them.

The last of these examples is a classic one of functional adaptation in living beings, and I have cited it only to emphasize how arbitrary and pointless it would be to deny that the natural organ, the eye, represents the materialization of a "purpose"—that of picking up images—while this is indisputably also the origin of the camera. It would be the more absurd to deny it since, in the last analysis, the purpose which "explains" the camera can only be the same as the one to which the eye owes its structure. Every artifact is a product made by a living being which through it expresses, in a particularly conspicuous manner, one of the fundamental characteristics common to all living beings without exception: that of being *objects endowed with a purpose or project,* which at the same time they exhibit in their structure and carry out through their performances (such as, for instance, the making of artifacts).

Rather than reject this idea (as certain biologists have tried to do) it is indispensable to recognize that it is essential to the very definition of living beings. We shall maintain that the latter are distinct from all other structures or systems present in the universe through this characteristic property, which we shall call *teleonomy.*

But it must be borne in mind that, while necessary to the definition of living beings, this condition is not sufficient, since it does not propose any objective criteria for distinguishing between living beings themselves and the artifacts issuing from their activity.

It is not enough to point out that the project which gives rise to an artifact belongs to the animal that created it, and not to the artificial object itself. This obvious notion is also too subjective, as the difficulty of utilizing it in the computer program would prove: for upon what basis would the machine be able to decide that the project of picking up images—the project represented by the camera—belongs to some object other than the camera itself? By examining nothing beyond the finished structure and by simply analyzing its performance it is possible to identify the project, but not its author or source.

To achieve this we must have a program which studies not only the actual object but its origin, its history, and, for a start, how it has been put together. Nothing, in principle at least, stands in the way of formulating such a program. Even if it were rather crudely compiled, we would be able with it to discern a radical difference between any artifact, however highly perfected, and a living being. The machine could not fail to note that the macroscopic structure of an artifact (whether a honeycomb, a dam built by beavers, a paleolithic hatchet, or a spacecraft) results from the application to the materials constituting it of forces *exterior* to the object itself. Once complete, this macroscopic structure attests, not to inner forces of cohesion between atoms or molecules constituting its material (and conferring upon it only its general properties of density, hardness, ductility, etc.), but to the *external* forces that have shaped it.

On the other hand, the program will have to register the fact that a living being's structure results from a totally different process, in that it owes almost nothing to the action of outside forces, but everything, from its overall shape down to its tiniest detail, to "morphogenetic" interactions within the object itself. It is thus a structure giving proof of an autonomous determinism: precise, rigorous, implying a virtually total "freedom" with respect to outside agents or conditions—which are capable, to be sure, of impeding this development, but not of governing or guiding it, not of prescribing its organizational scheme to the living object. Through the autonomous and spontaneous character of the morphogenetic processes that build the macroscopic structure of living beings, the latter are absolutely distinct from artifacts, as they are, furthermore, from the majority of natural objects whose macroscopic morphology largely results from the influence of external agents. To this there is a single exception: that, once again, of crystals, whose characteristic geometry reflects microscopic interactions occurring within the object itself. Hence, utilizing this criterion alone, crystals would have to be classified together with living beings, while artifacts and natural objects, alike fashioned by outside agents, would comprise another class.

That this last criterion, after those of regularity and repetition, should point to a similarity between crystalline structures and the structures of living beings might well set our programmer to thinking. Though unversed in modern biology, he would be obliged to wonder whether the internal forces which confer their macroscopic structure upon living beings might be of the same nature as the microscopic interactions responsible for crystalline morphologies. That this is indeed the case constitutes one of the main themes to be developed in the ensuing chapters of this essay. But for the moment we are looking for the most general criteria to define the macroscopic properties that set living beings apart from all other objects in the universe.

Having "discovered" that an internal, autonomous determinism guarantees the formation of the extremely complex structures of living beings, our programmer (with no training in biology, but an information specialist by profession) must necessarily see that such structures represent a considerable quantity of information whose source has still to be identified: for all expressed—and hence received—information presupposes a source.

Let us assume that, continuing his investigation, our programmer at last makes his final discovery: that the source of the information expressed in the structure of a living being is *always* another, structurally identical object. He has now identified the source and detected a third remarkable property in these objects: their ability to reproduce and to transmit *ne varietur* the information corresponding to their own structure. A very rich body of information, since it describes an organizational scheme which, along with being exceedingly complex, is preserved intact from one generation to the next. The term we shall use to designate this property is *invariant reproduction,* or simply *invariance.*

With their invariant reproduction we find living beings and crystalline structures once again sharing a property that renders them unlike all other known objects in the universe. Certain chemicals in supersaturated solution do not crystallize unless the solution has been inoculated with crystal seeds. We know as well that in cases of a chemical capable of crystallizing into two different systems, the structure of the crystals appearing in the solution will be determined by that of the seed employed. Crystalline structures, however, represent a quantity of information by several orders of magnitude inferior to that transmitted from one generation to another in the simplest living beings we are acquainted with. By this criterion—purely quantitative, be it noted—living beings may be distinguished from all other objects, crystals included.

Let us now forget our Martian programmer and leave him to mull things over undisturbed. This imaginary experiment has had no other aim than to compel us to "rediscover" the more general properties that characterize living beings and distinguish them from the rest of the universe. Let us now admit to a familiarity with modern biology, so as to go on to analyze more closely and to try to define more precisely, if possible quantitatively, the properties in question. We have found three: teleonomy, autonomous morphogenesis, and reproductive invariance.

Of them all, reproductive invariance is the least difficult to define quantitatively. Since this is the capacity to reproduce highly ordered structure, and since a structure's degree of order can be defined in units of information, we shall say that the "invariance content" of a given species is equal to the amount of information which, transmitted from one generation to the next, assures the preservation of the specific structural standard. As we shall see later on, with the help of a few assumptions it will be possible to arrive at an estimate of this amount.

That in turn will enable us to bring into better focus the notion most immediately and plainly inspired by the examination of the structures and performances of living beings, that of teleonomy. Analysis nevertheless reveals it to be a profoundly ambiguous concept, since it implies the subjective idea of "project." We remember the example of the camera: if we agree that this object's existence and structure realize the "project" of capturing images, we must also agree, obviously enough, that a similar project is accomplished with the emergence of the eye of a vertebrate.

But it is only as a part of a more comprehensive project that each individual project, whatever it may be, has any meaning. All the functional adaptations in living beings, like all the artifacts they produce, fulfill particular projects which may be seen as so many aspects or fragments of a unique primary project, which is the preservation and multiplication of the species.

To be more precise, we shall arbitrarily choose to define the essential teleonomic project as consisting in the transmission from generation to generation of the invariance content characteristic of the species. All the structures, all the performances, all the activities contributing to the success of the essential project will hence be called "teleonomic."

This allows us to put forward at least the *principle* of a definition of a species' "teleonomic level." All teleonomic structures and performances can be regarded as corresponding to a certain quantity of information which must be transmitted for these structures to be realized and these performances accomplished. Let us call this quantity "teleonomic information." A given species' "teleonomic level" may then be said to correspond to the quantity of information which, on the average and per individual, must be transferred to assure the generation-to-generation transmission of the specific content of reproductive invariance.

It will be readily seen that, in this or that species situated higher or lower on the animal scale, the achievement of the fundamental teleonomic project (i.e., invariant reproduction) calls assorted, more or less elaborate and complex structures and performances into play. The fact must be stressed that concerned here are not only the activities directly bound up with reproduction itself, but all those that contribute—be it very indirectly—to the species' survival and multiplication. For example, in higher mammals the play of the young is an important element of psychic development and social integration. Therefore this activity has teleonomic value, inasmuch as it furthers the cohesion of the group, a condition for its survival and for the expansion of the species. It is the degree of complexity of all these performances or structures, conceived as having the function of serving the teleonomic purpose, that we would like to estimate.

This magnitude, while theoretically definable, is not measurable in practice. Still, it may serve as a rule of thumb for ranking different species or groups upon a "teleonomic scale." To take an extreme example, imagine a bashful poet who, prevented by shyness from declaring his passion to the woman he loves, can only express it symbolically, in the poems he dedicates to her. Suppose that at last, conquered by these refined compliments, the lady surrenders to the poet's desire. His verses will have contributed to the success of his essential project, and information they contain must therefore be tallied in the sum of the teleonomic performances assuring transmission of genetic invariance.

Indisputably, no analogous performance figures in the successful accomplishment of the project in other animal species, the mouse for instance. But— and this is the important point—the genetic invariance content is about the same in the mouse and the human being (and in all mammals, for that matter). *The two magnitudes we have been trying to define are therefore quite distinct.*

Which leads us to consider a most important question concerning the relationship among the three properties we singled out as characteristic of living beings. The fact that the computer program identified them successively and independently does not prove that they are not simply three manifestations of a single, more basic, more secret property, inaccessible to any direct observation. Were this so, the drawing of distinctions among the properties, the seeking of different definitions for them, might be nothing but delusion and arbitrariness. Far from shedding light on the real problem, far from tracking down "the secret of life" and truly dissecting it, we would be engaged merely in exorcizing it.

It is perfectly true that these three properties—teleonomy, autonomous morphogenesis, and reproductive invariance—are closely interconnected in all living beings. Genetic invariance expresses and reveals itself only through, and thanks to, the autonomous morphogenesis of the structure that constitutes the teleonomic apparatus.

There is this to be observed right away: not all of these three concepts have the same standing. Whereas invariance and teleonomy are indeed characteristic "properties" of living beings, spontaneous structuration ought rather to be considered a mechanism. Further on we shall see that this mechanism intervenes both in the elaboration of teleonomic structures and in the reproduction of invariant information as well. That it finally accounts for the latter two properties does not, however, imply that they should be regarded as one. It remains possible—it is in fact methodologically indispensable—to maintain a distinction between them, and this for several reasons:

1. One can at least *imagine* objects capable of invariant reproduction but devoid of any teleonomic apparatus. Crystalline structures offer one example of this, at a level of complexity admittedly very much lower than that of all known living organisms.

2. The distinction between teleonomy and invariance is more than a mere logical abstraction. It is warranted on grounds of chemistry. Of the two basic classes of biological macromolecules, one, that of proteins, is responsible for almost all teleonomic structures and performances; while genetic invariance is linked exclusively to the other class, that of nucleic acids.

3. Finally, as will be seen in the next chapter, this distinction is assumed, explicitly or otherwise, in all the theories, all the ideological constructions (religious, scientific, or philosophical) pertaining to the biosphere and to its relationship to the rest of the universe.

Living creatures are strange objects. At all times in the past, men must have been more or less confusedly aware of this. The development of the natural sciences beginning in the seventeenth century, their flowering in the nineteenth, instead of effacing this impression rather rendered it more acute. Over against the physical laws governing macroscopic systems, the very existence of living organisms seemed to constitute a paradox, violating certain of the fundamental principles modern science rests upon. Just which ones? That is not immediately clear. Hence the question is, precisely, to analyze the nature of this—or these—"paradoxes." This will give us occasion to specify the relative position, vis-à-vis physical laws, of the two essential properties that characterize living organisms: reproductive invariance and structural teleonomy.

Indeed at first glance invariance appears to constitute a profoundly paradoxical property, since the maintaining, the reproducing, the multiplying of highly ordered structures seems in conflict with the second law of thermodynamics. This law enjoins that no macroscopic system evolve otherwise than in a downward direction, toward degradation of the order that characterizes it.

However, this prediction of the second law is valid, and verifiable, only if we are considering the overall evolution of an *energetically isolated* system. Within such a system, in one of its phases, we may see ordered structures take shape and grow without that system's overall evolution ceasing to comply with the second law. The best example of this is afforded by the crystallization of a saturated solution. The thermodynamics of such a system are well understood. The local enhancement of order represented by the assembling of initially unordered molecules into a perfectly defined crystalline network is "paid for" by a transfer of thermal energy from the crystalline phase to the solution: the entropy—or disorder—of the system as a whole augments to the extent stipulated by the second law.

This example shows that, within an isolated system, a local heightening of order is compatible with the second law. We have pointed out, however, that the degree of order represented by even the simplest organism is incomparably higher than that which a crystal defines. We must now ask whether the conservation and invariant multiplication of such structures is also compatible with the second law. This can be verified through an experiment closely comparable with that of crystallization.

We take a milliliter of water having in it a few milligrams of a simple sugar, such as glucose, as well as some mineral salts containing the essential elements that enter into the chemical constituents of living organisms (nitrogen, phosphorus, sulfur, etc.). In this medium we grow a bacterium, for example *Escherichia coli* (length, 2 microns; weight, approximately 5×10^{-13} grams). Inside thirty-six hours the solution will contain several billion bacteria. We shall find that about 40 percent of the sugar has been converted into cellular constituents, while the remainder has been oxidized into carbon dioxide and water. By carrying out the entire experiment in a calorimeter, one can draw up the thermodynamic balance sheet for the operation and determine that, as in the case of crystallization, the entropy of the system as a whole (bacteria plus medium) has increased a little more than the minimum prescribed by the second law. Thus, while the extremely complex system represented by the bacterial cell has not been conserved but has multiplied several billion times, the thermodynamic debt corresponding to the operation has been duly settled.

No definable or measurable violation of the second law has occurred. Nonetheless, something unfailingly upsets our physical intuition as we watch this phenomenon, whose strangeness is even more appreciable than before the experiment. Why? Because we see very clearly that this process is bent or oriented in one exclusive direction: the multiplication of cells. These to be sure do not violate the laws of thermodynamics, quite the contrary. They not only obey them; they utilize them as a good engineer would, with maximum efficiency, to carry out the project and bring about the "dream" (as François Jacob has put it) of every cell: to become two cells.

Later we shall try to give an idea of the complexity, the subtlety, and the efficiency of the chemical machinery necessary to the accomplishment of a project demanding the synthesis of several hundred different organic constituents; their assembly into several thousand macromolecular species; and the mobilization and utilization, where necessary, of the chemical potential liberated by the oxidation of sugar: i.e., in the construction of cellular organelles. There is, however, no physical paradox in the invariant reproduction of these structures: invariance is bought at not one penny above its thermodynamic price, thanks to the perfection of the teleonomic apparatus which, grudging of calories, in its infinitely complex task attains a level of efficiency rarely approached by man-made machines. This apparatus is entirely logical, wonderfully rational, and perfectly adapted to its purpose: to preserve and reproduce the structural norm. And it achieves this, not by departing from physical laws, but by exploiting them to the exclusive advantage of its personal idiosyncrasy. It is the very existence of this purpose, at once both pursued and fulfilled by the teleonomic apparatus, that constitutes the "miracle." Miracle? No, the real difficulty is not in the physics of the phenomenon; it lies elsewhere, and deeper, involving our own understanding, our intuition of it. There is really, no paradox or miracle; but a flagrant *epistemological contradiction*.

The cornerstone of the scientific method is the postulate that nature is objective. In other words, the *systematic* denial that "true" knowledge can be got at by interpreting phenomena in terms of final causes—that is to say, of "purpose." An exact date may be given for the discovery of this canon. The formulation by Galileo and Descartes of the principle of inertia laid the groundwork not only for mechanics but for the epistemology of modern science, by abolishing Aristotelian physics and cosmology. To be sure, neither reason, nor logic, nor observation, nor even the idea of their systematic confrontation had been ignored by Descartes' predecessors. But science as we understand it today could not have been developed upon those foundations alone. It required the unbending stricture implicit in the postulate of objectivity—ironclad, pure, forever undemonstrable. For it is obviously impossible to imagine an experiment which could prove the *nonexistence* anywhere in nature of a purpose, of a pursued end.

But the postulate of objectivity consubstantial with science; it has guided the whole of its prodigious development for three centuries. There is no way to be rid of it, even tentatively or in a limited area, without departing from the domain of science itself.

Objectivity nevertheless obliges us to recognize the teleonomic character of living organisms, to admit that in their structure and performance they act projectively—realize and pursue a purpose. Here therefore, at least in appearance, lies a profound epistemological contradiction. In fact the central problem of biology lies with this very contradiction, which, if it is only apparent, must be resolved; or else proven to be utterly insoluble, if that should turn out indeed to be the case.

QUESTIONS FOR REFLECTION

1. Early in his essay, Monod entertains "regularity" and "repetition" as criteria to distinguish between the natural and the artificial. Do you think these criteria adequately distinguish the natural from the artificial? What alternative criteria would you propose?

2. A central idea Monod investigates is the contention that artificial objects have a purpose, reflecting the intention of those who made them. When is that not the case? Can you name any artificial objects that do not have an express purpose?

3. How might Monod's notion of "invariant reproduction" be applied to design?

4. Are we poets or engineers?

CRITICAL THINKING QUESTION

Are we poets or engineers? What is your answer to this question from the perspective of a student of design? How do you think philosophers and the general public think of designers and architects in terms of whether they are poets or engineers?

 FOR FURTHER READING

Dawkins, Richard. 2006. *The Selfish Gene: 30th Anniversary Edition.* New York: Oxford University Press.

6

What Is Meaning?

FIGURE 6.1
The Eiffel Tower of Paris, as the tallest building at the time it was built,
introduced a powerful visual connection throughout the city.

ARCH: Let's remember the line from Wallace Stevens' poem:

I am what is around me

We've been interpreting this line throughout our dialogues, returning to it as a point of departure for many of our themes, including our
discussion on place. We understood Stevens to be suggesting that
our identity—who we are—is tied up with where we are; identity is
relative to place.

PHILO: Yes.

What Do We Mean When We Say Objects Have Meaning?

ARCH: In Chapter 4, "What Is Place?," we discovered this tendency of designers and architects to assign meaning to places, resulting from a belief
that places can and do carry meaning. Places can carry meaning in
the way they are designed, but they also carry meaning as a result of
us occupying them.

PHILO: How so?

ARCH: Well, let's think about the studio space. Functionally, it's just a container. Most of the studios in our design building are pretty much
the same. There are some idiosyncratic aspects here and there, but
for practical purposes there's not much distinguishing them. All the
same, I have a favorite studio space I like to use for my classes, as I'm
sure you do for your classes.

PHILO: That's true.

ARCH: In fact, what's the first thing I say to all of my studios? I tell my students that they need to start filling up the space with work, to make it
a functioning studio where one can see creativity in action and ideas
at work. What's the first thing you did to your dorm room in college?

PHILO: You mean, a hundred years ago?

ARCH: Yes, can your memory go back that far?

PHILO: I put up posters and bought a plant to place on the windowsill.

ARCH: Why?

PHILO: To give it character.

ARCH: So that it would have meaning for you.

PHILO: Sure.

ARCH: And only for you, not anyone else.

PHILO: Why would I want to my dorm room to have meaning for someone else?

ARCH: That's exactly my point.

PHILO: That I put up posters in my dorm room?

ARCH: No, concentrate now. My point is that we generally believe or assume objects to have meaning, and we use objects to give meaning to the places we inhabit.

PHILO: OK. But, that seems a bit obvious, doesn't it?

ARCH: It isn't obvious at all!

PHILO: Why not?

ARCH: We may know *that* we hold objects to have meaning, and we may know *why* we use objects to give meaning to places we use, but do we know *how* objects and places come to carry meaning in the first place?

PHILO: I see your point.

ARCH: **Semiology** (the language of objects) is another central theme that flows from the questions: "I am what is around me" and "what is the meaning of place?" We can't discuss this subject without understanding how human perception and cognition function. In other words, we need to understand how humans form and retain memory and mental representations of their physical environment, whether it's natural or manmade.

PHILO: Yes, I agree. Go on.

Cave Drawings—Giving Meaning to Life's Objects

ARCH: Dear Philo, the example of early cave drawings has served us well in class, as it triggers discussion on a sensitive topic: the dominance of words over images and drawings. Our task as designers—whether we're designing buildings, furniture, appliances, apparel, or anything else—is to use these two modes of expression to communicate with those inside and outside of our profession, with people such as critics and clients. After all, the problem of communication is directly linked to that of the means (the vehicle, use of fashionable expression, and the medium). R. Jakobson establishes classical definitions of linguistic functions in his analysis of communication theory. Designers and architects must effectively use images and words together effectively as vehicles of expression.

Too often in the academic setting, the terms of reference are left vague, ill defined, and too personal to provide enough constructive criticism to push students' design projects forward into the next stage of development.

PHILO: Yes, that is a built-in issue for critical thinking, as we talked about in Chapter 1. As we said, critical thinking can be both in words and images. Although they are different modes of human communication, they are both cooperative and competitive, but always complementary.

ARCH: At this point I would like to recall a very useful definition of drawing by G. M. Cantacuzino.[1]

> Drawing is the means by which we represent on a two-dimensional surface an object or a creature. Drawing is the birthplace of writing. Before writing humans drew. The representation of models from nature led to progressive schematization of forms which become concepts and sounds. That is the root of the two categories of writing: pictographic writing and phonetic writing. Even after drawing separated itself from writing, it kept for a long time its descriptive and narrative character. Drawing therefore was from the beginning a means of expression between humans, a method of fixing and grasping forms.

PHILO: Yes, that is an interesting question, what was the meaning of those early cave drawings by human beings?

ARCH: A look at the early cave paintings in France and Spain will help with discussing this issue of meaning, why did these early hunter-gatherers make drawings? Was it born out of a utilitarian necessity? Were the drawings used to plan the next day's hunt? Or were they drawn out of a religious motivation, to express the power of humans over the soul of the animal, as some have suggested?

The earliest known European cave paintings date to 32,000 years ago. Their purpose is not known, but the evidence suggests that they were not merely decorations of living areas because the caves in which they have been found don't show signs of ongoing habitation.

FIGURE 6.2 There is much speculation about the purpose of early cave drawing such as those found in Lascaux, France, (left) and Altamira, Spain (right).

But Is It Art?

ARCH: The question we ask in this chapter brings us to another huge and confusing paradox: although we search for meaning in designed objects, we also consider architecture as a nonrepresentational art. Architecture is closer to music than the figurative arts of painting and sculpture. This simple fact is infamous for generating confusion among architects and designers alike. I will ask you a provocative question: given the fact that design and architecture have an obligation to function—as in "form follows function"—can they be regarded as art? And if they are part of the arts, are they "the least spiritual" due to the "weight of beams and bricks and mortar" as Arthur Schopenhauer is quoted in Nelson Goodman's essay "How Buildings Mean."[2]

> Arthur Schopenhauer ranked the several arts in a hierarchy, with literary and dramatic arts at the top, music soaring in a separate even higher heaven, and architecture sinking to the ground under the weight of beams and mortar. The governing principle seems to be some measure of spirituality, with architecture ranking lowest by vice of being grossly material.

PHILO: Yes, go on. I can agree with Schopenhauer so far. What is the problem?

ARCH: Goodman proceeds to defend design and architecture by pointing to the fact that[3]

> [I]n comparing architecture with the other arts, what may first strike us, despite Schopenhauer, is a close affinity with music: architectural and musical works, unlike paintings or plays or novels, are seldom descriptive or representational. With some interesting exceptions, architectural works do not denote—that is, do not describe, recount, depict, or portray. They mean, if at all, in other ways.

PHILO: That places a burden on the discussion of meaning of design and architectural works. Does it not?

ARCH: Yes, it does. That is one of the most misunderstood topics in design studios today. The misunderstanding is rooted in the confusion of the words: communication and signification. Roman Jakobson defines these two distinct functions of language as: denotation and signification. It would be useful at this point to review Roman Jakobson's Six Functions of Language.[4] Jakobson outlines six terms that illustrate how all types of communication work. He says that the function of the sign is to *communicate* ideas by means of *messages*. This implies an object, a thing spoken about or *referent, signs* and therefore *code,* a *means* or *medium* of transmission and obviously, and *emitter* (also called the *sender* by some users of this model) and a *receiver.*

On the basis of this diagram borrowed from communication theory, Jakobson established his classic definitions of six linguistic functions, and his analysis is still valid for all modes of communications. Furthermore, the problem of communication is linked to that of the means (the vehicle) or—to use a fashionable expression—the *medium.*[5]

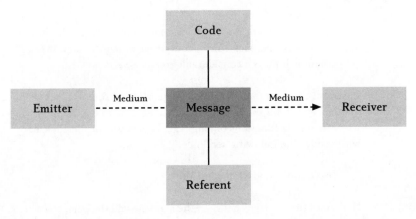

FIGURE 6.3
Jakobson's model of communication.

1. The *referential function.* "It defines the relations between the message and the object to which it refers. The fundamental problem is to formulate true, i.e., objective, observable, and verifiable, *information* concerning the referent."
2. The *emotive function.* Defines the relation between the message and the emitter.
3. The *connotative function* "is the relation between the message and the receiver, the aim of all communication being to elicit reaction from the receiver."
4. The *poetic or aesthetic function* is defined by R. Jakobson as the relationship between the message and itself.

   This is the aesthetic function. In the arts, the referent is the message, which thus ceases to be an instrument of communication and becomes an object.

   The arts and literature create message—objects, which as objects, and over and above the immediate signs which subtend them, are bearers of their own meaning, and belong to a specific Semiology that of stylization, hypostasis of the signifier, Symbolization, etc.

5. The *phatic function.* Affirms and maintains or halts communication.

6. The *metalinguistic function* "This defines the meaning of any signs which might not be understood by the receiver. This function refers one back to the code from which the sign takes its meaning. It plays a considerable role in all arts."

Based on the six functions of language, R. Jakobson provides us, in another article on the poetics of language, a simple example of the use of these six functions of language. This can be best made clear if we consider the following sentence:

I have two friends, John and Mary.

"It defines the relations between the message and the object to which it refers. The fundamental problem is to formulate true, i.e., objective, observable, and verifiable, information concerning the referent."

In this example, an object message can refer to the true facts: the speaker (the emitter) has only two friends. We may also assume, based on their names, that one is female and the other male. Those are facts about the world defined in this example. In terms of concrete information, that sentence could be interpreted as serving an emotional function. Based on the second function, we can hear the emitter confessing sadly to having only two friends. What a pity. Are we supposed to feel sorry for the speaker?

The first function is the *referential function.* Can design and architecture objects offer objective, observable, and verifiable information pertaining to the referent? The referent being the project we design; the referential function.

PHILO: Let's go on to the next definition.

ARCH: The *connotative function* "is the relation between the message and the receiver, the aim of all communication being to elicit reaction from the receiver." In the friend example used, the receiver might inquire, "Why did you place John ahead of Mary in that sentence message?" Let me ask you the following question: given the cultural code, which states that something first mentioned in any text is more important, we can assume that rank order can be intended to reflect importance and suggest power relationships. Are you telling me that John is a better friend than Mary?"

PHILO: In fact, this question goes to the heart of two linguistic functions: questioning the code, that is, the *metalinguistic function.*

This linguistic function refers us back to the code from which the sign takes its meaning. Do you mean to understand that John is a better friend than Mary because his name is placed first in the sentence? No, might the emitter respond. I (the emitter) did not intend any message by the order of the names. I only felt the ease and pleasure of the sound as I spoke those names.

ARCH: Well, let's see how this coincides with the definition of *poetic or aesthetic function* as defined by Jakobson. Let's look into how Jakobson defines the relationship between the message and itself.

PHILO: What do you mean by that?

ARCH: If I may say so, this is the most misunderstood word in our vocabulary: **poetics.**

In terms of our example, the order of those two words, *John* and *Mary,* does not matter to the emitter. What matters is the pleasure to the ear as ordered sounds are heard (refer back to architecture and music). This is the basis of all poetry, where the concrete sound is in front of an abstract meaning. This is known as "concrete poetry," which is the equivalent of "abstract expressionism" in the arts.

In other words, the sequence of the words *John* and *Mary* was poetic, with no intent to communicate meaning about the emitter's preference in any way. It was a poetic gesture towards the "formal" pleasure of sound. That is all! No functional communication was intended. Can we not say that here is the source of art for art's sake?

What does this mean, "formal pleasure of sound"? It means that formally it does not matter which name comes first, all that matters here is the pure order of the sounds, not their meaning. It sounds better to the speaker (poet) to say John before Mary. It falls in a poetic rhythm of sounds (iambic, for example). That is all.

Now that we better understand how modes of communication function, let's take a closer look at a more specific language: the language of objects.

Roland Barthes: Objects as Signs

ARCH: Allow me again to refer here in the discussion of "What is Meaning?" with the second line in Wallace Steven's poem *Theory,* which was introduced in Chapter 1.

> One is not a duchess
> A hundred yards from a carriage

Rolland Barthes' essay can be paraphrased as "One is not a Parisian a hundred miles from the Eiffel Tower."

This speaks of a social code based on measurement of a spatial distance, or **proxemics** of personal space. It is a denotative code, where the object is a prop in a social narrative. Therefore, I know who I am by the place where I live or the land I control (one's personal power).

Barthes writes that architectural objects belong to the group of objects. Gestures and pictorial images, whose origins are utilitarian and functional, were not originally intended for communication. They are objects of everyday use by people, in a derivative way, to signify something. He called them *sign-functions.* Their essence, and original reason for creation, was not to send messages. In this way they are not like words, which are arbitrary symbols, but instead serve specific functional purposes.

We should refocus on Rolland Barthes' quotations: "architecture is always dream and function" and "use never does anything but shelter meaning ... the emergence of a 'new category' ... that of concrete abstraction."

PHILO: What is **concrete abstraction?**

ARCH: A close reading of the essay provides a complete program for an approach to architecture, and central to this program is a set of attitudes toward abstraction, meaning, and thinking. There is a theory of cognition, a set of prescriptions, on how to approach the designed object. Whether it's the tower or the city of Paris itself, significant discourse develops on almost every major theme of contemporary architectural relevance.

PHILO: Barthes is from a along line of thinkers and writers, primarily of the Western tradition. These thinkers believe that life is less a search for pleasure than it is a quest for order and meaning. Of course these two realms, pleasure and meaning, are not entirely divorced from one another.

Barthes writes that, "the [Eiffel] Tower looks at Paris." To visit the Tower is to ascend to the balcony in order to perceive, comprehend, and savor a certain essence of Paris. The vantage point from the Tower permits one to transcend sensation and see built objects organized in a structure that reveals a new category: concrete abstraction.

It is significant that Barthes places the word concrete in front (concrete being the object), and the Tower is first a sensible (sense data) experience, and only after an abstraction does it become a symbol. Here we find ourselves at the heart of the matter. The tower allows one to take a step back and analyze Paris from the new perspective it creates. The very existence of the Tower allows for the possibility of detachment. As an epistemological strategy, detachment is a tradition that runs throughout Western thinking.

The appeal of science in the twentieth century and the many quests for objectivity lie at the heart of architectural systematizing. But once again, this is one of those wonderful paradoxes that are so much a part of Barthes' thinking. The very tower, which makes objectivity possible by generating distance, also provides for an understanding and basis of wholism.

ARCH: What do you mean by wholism, Philo?

PHILO: **Wholism** accounts for both objectivity and distance and prevents one from falling into the analytic trap of looking only at one part at a time.

ARCH: I see. So before the Tower, only a privileged few had access to the spire of Notre Dame. Other rare cases of detached perspectives could be seen from hot air balloons, but this was not a regular experience for the commoner. Before the Eiffel Tower, Paris could be grasped in its entirety only by leap of the imagination. But now, all parts can be seen at once and their relation to each other is revealed. The strategy of viewing from above, in terms of plans and models, has always been a useful tool for architects.

PHILO: Even the ancient Egyptian hieroglyphs for the city, the crossroads etched within walls, recognize the power of this point of view. This distance perspective quite literally provides an overview, which serves to gain meaning and understanding.

ARCH: Yes, for Barthes humans are active agents constantly inserting meaning into the world; we are all lovers of signification. Knowledge and meaning are the result of an "infinite circuit of functions . . . of glance, object, and symbol."

Barthes is speaking about the cycle of perception and cognition. This cycle allows humans to construct a representation of reality, in the Piagetian sense. Jean Piaget suggests that knowledge of the world is composed of two aspects: one is essentially figurative, relating to percepts, images, and sense data of successive states of momentary configurations of the world through direct and immediate contact.

The second aspect is operative. This term refers to operations that intervene between successive states. During these states the person transforms parts of the world into reconstructable patterns or schemes.

Barthes talks about "glance" and "object." Visual perception is only one form of figurative knowledge, whereas thinking and intelligence are based on the operative mode.

To know the world is to be in it and move through it. The Tower not only allows but also encourages this to happen.

ARCH: What does Barthes mean when he writes that "the Tower is much more a crystallizer than a true object"? Why is the word *crystallizer* placed in opposition to the term *true object*? If by *true object* he means a tangible thing that can be seen, touched, smelled, then the opposite of a true object would be an idea—a mental thing, a *concrete abstraction*.

PHILO: Critical thinking encourages us to ask: in what way is it a crystallizer? Because it helps the mind to construct new categories of cognition to "reconstitute memory and sensation. In this struggle we are required to identify and divide . . . to group and separate . . ."

ARCH: What Barthes is telling us is that the process of thinking and acquiring knowledge, in general, is similar to the task of forming a spatial image of Paris. Taking the journey to the top of the Tower creates a cognitive map. What is crystallized is an abstract map of Paris because it is only from up there that we can decipher, recognize known sites, and connect them spatially through the structure of their relationships.

PHILO: He is describing a process of organizing, categorizing, and ordering reality.

When Barthes says that "architecture is always dream and function!" and "use never does anything but shelter meaning," he is paying homage to both philosophical dualism and the central conviction that we are beings that think even before we are beings that are extended in space.

ARCH: This is significant for our relationship to architecture, just as it is for all the other spheres of existence.

PHILO: Descartes said the same thing, and in many ways, the sentiment is similar to Gaston Bachelard's assertion, that the "house is shelter for the daydreamer."

ARCH: Yes! Because of this origin, Barthes sees these objects as having a dual linguistic role. One is to first represent and denote the original function. The second is a disguised connotative role in which "the function becomes pervaded with meaning." What does that mean? (See the Six Functions of Language.)

PHILO: Why are you wondering about that? Is it not clear that the first obligation of design and architecture is to function as we discussed in Chapter 2, "What Is Form? What Is Function?" The fact that meaning (any possible meaning) is rooted in function is not a surprise. Barthes is very clear when he writes, "Use never does anything but shelter meaning."

ARCH: Well then, Barthes also writes that this phenomenon is inevitable. As soon as there is society, every usage is converted into a sign of itself. Yes, a door is a door, a penetration through a wall, a fire exit, a means of keeping the wind outside, but when an object can give images of hesitation, temptation, desire, security, welcome, and respect (as it does for Gaston Bachelard), then this second-order linguistic role becomes grafted on top of its primary role as a functional object.

PHILO: Yes, I have always thought these two thinkers, Barthes and Bachelard, got it right when attempting to identify the language of objects.

ARCH: Barthes calls these objects and gestures *semiological signs,* and he points out that they differ significantly from verbal and written signs. This is a very important distinction between verbal language and the language of objects. For Barthes, the two roles of the usable object are interwoven. In the case of the Tower, its inutility has always been considered something of a scandal, but it is this very uselessness that frees the object from its denotative utilitarian role and enables it to take on the second connotative role. It's "as if the function of art were to reveal the profound uselessness of objects." But Barthes cautions against completely ignoring the utilitarian function, however naive or obscure. "And yet here as in the case of the Tower the naive utilitarianism of the enterprise is not separate from the oneiric, infinitely powerful function." To satisfy this function, certain formal properties of the Tower are quite important. "Reduced to a single line whose sole function is to join, as the poet says, base and summit or again, heaven and earth." And then there is the relationship to use, "as if the function of art were to reveal the profound uselessness of objects."

PHILO: Well then, dear Arch, what can we make out of Barthes' proposition that "the Tower is friendly"? Does this suggest that the Eiffel Tower is a social event/object? I would stress that aspect of it from my point of view.

ARCH: Yes, of course. "The Tower is friendly ... all this night too it will be there connecting me above Paris to each of my friends that I know are seeing it." The Tower, builds a community. More importantly, it builds a community based on shared percepts. Isn't this the real function of a landmark in these media-dominated times? If city life is lived within the paradox of "the close stranger and distant friend"—where physical and psychological space rarely correlate and the people who have significance in your life are not the people physically close to you: in the elevator, on the subway, and crowded city street—then the Tower plays a significant part in the social life of the group. The Tower functions as a primary generator of relationships between people. Barthes also calls the Tower a "rite of initiation" and a "rite of inclusion" for a young man from the provinces. But this is an initiation into what, exactly? How does this activate inclusion, and into which secret fraternity? It is an initiation and inclusion into select groups of citizens who together compose parts of the clear cognitive spatial image of the city. Knowing that concrete abstraction is privy to knowledge, one belongs to the group.

PHILO: The last two themes deal with what Barthes calls "the Tower itself." (This is connected to the self-referential function of object language based on Jakobson) The Tower will live its life as an object before being mobilized as a symbol.

ARCH: The technical order of the Tower engages the visitor in a number of interactions, which are so rich that they result in the viewer's becoming an "engineer by proxy." It's possible to see how the thing is made, while at the same time one becomes aware of the fallibility of perception—a straight line that isn't really a straight line. The very transparency of the Tower leads one inevitably to think about certain traditional architectural concerns, like the separation of inside and outside and the issue of verticality.

PHILO: If meaning is the dialectic between sensation and thinking, then the essay itself is a model that provides lessons and examples on how these activities can best proceed. What are some of these lessons? Paradox and binary processes should be at the heart of our attempts at meaning. "Maupassant eats there but doesn't like the food" and "the Tower sees and is seen, the surprise of seeing how this rectilinear form, which is consumed in every corner of Paris as a pure line, is composed of countless segments, interlinked, crossed and divergent." Take a step back and look at the whole, whether it's the Tower (as a whole) or the parts themselves. Take a step forward and examine the details.

CRITICAL READING PASSAGE

"The Eiffel Tower," from *Mythologies*
Roland Barthes
1957

ABOUT THE AUTHOR

Roland Barthes (1915–1980) was a French writer and philosopher who may also be said to be one of earliest critics of popular culture. Barthes engaged in many types of cultural production, from literature and fashion to architecture, advertising and design. Because of the many areas in which he wrote, it is challenging to categorize Barthes' work under one type of intellectual movement. Nonetheless, he is often considered part of the structuralist movement in twentieth century thought. Structuralism was a form of inquiry originated in large part by the anthropologist Claude Levi-Strauss (b. 1908), who applied discoveries in the then very young discipline of linguistics to ethnographic study of so-called "primitive cultures."

The application of linguistics to primitive cultures revealed to Levi-Strauss that *all* cultures obeyed the same kind of logic—or structure—in creating cultural meaning. The role of myths, for example, that every culture possesses, so argued the structuralists, demonstrated that every culture participates in collective meaning-making.

Barthes wrote a number of essays from 1954 to 1956 analyzing structures of meaning in contemporary French culture, focusing very much on the symbolic function of concrete objects—wrestling, toys, red wine, "the Brain of Einstein," etc. The essays were collected under the title *Mythologies* and published in French in 1957. Though Barthes wrote the essay "The Eiffel Tower" in 1964, it is considered one of the contemporary myths he treated in his earlier work. Note how Barthes attends to the symbolic value of the Eiffel Tower and its role in how the French construct the meaning of their cultural identity.

Maupassant often lunched at the restaurant in the tower, though he didn't care much for the food: *It's the only place in Paris,* he used to say, *where I don't have to see it.* And it's true that you must take endless precautions, in Paris, not to see the Eiffel Tower; whatever the season, through mist and cloud, on overcast days or in sunshine, in rain—wherever you are, whatever the landscape of roofs, domes, or branches separating you from it, *the Tower is there;* incorporated into daily life until you can no longer grant it any specific attribute, determined merely to persist, like a rock or the river, it is as literal as a phenomenon of nature whose meaning can be questioned to infinity but whose existence is incontestable. There is virtually no Parisian glance it fails to *touch* at some time of day; at the moment I begin writing these lines about it, the Tower is there, in front of me, framed by my window; and at the very moment the January night blurs it, apparently trying to make it invisible, to deny its presence, two little lights come on, winking gently as they revolve at its very tip: all this night, too, it will be there, connecting me above Paris to each of my friends that I know are seeing it: with it we all comprise a shifting figure of which it is the steady center: the Tower is friendly.

The Tower is also present to the entire world. First of all as a universal symbol of Paris, it is everywhere on the globe where Paris is to be stated as an image; from the Midwest to Australia, there is no journey to France which isn't made, somehow, in the Tower's name, no schoolbook, poster, or film about France which fails to propose it as the major sign of a people and of a place: it belongs to the universal language of travel. Further: beyond its strictly Parisian statement, it touches the most general human image-repertoire: its simple, primary shape confers upon it the vocation of an infinite cipher: in turn and according to the appeals of our imagination, the symbol of Paris, of modernity, of communication, of science or of the nineteenth century, rocket, stem, derrick, phallus, lightning rod or insect, confronting the great itineraries of our dreams, it is the inevitable sign; just as there is no Parisian glance which is not compelled to encounter it, there is no fantasy which fails, sooner or later, to acknowledge its form and to be nouished by it; pick up a pencil and let your hand, in other words your thoughts, wander, and it is often the Tower which will appear, reduced to that simple line whose sole mythic function is to join, as the poet says, *base and summit,* or again, *earth and heaven.*

This pure—virtually empty—sign—is ineluctable, *because it means everything.* In order to negate the Eiffel Tower (though the temptation to do so is rare, for this symbol offends nothing in us), you must, like Maupassant, get up on it and, so to speak, identify yourself with it. Like man himself, who is the only one not to know his own glance, the Tower is the only blind point of the total optical system of which it is the center and Paris the circumference. But in this movement which seems to limit it, the Tower acquires a new power: an object when we look at it, it becomes a lookout in its turn when we visit it, and now constitutes as an object, simultaneously extended and collected beneath it, that Paris which just now was looking at it. The Tower is an object which sees, a glance which is seen; it is a complete verb, both active and passive, in which no function, no *voice* (as we say in grammar, with a piquant ambiguity) is defective. This dialectic is not in the least banal, it makes the Tower a singular monument; for the world ordinarily produces either purely functional organisms (camera or eye) intended to see things but which then afford nothing to sight, what *sees* being mythically linked to what remains *hidden* (this is the theme of the voyeur), or else spectacles which themselves are blind and are left in the pure passivity of the visible. The Tower (and this is one of its mythic powers) transgresses this separation, this habitual divorce of *seeing* and *being seen;* it achieves a sovereign circulation between the two functions; it is a complete object which has, if one may say so, both sexes of sight. This radiant position in the order of perception gives it a prodigious propensity to meaning: the Tower attracts meaning, the way a lightning rod attracts thunderbolts; for all lovers of signification, it plays a glamorous part, that of a pure signifier i.e., of a form in which men unceasingly put *meaning* (which they extract at will from their knowledge, their dreams, their history), without this meaning thereby ever being finite and fixed: who can say what the Tower will be for humanity tomorrow? But there can be no doubt it will always be something, and something of humanity itself. Glance, object, symbol, such is the infinite circuit of functions which permits it always to be something other and something much more than the Eiffel Tower.

In order to satisfy this great oneiric function, which makes it into a kind of total monument, the Tower must escape reason. The first condition of this victorious flight is that the Tower be an utterly *useless* monument. The Tower's inutility has always been obscurely felt to be a scandal, i.e., a truth, one that is precious and inadmissible. Even before it was built, it was blamed for being useless, which, it was believed at the time, was sufficient to condemn it; it was not in the spirit of a period commonly dedicated to rationality and to the empiricism of great bourgeois enterprises to endure the notion of a useless object (unless it was declaratively an *objet d'art,* which was also unthinkable in relation to the Tower); hence Gustave Eiffel, in his own defense of his project in reply to the Artists' Petition, scrupulously lists all the future uses of the Tower; they are all, as we might expect of an engineer, scientific uses: aerodynamic measurements, studies of the resistance of substances, physiology of the climber, radio-electric research, problems of telecommunication, meteorological observations, etc. These uses are doubtless incontestable, but they seem quite ridiculous alongside the overwhelming myth of the Tower, of the human meaning which it has assumed throughout the world. This is because here the utilitarian excuses, however ennobled they may be by the myth of Science, are nothing in comparison to the great imaginary function which enables men to be strictly human. Yet, as always, the gratuitous meaning of the work is never avowed directly: it is rationalized under the rubric of *use:* Eiffel saw hit Tower in the form of a serious object, rational, useful; men return it to him in the form of a great baroque dream which quite naturally touches on the borders of the irrational.

This double movement is a profound one: architecture is always dream and function, expression of a utopia and instrument of a convenience. Even before the Tower's birth, the nineteenth century (especially in America and in England) had often dreamed of structures whose height would be astonishing, for the century was given to technological feats, and the conquest of the sky once again preyed upon humanity. In 1881, shortly before the Tower, a French architect had elaborated the project of a sun tower; now this project, quite mad technologically, since it relied on masonry and not on steel, also put itself under the warrant of a thoroughly empirical utility; on the one hand, a bonfire placed on top of the structure was to illuminate the darkness of every nook and cranny in Paris by a system of mirrors (a system that was undoubtedly a complex one!), and on the other, the last story of this sun tower (about 1,000 feet, like the Eiffel Tower) was to be reserved for a kind of sunroom, in which invalids would benefit from an air "as pure as in the mountains." And yet, here as in the case of the Tower, the naïve utilitarianism of the enterprise is not separate from the oneiric, infinitely powerful function which, actually, inspires its creation: use never does anything but shelter meaning. Hence we might speak, among men, of a true Babel complex: Babel was supposed to *serve* to communicate with God, and yet Babel is a dream which touches much greater depths than that of the theological project; and just as this great ascensional dream, released from its utilitarian prop, is finally what remains in the countless Babels represented by the painters, as if the function of art were to reveal the profound uselessness of objects, just so the Tower, almost immediately disengaged from the scientific considerations which had authorized its birth (it matters very little here that the Tower should be in fact useful), has arisen from a great human dream in which movable and infinite meanings are mingled: it has reconquered the basic uselessness which makes it live in men's imagination. At first, it was sought—so paradoxical is the notion of an empty monument—to make it into a "temple of Science"; but this is only a metaphor; as a matter of fact, the Tower is *nothing,* it achieves a kind of zero degree of the monument; it participates in no rite, in no cult, not even in Art; you cannot visit the Tower as a museum: there is nothing to see *inside* the Tower. This empty monument nevertheless receives each year twice as many visitors as the Louvre and considerably more than the largest movie house in Paris.

Then why do we visit the Eiffel Tower? No doubt in order to participate in a dream of which it is (and this is its originality) much more the crystallizer than the true object. The Tower is not a usual spectacle; to enter the Tower, to scale it, to run around its courses, is, in a manner both more elementary and more profound, to accede to a *view* and to explore the interior of an object (though an openwork one), to transform the touristic rite into an adventure of sight and of the intelligence. It is this double function I should like to speak of briefly, before passing in conclusion to the major symbolic function of the Tower, which is its final meaning.

The Tower looks at Paris. To visit the Tower is to get oneself up onto the balcony in order to perceive, comprehend, and savor a certain essence of Paris. And here again, the Tower is an original monument. Habitually, belvederes are outlooks upon nature, whose elements—waters, valleys, forests—they assemble beneath them, so that the tourism of the "fine view" infallibly implies a natur-ist mythology. Whereas the Tower overlooks not nature but the city; and yet, by its very position of a visited outlook, the Tower makes the city into a kind of nature; it constitutes the swarming of men into a landscape, it adds to the frequently grim urban myth a romantic dimension, a harmony, a mitigation; by it, starting from it, the city joins up with the great natural themes which are offered to the curiosity of men: the ocean, the storm, the mountains, the snow, the rivers. To visit the Tower, then, is to enter into contact not with a histori-cal Sacred, as is the case for the majority of monuments, but rather with a new nature, that of human space: the Tower is not a trace, a souvenir, in short a culture; but rather an immediate, consumption of a humanity made natural by that glance which transforms it into space.

One might say that for this reason the Tower materializes an imagination which has had its first expression in literature (it is frequently the function of the great books to achieve in advance what technology will merely put into execution). The nineteenth century, fifty years before the Tower, produced indeed two works in which the (perhaps very old) fantasy of a panoramic vision received the guarantee of a major poetic writing (*écriture*): these are, on the one hand, the chapter of *Notre-Dame de Paris* (*The Hunchback of Notre Dame*) devoted to a bird's-eye view of Paris, and on the other, Michelet's *Tableau chro-nologique*. Now, what is admirable in these two great inclusive visions, one of Paris, the other of France, is that Hugo and Michelet clearly understood that to the marvelous mitigation of altitude the panoramic vision added an incom-parable power of *intellection*: the bird's-eye view, which each visitor to the Tower can assume in an instant for his own, gives us the world to *read* and not only to perceive; this is why it corresponds to a new sensibility of vision; in the past, to travel (we may recall certain—admirable, moreover—promenades of Rousseau) was to be thrust into the midst of sensation, to perceive only a kind of tidal wave of things; the bird's-eye view, on the contrary, represented by our romantic writers as if they had anticipated both the construction of the Tower and the birth of aviation, permits us to transced sensation and to see things *in their structure*. Hence it is the advent of a new perception, of an intellectualist mode, which these literatures and these architectures of vision mark out (born in the same century and probably from the same history): Paris and France become under Hugo's pen and Michelet's (and under the glance of the Tower) intelligible objects, yet without—and this is what is new—losing anything of their materiality: a new category appears, that of concrete abstraction; this, moreover, is the meaning which we can give today to the word *structure:* a corpus of intelligent forms.

Like Monsieur Jourdain confronted with prose, every visitor to the Tower makes structuralism without knowing it (which does not keep prose and structure from existing all the same); in Paris spread out beneath him, he spontaneously distinguishes separate—because known—points—and yet does not stop linking them, perceiving them within a great functional space: in short, he separates and groups: Paris offers itself to him as an object virtually *prepared,* exposed to the intelligence, but which he must himself construct by a final activity of the mind: nothing less passive than the *overall view* the Tower gives to Paris. This activity of the mind, conveyed by the tourist's modest glance, has a name: decipherment.

What, in fact, is a panorama? An image we attempt to decipher, in which we try to recognize known sites, to identify landmarks. Take some view of Paris taken from the Eiffel Tower; here you make out the hill sloping down from Chaillot, there the Bois de Boulogne; but where is the Arc de Triomphe? You don't see it, and this absence compels you to inspect the panorama once again, to look for this point which is missing in your structure; your knowledge (the knowledge you may have of Parisian topography) struggles with your perception, and in a sense, that is what intelligence is: to *reconstitute,* to make memory and sensation cooperate so as to produce in your mind a simulacrum of Paris, of which the elements are in front of you, real, ancestral, but nonetheless disoriented by the total space in which they are given to you, for this space was unknown to you. Hence we approach the complex, dialectical nature of all panoramic vision; on the one hand, it is a euphoric vision, for it can slide slowly, lightly the entire length of a continuous image of Paris, and initially no "accident" manages to interrupt this great layer of mineral and vegetal strata, perceived in the distance in the bliss of altitude; but, on the other hand, this very continuity engages the mind in a certain struggle, it seeks to be deciphered, we must find *signs* within it, a familiarity proceeding from history and from myth; this is why a panorama can never be consumed as a work of art, the aesthetic interest of a painting ceasing once we try to *recognize* in it particular points derived from our knowledge; to say that there is a beauty to Paris stretched out at the feet of the Tower is doubtless to acknowledge this euphoria of aerial vision which recognizes nothing other than a nicely connected space; but it is also to mask the quite intellectual effort of the eye before an object which requires to be divided up, identified, reattached to memory; for the bliss of sensation (nothing happier than a lofty outlook) does not suffice to elude the questioning nature of the mind before any image.

This generally intellectual character of the panoramic vision is further attested by the following phenomenon, which Hugo and Michelet had moreover made into the mainspring of their bird's-eye views: to perceive Paris from above is infallibly to imagine a history; from the top of the Tower, the mind finds itself dreaming of the mutation of the landscape which it has before its eyes; through the astonishment of space, it plunges into the mystery of time, lets itself be affected by a kind of spontaneous anamnesis: it is duration itself which becomes panoramic. Let us put ourselves back (no difficult task) at the level of an average knowledge, an ordinary question put to the panorama of Paris; four great moments immediately leap out to our vision, i.e., to our consciousness. The first is that of prehistory; Paris was then covered by a layer of water, out of which barely emerged a few solid points; set on the Tower's first floor, the visitor would have had his nose level with the waves and would have seen only some scattered islets, the Etoile, the Pantheon, a wooded island which was Montmartre and two blue stakes in the distance, the towers of Notre-Dame, then to his left, bordering this huge lake, the slopes of Mont Valérien; and conversely, the traveler who chooses to put himself today on the heights of this eminence, in foggy weather, would see emerging the two upper stories of the Tower from a liquid base; this prehistoric relation of the Tower and the water has been, so to speak, symbolically maintained down to our own days, for the Tower is partly built on a thin arm of the Seine filled in (up to the Rue de l'Université) and it still seems to rise from a gesture of the river whose bridges it guards. The second history which lies before the Tower's gaze is the Middle Ages; Cocteau once said that the Tower was the Notre-Dame of the Left Bank; though the cathedral of Paris is not the highest of the city's monuments (the Invalides, the Pantheon, Sacré-Coeur are higher), it forms with the tower a pair, a symbolic couple, recognized, so to speak, by Tourist folklore, which readily reduces Paris to its Tower and its Cathedral: a symbol articulated on the opposition of the past (the Middle Ages always represent a dense time) and the present, of stone, old as the world, and metal, sign of modernity. The third moment that can be read from the Tower is that of a broad history, undifferentiated since it proceeds from the Monarchy to the Empire, from the Invalides to the Arc de Triomphe: this is strictly the History of France, as it is experienced by French schoolchildren, and of which many episodes, present in every schoolboy memory, touch Paris. Finally, the Tower surveys a fourth history of Paris, the one which is being made now; certain modern monuments (UNESCO, the Radio-Télévision building) are beginning to set signs of the future within its space; the Tower permits harmonizing these unaccommodated substances (glass, metal), these new forms, with the stones and domes of the past; Paris, in its duration, under the Tower's gaze, composes itself like an abstract canvas in which dark oblongs (derived from a very old past) are contiguous with the white rectangles of modern architecture.

Once these points of history and of space are established by the eye, from the top of the Tower, the imagination continues filling out the Parisian panorama, giving it its structure; but what then intervenes are certain human functions; like the devil Asmodeus, by rising above Paris, the visitor to the Tower has the illusion of raising the enormous lid which covers the private life of millions of human beings; the city then becomes an intimacy whose functions, i.e., whose connections he deciphers; on the great polar axis, perpendicular to the horizontal curve of the river, three zones stacked one after the other, as though along a prone body, three functions of human life: at the top, at the foot of Montmartre, pleasure; at the center, around the Opéra, materiality, business, commerce; toward the bottom, at the foot of the Pantheon, knowledge, study; then, to the right and left, enveloping this vital axis like two protective muffs, two large zones of habitation, one residential, the other blue-collar; still farther, two wooded strips, Boulogne and Vincennes, It has been observed that a kind of very old law incites cities to develop toward the west, in the direction of the setting sun; it is on this side that the wealth of the fine neighborhoods proceeds, the east remaining the site of poverty; the Tower, by its very implantation, seems to follow this movement discreetly; one might say that it accompanies Paris in this westward shift, which our capital does not escape, and that it even invites the city toward its pole of development, to the south and to the west, where the sun is warmer, thereby participating in that great mythic function which makes every city into a living being: neither brain nor organ, situated a little apart from its vital zones, the Tower is merely the witness, the gaze which discreetly fixes, with its slender signal, the whole structure—geographical, historical, and social—of Paris space. This deciphering of Paris, performed by the Tower's gaze, is not only an act of the mind, it is also an initiation. To climb the Tower in order to contemplate Paris from it is the equivalent of that first journey, by which the young man from the provinces went up to Paris, in order to conquer the city. At the age of twelve, young Eiffel himself took the diligence from Dijon with his mother and discovered the "magic" of Paris. The city, a kind of superlative capital, summons up that movement of accession to a superior order of pleasures, of values, of arts and luxuries; it is a kind of precious world of which knowledge makes the man, marks an entrance into a true life of passions and responsibilities; it is this myth—no doubt a very old one—which the trip to the Tower still allows us to suggest; for the tourist who climbs the Tower, however mild he may be, Paris laid out before his eyes by an individual and deliberate act of contemplation is still something of the Paris confronted, defied, possessed by Rastignac. Hence, of all the sites visited by the foreigner or the provincial, the Tower is the first obligatory monument; it is a Gateway, it marks the transition to a knowledge: one must sacrifice to the Tower by a rite of inclusion from which, precisely, the Parisian alone can excuse himself; the Tower is indeed the site which allows one to be incorporated into a race, and when it regards Paris, it is the very essence of the capital it gathers up and proffers to the foreigner who has paid to it his initiational tribute.

From Paris contemplated, we must now work our way back toward the Tower itself: the Tower which will live its life as an object (before being mobilized as a symbol). Ordinarily, for the tourist, every object is first of all an *inside,* for there is no visit without the exploration of an enclosed space: to visit a church, a museum, a palace is first of all to shut oneself up, to "make the rounds" of an interior, a little in the manner of an owner: every exploration is an appropriation; this tour of the *inside* corresponds, moreover, to the question raised by the *outside:* the monument is a riddle, to enter it is to solve, to possess it; here we recognize in the tourist visit that initiational function we have just invoked apropos of the trip to the Tower; the cohort of visitors which is enclosed by a monument and processionally follows its internal meanders before coming back outside is quite like the neophyte who, in order to accede to the initiate's status, is obliged to traverse a dark and unfamiliar route within the initatory edifice. In the religious protocol as in the tourist enterprise, being enclosed is therefore a function of the rite. Here, too, the Tower is a paradoxical object: one cannot be shut up within it since what defines the Tower is its longilineal form and its open structure: How can you he enclosed within emptiness, how can you visit a line? Yet incontestably the Tower is visited: we linger within it, before using it as an observatory. What is happening? What becomes of the great exploratory function of the *inside* when it is applied to this empty and depth-less monument which might be said to consist entirely of an exterior substance?

In order to understand how the modern visitor adapts himself to the paradoxical monument which is offered to his imagination, we need merely observe what the Tower gives him, insofar as one sees in it an object and no longer a lookout. On this point, the Tower's provisions are of two kinds. The first is of a technical order; the Tower offers for consumption a certain number of performances, or, if one prefers, of paradoxes, and the visitor then becomes an engineer by proxy; these are, first of all, the four bases, and especially (for enormity does not astonish) the exaggeratedly oblique insertion of the metal pillars in the mineral mass; this obliquity is curious insofar as it gives birth to an upright form, whose very verticality absorbs its departure in slanting forms, and here there is a kind of agreeable challenge for the visitor; then come the elevators, quite surprising by their obliquity, for the ordinary imagination requires that what rises mechanically slide along a vertical axis; and for anyone who takes the stairs, there is the enlarged spectacle of all the details, plates, beams, bolts, which *make* the Tower, the surprise of seeing how this rectilinear form, which is consumed in every corner of Paris as a pure line, is composed of countless segments, interlinked, crossed, divergent: an operation of reducing an appearance (the straight line) to its contrary reality (a lacework of broken substances), a kind of demystification provided by simple enlargement of the level of perception, as in those photographs in which the curve of a face, by enlargement, appears to be formed of a thousand tiny squares variously illuminated. Thus the Tower-as-object furnishes its observer, provided he insinuates himself into it, a whole series of paradoxes, the delectable contraction of an appearance and of its contrary reality.

The Tower's second provision, as an object, is that, despite its technical singularity, it constitutes a familiar "little world"; from the ground level, a whole humble commerce accompanies its departure: vendors of postcards, souvenirs, knicknacks, balloons, toys, sunglasses, herald a commercial life which we rediscover thoroughly installed on the first platform. Now any commerce has a space-taming function; selling, buying, exchanging—it is by these simple gestures that men truly dominate the wildest sites, the most sacred constructions. The myth of the moneylenders driven out of the Temple is actually an ambiguous one, for such commerce testifies to a kind of affectionate familiarity with regard to a monument whose singularity no longer intimidates, and it is by a Christian sentiment (hence to a certain degree a special one) that the spiritual excludes the familiar; in Antiquity, a great religious festival as well as a theatrical representation, a veritable sacred ceremony, in no way prevented the revelation of the most everyday gestures, such as eating or drinking: all pleasures proceeded simultaneously, not by some heedless permissiveness but because the ceremonial was never savage and certainly offered no contradiction to the quotidian. The Tower is not a sacred monument, and no taboo can forbid a commonplace life to develop there, but there can be no question, nonetheless, of a trivial phenomenon here; the installation of a restaurant on the Tower, for instance (food being the object of the most symbolic of trades), is a phenomenon corresponding to a whole meaning of leisure; man always seems disposed—if no constraints appear to stand in his way—to seek out a kind of counterpoint in his pleasures: this is what is called comfort. The Eiffel Tower is a comfortable object, and moreover, it is in this that it is an object either very old (analogous, for instance, to the ancient Circus) or very modern (analogous to certain American institutions such as the drive-in movie, in which one can simultaneously enjoy the film, the car, the food, and the freshness of the night air). Further, by affording its visitor a whole polyphony of pleasures, from technological wonder to haute cuisine, including the panorama, the Tower ultimately reunites with the essential function of all major human sites: autarchy; the Tower can live on itself: one can dream there, eat there, observe there, understand there, marvel there, shop there; as on an ocean liner (another mythic object that sets children dreaming), one can feel oneself cut off from the world and yet the owner of a world.

QUESTIONS FOR REFLECTION

1. How does Barthes argue that the Eiffel Tower fulfills a symbolic function?

2. What symbolic effect does the Eiffel Tower have on the identity of Paris and French culture in general?

3. Do you agree with Barthes that cultural objects have an everyday use as well as a symbolic function?

4. What "myths" currently populate our culture?

 FOR FURTHER READING

Goodman, Nelson. "How Buildings Mean." *Critical Inquiry*. June 1985.

Sontag, Susan. "Against Interpretation." *Against Interpretation and Other Essays*. New York: Farrar, Strauss and Giroux, 1986, pp. 3–14.

7

What Is Time?

FIGURE 7.1
Marcel Duchamp's *Nude Descending a Staircase, No. 2*
depicts movement over time.

ARCH: For me as an architect, this chapter is an attempt to capture the nature of our essential endeavors, which is to measure "space and time." We architects and, if I may say so, philosophers have been indoctrinated (for better or for worse) to experience the world in terms of 3D, or the so called fourth dimension: time. The new advanced physics we have read about identifies at least eleven dimensions.

We ignore time in favor of space! Time is a very difficult subject for architects. It may even be counter to our very own bodily experience. We can recall Gaston Bachelard's famous line: "Inhabited space transcends geometrical space."

PHILO: Why is time more difficult than other topics?

ARCH: Capturing "lived in" space, as experienced by individuals both singly or as members of groups, is a difficult task in design at any scale. This because at the foundation of constructive activity is an act of geometry (in which we stop time) to grasp and measure space.

PHILO: Please tell the story.

Stopping Time, Mastering Space

ARCH: Michel Serres, in an essay titled "The Birth of Geometry," tells the story of Thales, the first Greek geometer to visit Egypt with the task to measure the heights of the pyramids. In order to measure from a distance he placed a stick in the sand and waited until the face of the pyramid had *no shadow* on the ground. At that moment he measured the shadow of the stick. This enabled him to draw two similar triangles to establish the height of the pyramid at a distance. Serres argues that was the birth of geometry, when time (the movement of the sun) was put on hold in order to measure the height of the pyramid and measure space in general.

Because, again, from time immemorial we (architects) were taught that in order to capture and measure space, we have to stop time, as architecture was supposed to deny the transitory nature of existence.

Architecture's main purpose for existing was to function mnemonically, that is, to function as the cultural responsibility towards group memory. The classic cliché has been that architecture is timeless and tends to a "timeless ideal" condition. Of course we can update that ancient model for our time, when "flux" is the dominant model of understanding reality, as opposed to the Greek early model of fixity. Geometry, the main tool of architects, was the operational method of constructing a view of ever changing external reality. I will try to summarize as best I can with this ancient Greek philosophical dispute as follows. It is a tall order for designers and architects to live in real time when it is immortality we crave in our work, (or at least we did until recently). We know better now. In cyberspace they say: "If you are not in real time, you don't exist" (more about that later in this chapter).

The Transitory Nature of Existence: The Greek Dilemma

PHILO: Really, would you explain that?

ARCH: That might be a story I should let you tell.

PHILO: Because we are addressing this to design students why don't you tell it, and I will comment if necessary.

ARCH: Well, here we have it. The dialectical theme that took shape twenty-five hundred years ago is still around and in full force, present in our culture and architectural discourse. This dialogue among the early Greeks should be quite familiar by now to students of design with meaning of such terms and oppositions as: *being* (fixity) and *becoming* (change over time); that is, permanence and change, space and time, geometric form as timeless truth or truth through acts of piling and shaping stone. This is the dialogue between Heraclitus and Parmenides. Their thoughts, doubts, and solutions arose from the unhappy observation of the changeableness of things and the fear that in such a world no certain knowledge is possible (if reality is constantly changing). In short, Heraclitus found change over time the true nature of existence whereas Parmenides argued for a fixed and timeless universe.

The Perception of Change

PHILO: Yes, Arch, I know that story. The world has moved on well beyond the classical Greek model of fixity. The other Greek world view of Heraclitus, where we were told that the world is in perpetual flux, has been gaining the upper hand in the contemporary paradigm, and that is the world view of the young.

ARCH: Well, if I may point out, design and architecture have been trying to keep up with these shifting definitions of time since the emergence of the modern approach to time and space in the view of Einstein's theoretical model.

In the twenty-first century, we must escape this ancient naive dialectic. Architecture exists in both time and space, to both of which we attribute meaning. Stones don't speak. We give them a voice. The ancients knew that. Aristotle asked the question, "What causes the bronze to become a statue? What produces this change is its maker?"Aristotle called it the "efficient cause" and space, but it is always an act of construction.

PHILO: Well that is liberating. We will have the students read Bergson.

ARCH: Yes they will read "The Perception of Change." This essay, along with many others, reveals our collective emergent ideological tilt towards Heraclitus and the resultant natural affinity we find in ourselves with the metaphoric possibilities of the word *time*.

Bergson's cardinal third rule is: "State problems and solve them in terms of time, not of space." In other words, reference all descriptions of reality to the time dimension because only then do we account for change.

PHILO: Do you mean the understanding of time has radically changed in modern thought? I could have said that as well within philosophy. But how does such a shift in the scientific understanding of time affect the outlook of time and space in architecture and design?

ARCH: First of all, it distinguishes the sense of time between individual perception of time and collective understanding, or should I say agreement of time.

PHILO: What do you mean? Time is time. How can it be different for individuals and groups?

ARCH: Well, you might want to see "The Culture of Time and Space, 1880–1918," but let's move on. You see? I just used a temporal metaphor.

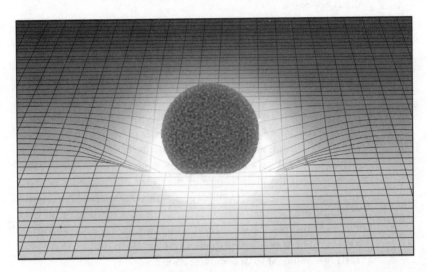

FIGURE 7.2 Space and time deform relative to the mass of the ball at the center.

Contradictions of Time and Space

PHILO: Seems to me more like a spatial metaphor, or rather, an example of how time is measured in terms of space. We "move on" into the future by covering a measured distance.

Our discussion just now reminds me of another reason why Le Corbusier came up with the notion of the *promenade architecturale*, the idea that the spectator's movement through designed space completes the meaning of that space and constitutes the experience of place. For Le Corbusier, the dependence on the spectator's movement helped to conceive of architecture as nonstatic.

ARCH: That's right. The *promenade architecturale* introduces time as one of architecture's dimensions.

PHILO: It occurs to me there are other, sometimes contradictory, instances of architecture incorporating time as one of its design dimensions.

ARCH: Which ones are you thinking of?

PHILO: A somewhat scandalous, but no less historical, example is that of Albert Speer.

ARCH: He is the architect Adolf Hitler appointed his planner-in-chief during World War II.

PHILO: Yes, Speer is infamous for being the Nazi's chief architect. His position in modern architecture is most peculiar. Though he lived during modernism, he wasn't a modernist. He was interested in the classical period, much as Le Corbusier was. But instead of arguing that modern architecture should model itself off the *way* classical architecture established itself as a standard in the manner Le Corbusier held, Speer believed the architecture of the Third Reich should be built with the same materials that allowed classical architecture to become the beautiful ruins they were. In fact, one of the structures Speer held as an example was the Parthenon, which we already talked about in Chapter 2. For Speer, the Parthenon's beauty lay in the fact that it was a lasting monument to Greek civilization.

ARCH: That is why Speer rejected modern architecture's use of metal, concrete, and glass. He viewed them as inferior materials that would not allow buildings to become beautiful ruins. He even wrote an essay in 1938 called the *Ruinenwertstheorie*—the *Theory of the Value of Ruins*—in which he advocated the use of stone to realize the goal of architecture one day becoming beautiful ruins.

PHILO: Interestingly enough, Speer believed architecture should have a consciousness of time, of the fact that it would fall into ruin one day, but only so that it could one day appear as a monument to a great civilization.

ARCH: Which is where you find the contradiction.

PHILO: Yes, for Speer, architecture could overcome time and become a monument, but only by exposing itself to the destruction that the passing of time brings to all things.

ARCH: Speer thus imagined in his design what his buildings would look like as ruins. He gave more weight to how a building would look as a ruin than how it looked in the present. You might say Speer's design philosophy was one of the first examples of planned obsolescence.

PHILO: I suppose, in a sense. Except I think Speer thought his buildings would only take on real significance once they became ruins.

ARCH: Well, that's certainly one additional example of how time functions as a dimension of design. You mentioned thinking of at least one other.

PHILO: It's funny you mentioning just now "planned obsolescence" because that's the other example I had in mind.

ARCH: How is it that different from the example of Speer?

PHILO: Well, as I'm sure you know, "planned obsolescence" is a term that comes out of industrial design, rather than architecture. In fact, the industrial designer Brooks Stevens is credited with coining the term, having used it as the title of an address he gave at an advertising conference in 1954. Stevens defined planned obsolescence as "instilling in the buyer the desire to own something a little newer, a little better, a little sooner than is necessary."[1]

ARCH: I can see how this connects to time and why it interests you in particular, because planned obsolescence reveals a certain understanding of time in design that is tied to commodity production. You have been consistent in our conversations in reminding us of how design production is inseparable from capitalist production, which includes not only the making of commodities but the social relationships the manufacturing of commodities entails.

PHILO: Yes, that has been my particular interest in the questions we have been posing throughout our discussions. For me, critical thinking in design depends on a fundamental reflection on the social, political, and historical conditions out of which design problems appear. These are not just intellectual problems one can either decide to entertain or ignore.

ARCH: Fair enough. But I feel you're about to expand our discussion now to questions concerning the designer's responsibility in terms of these conditions you list.

PHILO: I have to admit I am tempted to go in that direction, yes.

ARCH: The only problem is that we've already devoted space for that discussion a little later on in our dialogues. For the moment, why don't you just say more about how you see time related to design production in terms of planned obsolescence.

PHILO: Well, planned obsolescence reveals a view of time based on a product's consumption by a consumer. When the product has been "used up," so to speak, by the consumer within a timeframe decided in advance by the producer, there will already be another product waiting for the consumer to buy to replace the original product.

ARCH: It's true that we see this clearly enough with computer production. Every season, the computers we're offered are supposedly the fastest, most cutting-edge, etc., etc. Yet, just when I buy a new computer, I see there's already a newer model released right after. Then I'm forced to upgrade yet again.

PHILO: Again, that's how the industry works. As soon as one model of processing chip is released, engineers are already at work designing a newer one. Industrial design is no different. There's always a new design on the horizon that will make the product you *just bought* a month ago seem terribly outdated.

ARCH: Well, it would be difficult to make money if one always fulfilled a consumer's need fully.

PHILO: Fulfilling a need is one thing. But designing a product in such a way so as to create new needs when the others have been fulfilled just fine already is another thing altogether.

ARCH: I take your point.

PHILO: I know you're interested more in the traditional philosophical point to these discussions, so let me say it this way: What planned obsolescence shows is the existence of another kind of temporality that is culturally specific and qualitatively different from other kinds of temporality. Our question is, "What is time?" Well, the answer, as always, is: it depends. The time of commodity production is different from the time of agrarian production.

ARCH: Well, maybe not anymore. But I understand what you're saying. At one point in history, the experience of time was different in the cities from on the farm.

PHILO: That's right. Now, we have corporate food production, so maybe the distinction is not that great anymore. But at one time, agrarian societies followed what the French theorist Guy Debord called "cyclical time," the time of the seasons. Production obeyed cyclical time, which he characterizes as more natural than the time of commodity production, which he calls "pseudocyclical time."

ARCH: In his famous book, *The Society of the Spectacle* (1967), as well as the film he made in 1973, which he gave the same name?[2]

PHILO: Yes, according to Debord, commodity production gives us a feeling of cyclical time, but the categories of that experience—night, day, work week, weekend, vacations—are actually just pseudo experiences of time. They aren't direct experiences of time, but time experienced as a by-product of our labor schedule and the production/consumption of products.

ARCH: I'll grant you those points that you've made with reference to Debord. But Debord does not say that's all there is. After all, he belonged to the Situationists, who believed, true to their name, that it was possible to break with the temporality belonging to commodity production by designing "situations," encounters that broke free from the rules and regulations of modern life.

PHILO: That's true. They did believe in that. And they also believed it was possible through new forms of design. In fact, many of them were filmmakers, like Debord, but others, like Constant, were architects and artists.

CRITICAL READING PASSAGE

Chapter 5, "The Perception of Change"
from *The Creative Mind: An Introduction to Metaphysics*
Henri Bergson
1911

ABOUT THE AUTHOR

French philosopher Henri Bergson (1859–1941) was widely influential during his lifetime. His work on the relationship between matter, the image, and time gave rise to a number of concepts that were taken up by many twentieth-century thinkers, as well as artists and designers. Bergson's notions of multiplicity and virtuality, for example, have been put to use in much of contemporary architectural design and theory, including so-called "organic architecture" and "mass-produced customization."

Bergson first delivered this chapter's critical reading passage, "The Perception of Change," at Oxford University in 1911. In this text, Bergson argues that we habitually think of change as movement from one position to another. A person moves from a position sitting to a standing position, or he or she might run across a field. According to Bergson, we tend to think that the person occupies different intermediary positions along the way. The problem with this conception, however, is that it reduces movement—and, therefore, change—to individual bits of space. Conceiving change in this way reduces time to space, argue Bergson. Thus, one provocative claim Bergson makes is that there is movement, but no underlying thing—a person, an object—that moves. Movement and change are indivisible.

THE PERCEPTION OF CHANGE

My first words are words of thanks to the University of Oxford for the great honor she has done me in inviting me to address her. I have always thought of Oxford as one of the few sanctuaries where, reverently maintained, passed on by each generation to the next the warmth and radiance of ancient thought are preserved. But I also know that this attachment to antiquity does not prevent your University from being very modern and very much alive. More especially in what concerns philosophy, am I struck to see with what profundity and what originality the ancient philosophers are studied here (did not one of your most eminent masters only recently touch up the interpretation of the Platonic theory of Ideas on its essential points?); and I am also struck, on the other hand, by the fact that Oxford is in the vanguard of the philosophical movement with the two extreme conceptions of the nature of truth: integral rationalism and pragmatism. This alliance of past and present is fruitful in all fields, nowhere more so than in philosophy. To be sure, we have something new to do and perhaps the moment has come to be fully alive to it; but the fact that it is new does not mean that it must be revolutionary. Let us rather study the ancients, become imbued with their spirit and try to do, as far as possible, what they themselves would be doing were they living among us. Endowed with our knowledge (I do not refer so much to our mathematics and physics which would perhaps not radically alter their way of thinking, but especially our biology and psychology), they would arrive at very different results from those they obtained. That is what particularly strikes me in the problem I have undertaken to deal with here, that of change.

I chose it, because I consider it fundamental, and because I believe that if one were convinced of the reality of change and if one made an effort to grasp it, everything would become simplified, philosophical difficulties, considered insurmountable, would fall away. Not only would philosophy gain by it, but our everyday life—I mean the impression things make upon us and the reaction of our intelligence, our sensibility and our will upon things—would perhaps be transformed and, as it were, transfigured. The point is that usually we look at change but we do not see it. We speak of change, but we do not think about it. We say that change exists, that everything changes, that change is the very law of things: yes, we say it and we repeat it; but those are only words, and we reason and philosophize as though change did not exist. In order to think change and see it, there is a whole veil of prejudices to brush aside, some of them artificial, created by philosophical speculation, the others natural to common sense. I believe we shall end by coming to an agreement about them, and shall thus form a philosophy in which every one will collaborate, upon which everyone will be able to agree. That is why I should like to fix two or three points upon which it seems to me agreement has already been reached; it will gradually be extended to the rest of them. The first lecture therefore will deal less with change itself than with the general characteristics of a philosophy attached to the intuition of change.

Here, first of all, is a point upon which every one will agree. If the senses and the consciousness had an unlimited scope, if in the double direction of matter and mind the faculty of perceiving was indefinite, one would not need to conceive any more than to reason. Conceiving is a make-shift when perception is not granted us, and reasoning is done in order to fill up the gaps of perception or to extent its scope. I do not deny the utility of abstract and general ideas—any more than I question the value of bank-notes. But just as the note is only a promise of gold so a conception has value only through the eventual perceptions it represents. It is not, of course, merely a question of the perception of a thing, or a quality, or a state. One can conceive an order, a harmony, and more generally a *truth,* which then becomes a *reality.* I say that we agree on this point. Everyone could see for himself, in fact, that the most ingeniously assembled conceptions and the most learnedly constructed reasonings collapse like a house of cards the moment the fact—a single fact really seen—collides with these conceptions and these reasonings. There is not a single metaphysician, moreover, not one theologian, who is not ready to affirm that a perfect being is one who knows all things intuitively without having to go through reasoning, abstraction and generalization. There is no difficulty therefore about the first point.

And there will not be any more about the second, which we come to now. The insufficiency of our faculties of perception—an insufficiency verified by our faculties of conception and reasoning—is what has given birth to philosophy. The history of doctrines attests it. The conceptions of the earliest Greek thinkers were certainly very close to perception, since it was by the transformations of a sensible element like water, air or fire, that they completed the immediate sensation. But from the time the philosophers of the school of Elea, criticizing the idea of transformation, had shown or thought they had shown the impossibility of keeping so close to the sense-data, philosophy started off along the road it has since traveled, the road leading to a "supra-sensible" world: one was to explain things henceforth with pure "ideas." It is true that for the ancient philosophers the intelligible world was situated outside and above the one our senses and consciousness perceive: our faculties of perception showed us only shadows projected in time and space by immutable and eternal Ideas. For the moderns, on the contrary, these essences are constitutive of sensible things themselves; they are veritable substances, of which phenomena are only the surface covering. But all of them, ancient and modern, are agreed in seeing in philosophy a substitution of the concept for the percept. They all appeal from the insufficiency of our senses and consciousness to the faculties of the mind no longer perceptive, I mean to the functions of abstraction, generalization and reasoning.

On the second point we can therefore be agreed. I come then to the third, which, I imagine, will not occasion any discussion either.

If such is really the philosophical method, there is not, there cannot be *a* philosophy as there is *a* science; on the contrary there will always be as many different philosophies as there are original thinkers. How could it be otherwise? No matter how abstract a conception may be it always has its starting point in a perception. The intellect combines and separates; it arranges, disarranges and co-ordinates; it does not create. It must have a matter, and this matter can only reach it through the senses or the consciousness. A philosophy which constructs or completes reality with pure ideas will therefore only be substituting for or adding to our concrete perceptions as a whole, some particular one of them it has elaborated, thinned down, refined and thereby converted into abstract and general idea. But there will always be something arbitrary in its choice of that privileged perception, for positive science has taken for itself all that is incontestably common to different things; or in other words *quantity,* and all that remains for philosophy therefore is the domain of *quality,* where everything is heterogeneous to everything else, and where a part will never represent the whole except in virtue of a contestable if not arbitrary decree. One can always oppose other decrees to this one. And many different philosophies will spring up, armed with different concepts. They will struggle indefinitely with one another.

Here, then, is the question which arises, and which I consider essential. Since any attempt at purely conceptual philosophy calls forth antagonistic efforts, and since, in the field of pure dialectics there is no system to which one cannot oppose another, should we remain in that field or, (without, of course, ceasing to exercise our faculties of conception and reasoning), ought we not rather return to perception, getting it to expand and extend? I was saving that it is the insufficiency of natural perception which has driven philosophers to complete perception by conception—the latter having as its function to fill in the spaces between the data of the senses or of consciousness and in that way to unify and systematize our knowledge of things. But the examination of doctrines shows us that the faculty of conceiving, as it advances in this work of integration, is forced to eliminate from the real a great number of qualitative differences, to extinguish in part our perceptions, and to weaken our concrete vision of the universe. For the very reason that each philosophy is led, willy-nilly, to proceed in this way, it gives rise to opposing philosophies, each of which picks up something of what the other has dropped. The method, therefore, goes contrary to the purpose: it should in theory extend and complete perception; it is obliged in fact to require that many perceptions stand aside so that some one of them may become representative of the others.—But suppose that instead of trying to rise above our perception of things we were to plunge into it for the purpose of deepening and widening it. Suppose that we were to insert our will into it, and that this will, expanding, were to expand our vision of things. We should obtain this time a philosophy where nothing in the data of the senses or the consciousness would be sacrificed; the no quality, no aspect of the real would be substituted for the rest ostensibly to explain it. But above all we should have a philosophy to which one could not oppose others, for it would have left nothing outside of itself that other doctrines could pick up; it would have taken everything. It would have taken every thing that is given, and even more, for the senses and consciousness, urged on by this philosophy to an exceptional effort, would have given it more than they furnish naturally. To the multiplicity of systems contending with one another, armed with different concepts, would succeed the unity of a doctrine capable of reconciling all thinkers in the same perception—a perception which moreover would grow ever larger, thanks to the combined effort of philosophers in a common direction.

It will be said that this enlarging is impossible. How can one ask the eyes of the body, or those of the mind, to see more than they see? Our attention can increase precision, clarify and intensify; it cannot bring forth in the field of perception what was not there in the first place. That's the objection.—It is refuted in my opinion by experience. For hundreds of years, in fact, there have been men whose function has been precisely to see and to make us see what we do not naturally perceive. They are the artists.

What is the aim of art if not to show us, in nature and in the mind, outside of us and within us, things which did not explicitly strike our senses and our consciousness? The poet and the novelist who express a mood certainly do not create it out of nothing; they would not be understood by us if we did not observe within ourselves, up to a certain point, what they say about others. As they speak, shades of emotion and thought appear to us which might long since have been brought out in us but which remained invisible; just like the photographic image which has not yet been plunged into the bath where it will be revealed. The poet is this revealing agent. But nowhere is the function of the artist shown as clearly as in that art which gives the most important place to imitation, I mean painting. The great painters are men who possess a certain vision of things which has or will become the vision of all men. A Corot, a Turner—not to mention others—have seen in nature many an aspect that we did not notice. Shall it be said that they have not seen but created, that they have given us products of their Imagination, that we adopt their inventions because we like them and that we get pleasure from looking at nature through the image the great painters have traced for us? It is true to a certain extent; but, if it were only that, why should we say of certain works—those of the masters—that they are true? Where would the difference be between great art and pure fancy? If we reflect deeply upon what we feel as we look at a Turner or a Corot, we shall find that, if we accept them and admire them, it is because we had already perceived something of what they show us. But we had perceived without seeing. It was, for us, a brilliant and vanishing vision, lost in the crowd of those visions, equally brilliant and equally vanishing, which become overcast in our ordinary experience like "dissolving views" and which constitute, by their reciprocal interference, the pale and colorless vision of things that is habitually ours. The painter has isolated it; he has fixed it so well on the canvas that henceforth we shall not be able to help seeing in reality what he himself saw.

Art would suffice then to show us that an extension of the faculties of perceiving is possible. But how does this extension work?—Let us notice that the artist has always been considered an "idealist." We mean by that that he is less preoccupied than ourselves with the positive and material side of life. He is, in the real sense of the word, "absent-minded." Why then, being detached from reality to a greater degree, does he manage to see in it more things? We should not understand why if the vision we ordinarily have of external objects and of ourselves were not a vision which we had been obliged to narrow and drain by our attachment to reality, our need for living and acting. As a matter of fact, it would be easy to show that the more we are preoccupied with living, the less we are inclined to contemplate, and that the necessities of action tend to limit the field of vision. I cannot go into a demonstration of this point; I am of the opinion that an entirely new light would illuminate many psychological and psychophysiological questions if we recognized that distinct perception it merely cut, for the purposes of practical existence, out of a wider canvas. In psychology and elsewhere, we like to go from the part to the whole, and our customary system of explanation consists in reconstructing ideally our mental life with simple elements, then in supposing that the combination of these elements has really produced our mental life. If things happened this way, our perception would as a matter of fact be inextensible; it would consist of the assembling of certain specific materials, in a given quantity, and we should never find anything more in it than what had been put there in the first place.

But the facts, taken as they are, without any mental reservation about providing a mechanical explanation of the mind, suggest an entirely different interpretation. They show us, in normal psychological life, a constant effort of the mind to limit its horizon, to turn away from what it has a material interest in not seeing. Before philosophizing one must live; and life demands that we put on blinders, that we look neither to the right, nor to the left nor behind us, but straight ahead in the direction we have to go. Our knowledge, far from being made up of a gradual association of simple elements, is the effect of a sudden dissociation: from the immensely vast field of our virtual knowledge, we have selected, in order to make it into actual knowledge, everything which concerns our action upon things; we have neglected the rest. The brain seems to have been constructed with a view to this work of selection. That could easily be shown by the way in which the memory works. Our past, as we shall see in our next lecture, is necessarily automatically preserved. It survives complete. But our practical interest is to thrust it aside, or at least to accept of it only what can more or less usefully illuminate and complete the situation in the present. The brain serves to bring about this choice: it actualizes the useful memories, it keeps in the lower strata of the consciousness those which are of no use. One could say as much for perception. The auxiliary of action, it isolates that part of reality as a whole that interests us; it shows us less the things themselves than the use we can make of them. It classifies, it labels them beforehand; we scarcely look at the object, it is enough for us to know to which category it belongs. But now and then, by a lucky accident, men arise whose senses or whose consciousness are less adherent to life. Nature has forgotten to attach their faculty of perceiving to their faculty of acting. When they look at a thing, they see it for itself, and not for themselves. They do not perceive simply with a view to action; they perceive in order to perceive—for nothing, for the pleasure of doing so. In regard to a certain aspect of their nature, whether it be their consciousness or one of their senses, they are born *detached;* and according to whether this detachment is that of a certain particular sense, or of consciousness, they are painters or sculptors, musicians or poets. It is therefore a much more direct vision of reality that we find in the different arts; and it is because the artist is less intent on utilizing his perception that he perceives a grater number of things.

Well, what nature does from time to time, by distraction, for certain privileged individuals, could not philosophy of such a matter attempt, in another sense and another way, for everyone? Would not the role of philosophy under such circumstances be to lead us to a completer perception of reality by means of a certain displacement of our attention? It would be a question of *turning* this attention *aside* from the part of the universe which interests us from a practical viewpoint and *turning it back* toward what serves no practical purpose. This conversion of the attention would be philosophy itself.

At first glance it would seem that this has long since been done. More than one philosopher has in fact said that in order to philosophize he had to be detached, and that speculation was the reverse of action. We were speaking a few moments ago of the Greek philosophers: not one of them expressed the idea more forcefully than Plotinus. "All action," he said (and he even added "all fabrication") "weakens contemplation."

And, faithful to the spirit of Plato, he thought that the discovery of truth demanded a conversion of the mind, which breaks away from the appearances here below and attaches itself to the realities above: "Let us flee to our beloved homeland!"—But as you see, it was a question of "fleeing." More precisely, for Plato and for all those who understand metaphysics in that way, breaking away from life and converting one's attention consisted in transporting oneself immediately into a world different from the one we inhabit, in developing other faculties of perception than the senses and consciousness. They did not believe that this education of the attention might most frequently consist in removing its blinders, in freeing it from the contraction that it is accustomed to by the demands of life. They were not of the opinion that the metaphysician, for at least half of his speculations, should continue to look at what every one looks at: no, he had always to turn toward something else. That is why they invariably call upon faculties of vision other than those we constantly exercise in the knowledge of the external world and of ourselves.

And precisely because he disputed the existence of these transcendent faculties, Kant believed metaphysics to be impossible. One of the most profound and important ideas in the *Critique of Pure Reason* is this: if metaphysics is possible, it is through a vision and not through a dialectic. Dialectics leads to contrary philosophies: it demonstrates the thesis as well as the antithesis of antinomies. Only a superior intuition (which Kant calls an "intellectual" intuition), that is, a *perception* of metaphysical reality, would enable metaphysics to be constituted. The most obvious result of the Kantian *Critique* is thus to show that one could only penetrate into the beyond by a vision, and that a doctrine has value in this domain only to the extent that it contains perception: take this perception, analyze it, recompose it, turn it round and round in all directions, cause it to undergo the most subtle operations of the highest intellectual chemistry, you will never get from your crucible anything more than you have put into it; as much vision as you have put into it, just so much will you find; and reasoning will not have made you go one step *beyond* what you had perceived in the first place. That is what Kant brought out so clearly and that, it seems to me, is the greatest service he rendered to speculative philosophy. He definitively established that, if metaphysics is possible, it can be so only through an effort of intuition. — Only, having proved that intuition alone would be capable of giving us a metaphysics, he added: this intuition is impossible.

Why did he consider it impossible? Precisely because he pictured a vision of the kind — I mean a vision of reality "in itself" — that Plotinus had imagined, as those who have appealed to metaphysical intuition have imagined it. By that they all understood a faculty of knowing which would differ radically from consciousness as well as from the senses, which would even be orientated in the opposite direction. They have all believed that to break away from practical life was to turn one's back upon it.

Why did they believe that? Why did Kant, their adversary, share their mistake? How is it they one and all had this conception even if they drew opposite conclusions from it — they constructing a metaphysics, and he declaring metaphysics impossible?

They believed it because they imagined that our senses and consciousness, as they function in everyday life, make us grasp movement directly. They believed that by our senses and consciousness, working as they usually work, we actually perceive the change which takes place in things and in ourselves. Then, as it is incontestable that in following the usual data of our senses and consciousness we arrive in the speculative order at insoluble contradictions, they concluded that contradiction was inherent in change itself and that in order to avoid this contradiction one had to get out of the sphere of change and lift oneself above Time. Such is the position taken by the metaphysician as well as by those who, along with Kant, deny the possibility of metaphysics.

Metaphysics, as a matter of fact, was born of the arguments of Zeno of Elea on the subject of change and movement. It was Zeno who, by drawing attention to the absurdity of what he called movement and change, led the philosophers—Plato first and foremost—to seek the true and coherent reality in what does not change. And it is because Kant believed that our senses and consciousness are in fact exerted in a real Time, that is, in a Time which changes continuously, in a duration which endures; it is because, on the other hand, he took into account the relativity of the usual data of our senses and consciousness (a relativity which he laid down, furthermore, long before the transcendent conclusion of his endeavor that he considered metaphysics impossible without an entirely different kind of vision from that of the senses and the consciousness—a vision, moreover, no trace of which he found in man).

But if we could prove that what was considered as movement and change by Zeno first, and then by metaphysicians in general, is neither change nor movement, that of change they retained what does not change, and of movement what does not move, that they took for an immediate and complete perception of movement and change a crystallization of this perception, a solidification with an eye to practice—and if we could show on the other hand, that what Kant took for time itself was a time which neither flows nor changes nor endures; then, in order to avoid such contradictions as those which Zeno pointed out and to separate our everyday knowledge from the relativity to which Kant considered it condemned, we should not have to get outside of time (we are already outside of it!), we should not have to free ourselves or change (we are already only too free of it!); on the contrary, what we should have to do is to grasp change and duration in their original mobility. Then we should not only see many difficulties drop away one by one, and more than one problem disappear; but through the extension and revivification of our faculty of perceiving, perhaps also (though for the moment it is not a question of rising to such heights) through a prolongation which privileged souls will give to intuition, we should re-establish continuity in our knowledge as a whole—a continuity which would no longer be hypothetical and constructed, but experienced and lived. Is a work of this kind possible? That is what we shall seek to determine, at least as far as the knowledge of our surroundings is concerned, in our second lecture.

SECOND LECTURE

You gave me such sustained attention yesterday that you must not be surprised if I am tempted to take advantage of it today. I am going to ask you to make a strenuous effort to put aside some of the artificial schema we interpose unknowingly between reality and us. What is required is that we should break with certain habits of thinking and perceiving that have become natural to us. We must return to the direct perception of change and mobility. Here is an immediate result of this effort. *We shall think of all change, all movement, as being absolutely indivisible.*

Let us begin with movement. I have my hand at point *A*. I move it over to point *B*, traversing the interval *AB*. I say that this movement from *A* to *B* is by nature simple.

But of this each, one of us has the immediate sensation. No doubt while we are moving our hand from *A* to *B* we say to ourselves that we could stop it at an intermediary point, but in that case we should not have to do with the same movement. There would no longer be a single movement from *A* to *B*; there would be, by hypothesis, two movements, with an interval. Neither from within, through the muscular sense, nor from without through sight, should we still have the same perception. If I leave my movement from *A* to *B* as it is, I feel it undivided and must declare it to be indivisible.

It is true that, when I watch my hand going from *A* to *B* and describing the interval *AB*, I say; "The interval *AB* can be divided into as many parts as I wish, therefore the movement from *A* to *B* can be divided into as many parts as I like, since this movement is applied exactly upon this interval." Or again: "At each instant of its trajection, the mobile passes through a certain point, therefore one can distinguish in the movement as many stages as one likes, therefore the movement is infinitely divisible." But let us reflect for a moment. How could the movement *be applied upon* the space it traverses? How can something moving coincide with something immobile? How could the moving object *be* in a point of its trajectory passage? It *passes through,* or in other terms, it *could be there.* It would be there if it stopped; but if it should stop there, it would no longer be the same movement we were dealing with. It is always by a single bound that a passing is completed, when there is no break in the passage. The bound may last few seconds, or days, months, years: it matters little. The moment it is one single bound, it is indecomposable. Only, once the passage is effected, as the trajectory is space and space is indefinitely divisible, we imagine that movement itself is indefinitely divisible. We like to imagine it because, in a movement, it is not the change of position which interests us, it is the positions themselves, the one the movement has left, the one it will take, the one it would take if it stopped on the way. We need immobility, and the more we succeed in imagining movement as coinciding with the immobilities of the points of space through which it passes, the better we think we understand it. To tell the truth, there never is real immobility, if we understand by that an absence of movement. Movement is reality itself, and what we call immobility is a certain state of things analogous to that produced when two trains move at the same speed, in the same direction, on parallel tracks: each of the two trains is then immovable to the travelers seated in the other. But a situation of this kind which, after all, is exceptional, seems to us to be the regular and normal situation, because it is what permits us to act upon things and also permits things to act upon us: the travelers in the two trains can hold out their hands to one another through the door and talk to one another only if they are "immobile," that is to say, if they are going in the same direction at the same speed. "Immobility" being the prerequisite for our action, we set it up as a reality, we make of it an absolute, and we see in movement something which is superimposed. Nothing is more legitimate in practice. But when we transport this habit of mind into the domain of speculation, we fail to recognize the true reality, we deliberately create insoluble problems, we close our eyes to what is most living in the real.

I need not recall the arguments of Zeno of Elea. They all involve the confusion of movement with the space covered, or at least the conviction that one can treat movement as one treats space, divide it without taking account of its articulations. Achilles, they say, will never overtake the tortoise he is pursuing, for when he arrives at the point where the tortoise was the latter will have had time to go further, and so on indefinitely. Philosophers have refuted this argument in numerous ways, and ways so difficult that each of these refutations deprives the others of the right to be considered definitive. There would have been, nevertheless, a very simple means of making short work of the difficulty: that would have been to question Achilles. For since Achilles finally catches up to the tortoise and even passes it, he must know better than anyone else how he goes about it. The ancient philosopher who demonstrated the possibility of movement by walking was right: his only mistake was to make the gesture without adding a commentary. Suppose then we ask Achilles to comment on his race: here, doubtless, is what he will answer: "Zeno insists that I go from the point where I am to the point the tortoise has left, from that point to the next point it has left, etc., etc.; that is his procedure for making me run. But I go about it otherwise. I take a first step, then a second, and so on: finally, after a certain number of steps, I take a last one by which I skip ahead of the tortoise. I thus accomplish a series of indivisible acts. My course is the series of these acts. You can distinguish its parts by the number of steps it involves. But you have not the right to disarticulate it according to another law, or to suppose it articulated in another way. To proceed as Zeno does is to admit that the race can be arbitrarily broken up like the space which has been covered; it is to believe that the passage is in reality applied to the trajectory; it is making movement and immobility coincide and consequently confusing one with the other."

But that is precisely what our usual method consists in. We argue about movement as though it were made of immobilities and, when we look at it, it is with immobilities that we reconstitute it. Movement for us is a position, then another position, and so on indefinitely. We say, it is true, that there must be something else, and that from one position to another there is the *passage* by which the interval is cleared. But as soon as we fix our attention on this passage, we immediately make of it a series of positions, even though we still admit that between two successive positions one must indeed assume a passage. We put this passage off indefinitely the moment we have to consider it. We admit that it exists, we give it a name; that is enough for us: once that point has been satisfactorily settled we turn to the positions preferring to deal with them alone. We have an instinctive fear of those difficulties which the vision of movement as movement would arouse in our thought; and quite rightly, once we have loaded movement down with immobilities. If movement is not everything, it is nothing; and if to begin with we have supposed that immobility can be a reality, movement will slip through our fingers when we think we have it.

I have spoken of movement; but I could say the same for any change whatever. All real change is an indivisible change. We like to treat it as a series of distinct states which form, as it were, a line in time. That is perfectly natural. If change is continuous in us and also in things, on the other hand, in order that the uninterrupted change which each of us calls "me" may act upon the uninterrupted change that we call a "thing," these two changes must find themselves, with regard to one another, in a situation like that of the two trains referred to above. We say, for example, that an object changes color, and that change here consists in a series of shades which would be the constitutive elements of change and which, themselves, would not change. But in the first place, if each shade has any objective existence at all, it is an infinitely rapid oscillation, it is change. And in the second place, the perception we have of it, to the extent that it is subjective, is only an isolated, abstract aspect of the general state of our person, and this state as a whole is constantly changing and causing this so-called invariable perception to participate in its change; in fact, there is no perception which is not constantly being modified. So that color, outside of us, is mobility itself, and our own person is also mobility. But the whole mechanism of our perception of things, like the mechanism of our action upon things has been regulated in such a way as to bring about, between the external and the internal mobility, a situation comparable to that of our two trains—more complicated, perhaps, but of the same kind: when the two changes, that of the object and that of the subject, take place under particular conditions, they produce the particular appearance that we call a "state." And once in possession of "states," our mind recomposes change with them. I repeat, there is nothing more natural: the breaking up of change into states enables us to act upon things, and it is useful in a practical sense to be interested in the states rather than in the change itself. But what is favorable to action in this case would be fatal to speculation. If you imagine a change as being really composed of states, you at once cause insoluble metaphysical problems to arise. They deal only with appearances. You have closed your eyes to true reality.

I shall not press the point. Let each of us undertake the experiment, let him give himself the direct vision of a change, of a movement: he will have a feeling of absolute indivisibility. I come then to the second point, closely allied to the first. *There are changes, but there are underneath the change no things which change: change has no need of a support. There are movements, but there is no inert or invariable object which moves: movement does not imply a mobile.*

It is difficult to picture things in this way, because the sense 'par excellence' is the sense of sight, and because the eye has developed the habit of separating, in the visual field, the relatively invariable figures which are then supposed to change place without changing form, movement is taken as super-added to the mobile as an accident. It is, in fact, useful to have to deal in daily life with objects which are stable and, as it were, responsible, to which one can address oneself as to persons. The sense of sight contrives to take things in this way: as an advance-guard for the sense of touch, it prepares our action upon the external world. But we already have less difficulty in perceiving movement and change as independent realities if we appeal to the sense of hearing. Let us listen to a melody, allowing ourselves to be lulled by it; do we not have the clear perception of a movement which is not attached to a mobile, of a change without anything changing? This change is enough, it is the thing itself. And even if it takes time, it is still indivisible; if the melody stopped sooner it would no longer be the same sonorous whole, it would be another, equally indivis-ible. We have, no doubt, a tendency to divide it and to picture, instead of the uninterrupted continuity of melody, a juxtaposition of distinct notes. But why? Because we are thinking of the discontinuous series of efforts we should be making to recompose approximately the sound heard if we were doing the singing, and also because our auditory perception has acquired the habit of absorbing visual images. We therefore listen to the melody through the vision which an orchestra-leader would have of it as he watched its score. We picture notes placed next to one another upon an imaginary piece of paper. We think of a keyboard upon which some one is playing, of the bow going up and down, of the musicians, each one playing his part along with the others. If we do not dwell on these spatial images, pure change remains, sufficient unto itself, in no way divided, in no way attached to a "thing" which changes.

Let us come back, then, to the sense of sight. In further concentrating our attention upon it we perceive that even here movement does not demand a vehicle nor change a substance in the ordinary meaning of the word. A sugges-tion of this vision of material things already comes to us from physical science. The more it progresses the more it resolves matter into actions moving through space, into movements dashing back and forth in a constant vibration so that mobility becomes reality itself. No doubt science begins by assigning a support to this mobility. But as it advances, the support recedes; masses are pulverized into molecules, molecules into atoms, atoms into electrons or corpuscles: finally, the support assigned to movement appears merely as a convenient schema—a simple concession on the part of the scholar to the habits of our visual imagi-nation. But there is no need to go so far. What is the "mobile" to which our eye attaches movement as to a vehicle? Simply a colored spot which we know perfectly well amounts, in itself, to a series of extremely rapid vibrations. This alleged movement of a thing is in reality only a movement of movements.

But nowhere is the *substantiality* of change so visible, so palpable as in the domain of the inner life. Difficulties and contradictions of every kind to which the theories of personality have led come from our having imagined, on the one hand, a series of distinct psychological states, each one invariable, which would produce the variations of the ego by their very succession, and on the other hand an ego, no less invariable, which would serve as support for them. How could this unity and this multiplicity meet? How, without either of them having duration—the first because change is something superadded, the second because it is made up of elements which do not change—how could they constitute an ego which endures? But the truth is that there is neither a rigid, immovable substratum nor distinct states passing over it like actors on a stage. There is simply the continuous melody of our inner life—a melody which is going on and will go on, indivisible, from the beginning to the end of our conscious existence. Our personality is precisely that.

This indivisible continuity of change is precisely what constitutes true duration. I cannot here enter into the detailed examination of a question I have dealt with elsewhere. I shall confine myself therefore to saying, in reply to those for whom this "real duration" is something inexpressible and mysterious, that it is the clearest thing in the world: *real duration* is what we have always called *time,* but time perceived as indivisible. That time implies succession I do not deny. But that succession is first presented to our consciousness, like the distinction of a "before" and "after" set side by side, is what I cannot admit. When we listen to a melody we have the purest impression of succession we could possibly have—an impression as far removed as possible from that of simultaneity—and yet it is the very continuity of the melody and the impossibility of breaking it up which make that impression upon us. If we cut it up into distinct notes, into so many "befores" and "afters," we are bringing spatial images into it and impregnating the succession with simultaneity: in space, and only in space, is there a clear-cut distinction of parts external to one another. I recognize moreover that it is in spatialized time that we ordinarily place ourselves. We have no interest in listening to the uninterrupted humming of life's depths. And yet, that is where real duration is. Thanks to it, the more or less lengthy changes we witness within us and in the external world, take place in a single identical time.

Thus, whether it is a question of the internal or the external, of ourselves or of things, reality is mobility itself. That is what I was expressing when I said that there is change, but that there are not things which change.

Before the spectacle of this universal mobility there may be some who will be seized with dizziness. They are accustomed to terra firma; they cannot get used to the rolling and pitching. They must have "fixed" points to which they can attach thought and existence. They think that if everything passes, nothing exists; and that if reality is mobility, it has already ceased to exist at the moment one thinks it—it eludes thought. The material world, they say, is going to disintegrate, and the mind will drown in the torrent-like flow of things.—Let them be reassured! Change, if they consent to look directly at it without an interposed veil, will very quickly appear to them to be the most substantial and durable thing possible. Its solidity is infinitely superior to that of a fixity which is only an ephemeral arrangement between mobilities. I have come, in fact, to the third point to which I should like to draw your attention.

It is this: if change is real and even constitutive of reality, we must envisage the past quite differently from what we have been accustomed to doing through philosophy and language. We are inclined to think of our past as inexistent, and philosophers encourage this natural tendency in us. For them and for us the present alone exists by itself: if something of the past does survive it can only be because of help given it by the present, because of some act of charity on the part of the present, in short—to get away from metaphor—by the intervention of a certain particular function called memory, whose role is presumed to be to preserve certain parts of the past, for which exception is made, by storing them away in a kind of box.—This is a profound mistake! A useful one, I admit, perhaps necessary to action, but fatal to speculation. One could find in it, "in a nutshell" as you say, most of the illusions capable of vitiating philosophical thought.

Let us reflect for a moment on this "present" which alone is considered to have existence. What precisely is the present? If it is a question of the present instant—I mean, of a mathematical instant which would be to time what the mathematical point is to the line—it is clear that such an instant is a pure abstraction, an aspect of the mind; it cannot have real existence. You could never create time out of such instants any more than you could make a line out of mathematical points. Even if it does exist, how could there be an instant anterior to it? The two instants could not be separated by an interval of time since, by hypothesis, you reduce time to a juxtaposition of instants. Therefore they would not be separated by anything, and consequently they would be only one: two mathematical points which touch are identical. But let us put such subtleties aside. Our consciousness tells us that when we speak of our present we are thinking of a certain interval of duration. What duration? It is impossible to fix it exactly, as it is something rather elusive. My present, at this moment, is the sentence I am pronouncing. But it is so because I want to limit the field of my attention to my sentence. This attention is something that can be made longer or shorter, like the interval between the two points of a compass. For the moment, the points are just far enough apart to reach from the beginning to the end of my sentence; but if the fancy took me to spread them further my present would embrace, in addition to my last sentence, the one that preceded it: all I should have had to do is to adopt another punctuation. Let us go further: an attention which could be extended indefinitely would embrace, along with the preceding sentence, all the anterior phrases of the lecture and the events which preceded the lecture, and as large a portion of what we call our past as desired. The distinction we make between our present and past is therefore, if not arbitrary, at least relative to the extent of the field which our attention to life can embrace. The "present" occupies exactly as much space as this effort. As soon as this particular attention drops any part of what it held beneath its gaze, immediately that portion of the present thus dropped becomes *ipso facto* a part of the past. In a word, our present falls back into the past when we cease to attribute to it an immediate interest. What holds good for the present of individuals holds also for the present of nations: an event belongs to the past, and enters into history when it is no longer of any direct interest to the politics of the day and can be neglected without the affairs of the country being affected by it. As long as its action makes itself felt, it adheres to the life of a nation and remains present to it.

Consequently nothing prevents us from carrying back as far as possible the line of separation between our present and our past. An attention to life, sufficiently powerful and sufficiently separated from all practical interest, would thus include in an undivided present the entire past history of the conscious person—not as instantaneity, not like a cluster of simultaneous parts, but as something continually present which would also be something continually moving: such, I repeat, is the melody which one perceives as indivisible, and which constitutes, from one end to the other—if we wish to extend the meaning of the word—a perpetual present, although this perpetuity has nothing in common with immutability, or this indivisibility with instantaneity. What we have is a present which endures.

That is not a hypothesis. It happens in exceptional cases that the attention suddenly loses the interest it had in life: immediately, as though by magic, the past once more becomes present. In people who see the threat of sudden death unexpectedly before them, in the mountain climber falling down a precipice, in drowning men, in men being hanged, it seems that a sharp conversion of the attention can take place—something like a change of orientation of the consciousness which, up until then turned toward the future and absorbed by the necessities of action, suddenly loses all interest in them. That is enough to call to mind a thousand different "forgotten" details and to unroll the whole history of the person before him in a moving panorama.

Memory therefore has no need of explanation. Or rather, there is no special faculty whose role is to retain quantities of past in order to pour it into the present. The past preserves itself automatically. Of course, if we shut our eyes to the indivisibility of change, to the fact that our most distant past adheres to our present and constitutes with it a single and identical uninterrupted change, it seems that the past is normally what is abolished and that there is something extraordinary about the preservation of the past: we think ourselves obliged to conjure up an apparatus whose function would be to record the parts of the past capable of reappearing in our consciousness.

But if we take into consideration the continuity of the inner life and consequently of its indivisibility, we no longer have to explain the preservation of the past, but rather its apparent abolition. We shall no longer have to account for remembering, but for forgetting. The explanation moreover will be found in the structure of the brain. Nature has invented a mechanism for canalizing our attention in the direction of the future, in order to turn it away from the past—I mean of that part of our history which does not concern our present actions—in order to bring to it at most, in the form of "memories," one simplification or another of anterior experience, destined to complete the experience of the moment; it is in this that the function of the brain consists. We cannot here undertake the discussion of that theory which claims that the brain is useful for the preservation of the past, that it stores up memories like so many photographic plates from which we afterward develop proofs, or like so many phonograms destined to become sounds again. We have examined this thesis elsewhere. This doctrine was largely inspired by a certain metaphysics with which contemporary psychology and psycho-physiology are imbued, and which one accepts naturally; this accounts for its apparent clarity. But as we consider it more closely, we see what difficulties and impossibilities accumulate in it. Let us take the case most favorable to the thesis, that of a material object making an impression on the eye and leaving a visual memory in the mind. What can this memory possibly be, if it is really the result of the fixation in the brain of the impression received by the eye? The slightest movement on the part of the object or the eye and there would be not one image but ten, a hundred, a thousand images, as many and more than on a cinematographic film. Were the object merely considered for a certain time, or seen at various moments, the different images of that object could be counted by millions. And we have taken the simplest example! Let us suppose all those images are stored up; what good will they serve? which one shall we use? Let us grant that we have our reasons for choosing one of them, why, and how, shall we throw it back into the past when we perceive it? But to pass over these difficulties, how shall we explain the diseases of the memory? In those diseases which correspond to local lesions of the brain, that is in the various forms of aphasia, the psychological lesion consists less in an abolition of the memories than in an ability to recall them. An effort, an emotion, can bring suddenly to consciousness words believed definitely lost. These facts, with many others, unite to prove that in such cases the brain's function is to choose from the past, to diminish it, to simplify it, to utilize it, but not to preserve it. We should have no trouble in looking upon things from this angle if we had not acquired the habit of believing that the past is abolished. Then its partial reappearance creates the effect of an extraordinary event which demands an explanation. And that is why we imagine here and there in the brain, memory "pigeon-holes" for preserving fragments of the past—the brain moreover, being self-preserving. As though that were not postponing the difficulty and simply putting off the problem! As though, by positing that cerebral matter is preserved through time, or more generally that all matter endures, one did not attribute to it precisely the memory one claimed to explain by it! Whatever we do, even if we imagine that the brain stores up memories, we do not escape the conclusion that the past can preserve itself automatically.

This holds not only for our own past, but also for the past of any change whatsoever, always providing that it is a question of a single and therefore indivisible change: the preservation of the past in the present is nothing else than the indivisibility of change. It is true that, with regard to the changes which take place outside of us we almost never know whether we are dealing with a single change or one composed of several movements interspersed with stops (the stop never being anything but relative). We would have to be inside beings and things as we are inside ourselves before we could express our opinion on this point. But that is not where the importance lies. It is enough to be convinced once and for all that reality is change, that change is indivisible, and that in an indivisible change the past is one with the present.

Let us imbibe this truth and we shall see a good many philosophical enigmas melt away and evaporate. Certain great problems such as that of substance, of change, and of their relation to one another, will no longer arise, All the difficulties raised around these points—difficulties which caused substance to recede little by little to the regions of the unknowable—came from the fact that we shut our eyes to the indivisibility of change. If change, which is evidently constitutive of all our experience, is the fleeting thing most philosophers have spoken of, if we see in it only a multiplicity of states replacing other States, we are obliged to re-establish the continuity between these states by an artificial bond: but this immobile substratum of immobility, being incapable of possessing any of the attributes we know—since all are changes—recedes as we try to approach it: it is as elusive as the phantom of change it was called upon to fix. Let us, on the contrary, endeavor to perceive change as it is in its natural indivisibility: we see that it is the very substance of things, and neither does movement appear to us any longer under the vanishing form which rendered it elusive to thought, nor substance with the immutability which made it inaccessible to our experience. Radical instability and absolute immutability are therefore mere abstract views taken from outside of the continuity of real change, abstractions which the mind then hypostasizes into multiple *states* on the one hand, into *thing* or substance on the other. The difficulties raised by the ancients around the question of movement and by the moderns around the question of substance disappear, the former because movement and change are substantial, the latter because substance is movement and change.

At the same time that theoretical obscurities disappear we get a glimpse of the possible solution of more than one reputedly unsolvable problem. The discussions on the subject of free will would come to an end if we saw ourselves where we are really, in a concrete duration where the idea of necessary determination loses all significance, since in it the past becomes identical with the present and continuously creates with it—if only by the fact of being added to it—something absolutely new. And we could gradually acquire a deeper appreciation of the relation of man to the universe if we took into account the true nature of *states,* of *qualities,* in fact of everything which presents itself to us with the appearance of stability. In such a case the object and the subject should be, with regard to one another, in a situation analogous to that of the two trains we spoke of at the beginning: it is a certain regulating of mobility on mobility which produces the effect of immobility. Let us then become imbued with this idea, let us never lose sight of the particular relation of the object to the subject translated by a static vision of things: everything that experience teaches us of the one will increase the knowledge we had of the other, and the light the latter receives will in turn be able, by reflection, to illuminate the former.

But as I said in the beginning, pure speculation will not be the only thing to benefit by this vision of universal becoming. We shall be able to make it penetrate into our everyday life, and through it, obtain from philosophy satisfactions similar to those we receive from art, but more frequent, more continual and more accessible to the majority of men. Art enables us, no doubt, to discover in things more qualities and more shades than we naturally perceive. It dilates our perception, but on the surface rather than in depth. It enriches our present, but it scarcely enables us to go beyond it. Through philosophy we can accustom ourselves never to isolate the present from the past which it pulls along with it. Thanks to philosophy, all things acquire depth—more than depth, something like a fourth dimension which permits anterior perceptions to remain bound up with present perceptions, and the immediate future itself to become partly outlined in the present. Reality no longer appears then in the static state, in its manner of being; it affirms itself dynamically, in the continuity and variability of its tendency. What was immobile and frozen in our perception is warmed and set in motion. Everything comes to life around us, everything is revivified in us. A great impulse carries beings and things along. We feel ourselves uplifted, carried away, borne along by it. We are more fully alive and this increase of life brings with it the conviction that grave philosophical enigmas can be resolved or even perhaps that they need not be raised, since they arise from a frozen vision of the real and are only the translation, in terms of thought, of a certain artificial weakening of our vitality. In fact, the more we accustom ourselves to think and to perceive all things *sub specie durationis,* the more we plunge into real duration. And the more we immerse ourselves in it, the more we set ourselves back in the direction of the principle, though it be transcendent, in which we participate and whose eternity is not to be an eternity of immutability, but an eternity of life: how, otherwise, could we live and move in it? *In ea vivimus et movemur et sumus.*

Questions for Reflection

1. How does our sense of sight influence our tendency to reduce time to space, or to put it another way, spatialize time?

2. How does Bergson's definition of change support his theory of time?

3. What role does Bergson say art has in recovering a more authentic experience of time? How can design contribute to this recovery?

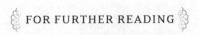 FOR FURTHER READING

Finney, Jack. *Time and Again.*

Kubler, Gregory. "The Shape of Time: Remarks on the History of Things."
"The Culture of Time and Space, 1880–1918": with a new preface

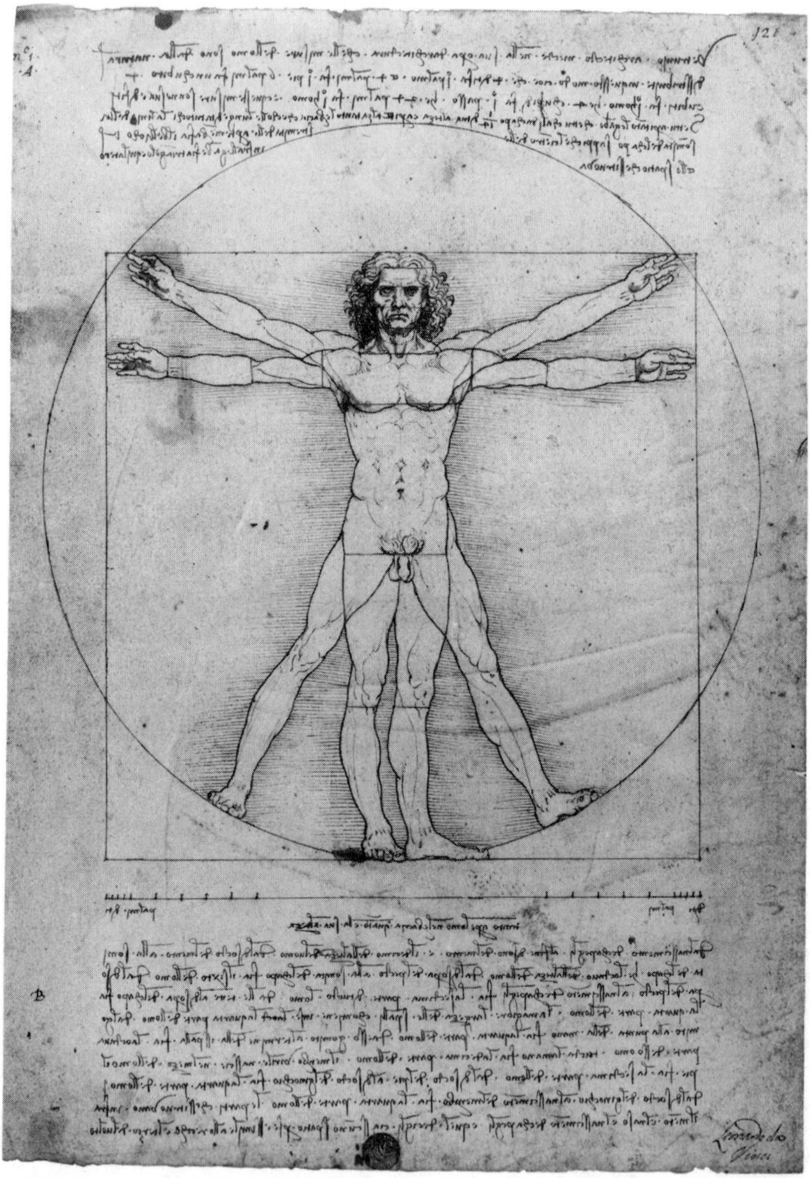

8

What Is the Body?

TOPICS

⟡ Standards of the body

⟡ The body in space

⟡ The static body and the dynamic body: from the Vitruvian
Man to the Promenade Architecturale

⟡ Designing and disciplining the body

FIGURE 8.1
Leonardo da Vinci's drawing of ideal proportions
of the human figure according to Vitruvius's 1st
century A.D. treatise "De Architectura"
(called "Vitruvian Man"), ca. 1492.

PHILO: A great deal of design depends on the human body.

ARCH: Do you mean to say "the body" or "a body?"

PHILO: I mean "the body" because the users of design are largely individual human beings.

Standards of the Body

ARCH: Obviously. Which human body do you have in mind? The Vitruvian Man illustrates an idealized geometric standard. Are you referring to a particular body or a *type* as the statistical standard size given in architectural standards book? Or are you referring to a model established by the dominant culture and applied as an ideal model? Along with an individual's actual size, can one also think of a person's unique social psychology as the body? Which of these attributes do you mean at this point?

PHILO: My primary concern is with examining closely uniquely human attributes. Shouldn't design be tailored specifically to the human body, the body for which it is intended?

Considering this reminds me of a fragment from the pre-Socratic philosopher Xenophones: "But if cattle and horses or lions had hands, or were able to draw with their hands and do the works that human beings do, horses would draw the forms of the gods like horses, and cattle like cattle, and they would make their bodies such as they each had themselves."[1]

ARCH: Yes, the human body has certain capabilities that make it distinct from other creatures. The most obvious is the hand with an opposing thumb and its ability to grasp a tool. We must also add the fact that humans walk upright on two feet. These two characteristics are generally assumed in all discussions about design. I would have thought that these are, by now, obvious, and they are part of any discussion.

PHILO: Of course. My question has to do with how design *imagines* the human body. Although custom design still exists in our day and age, most people don't commission a custom design for everything they use in life. I may order a bespoke suit that would accommodate the characteristics of my particular body, but I can't imagine commissioning a house that would function similarly anytime soon.

ARCH: Maybe you'll meet an architect who will cut you a deal.

PHILO: It'll have to be some deal. Are you offering?

ARCH: Maybe.

PHILO: Really, why?

ARCH: Because such a house would be expensive unless you as the client know what you need and like. In theory a house designed for any particular client does not have to be expansive if the architect and the client can find a way to meet the available budget. On the other hand you are right that only 2 percent of houses build in United States are designed by architects; the rest are built by developers using some statistical standards both of body and real estate market preferences.

PHILO: How can I have a house made to suit my personal needs?

ARCH: You're imagining a structure that would fit your body the way a custom designed glove might slip over your hand. A house that fits like a glove would fit only you and no one else.

PHILO: That's right.

ARCH: Well, it might work for the glove, but it won't work for much else. This glove metaphor for a perfect fit between a body and its external environment is naïve. Not even a suit you would fit that way. Your definition is closer to ergonomic design. That is the branch of engineering science in which biological science studies how to improve *the fit* between the physical demands of the chair, room, or workplace and the humans who sit, live, and/or perform work in such places. Is that what you mean by the perfect fit of the glove?

PHILO: Why not?

ARCH: Though our clothes are designed with the assumption that our bodies are perfectly symmetrical, they are of course not so. My right foot is longer than my left foot, which makes buying shoes a little difficult, but most people's feet are uneven. Same for my right arm; it's a different length than my left arm. When I buy suits, the tailor accounts for this discrepancy and alters the suit jacket's respective sleeves accordingly. The philosopher Ludwig Wittgenstein discusses this idea of tailoring.[2]

Say your shoulders are uneven. One slopes down lower than the other. This makes buying a suit off the rack difficult because the standard sizes and cuts don't account for this difference specific to your body. So you go to a custom tailor and have a suit made just for you. They add extra padding in one of the jacket's shoulders or take away some padding from the other so that it appears you body is symmetrical.

PHILO: And you're saying this isn't possible with a house?

FIGURE 8.2
This photograph of a dancer depicts the relationship between the body in motion and an outer skin. (Photo by Barbara Morgan; Martha Graham, *Lamentation*.)

ARCH: Yes and no. Even a custom tailored suit has more dimensions, so to speak, than just shape and size fitted to the body. A custom designed house for an individual is still possible but much more complex than you make it sound. That is because human beings are not only physical bodies but also minds. The way in which you state the problem makes it appear that you are only concerned with the physical body. Are you a pure materialist philosophically?

PHILO: Of course not. You should know that by now. To be clear this discussion takes place under the topic of the Standards of the Body. We will discuss the social and psychological standards of the symbolic "body" very soon under the topic Designing and Disciplining the Body.

ARCH: There is another topic that we should mention briefly before we continue our discussion. The word *body* is understood in the philosophical question known as the "mind-body problem."

PHILO: Yes, I know all about it. Is that why you asked me if I am a hard-core materialist?

ARCH: You sound like one when you talk about a house fitting the body like a glove. Students should minimally be aware of the philosophical Gordian knot as they consider the question "What is a Body?" I grant you that in this brief trigger dialogue about *the body* we couldn't possibly exhaust the topic. We should hold off this discussion for later. It might make a good critical thinking exercise to ask students to read and research the way Descartes defined mind-body problem and the phenomenological approach to *the body* of Merleau-Ponty. I feel that this is important because much of design pedagogy in the last 20 years has been influenced by phenomenology.

PHILO: OK. Let's get back to our discussion about you designing a house for me. Are you trying to avoid the issue? Where were we? I asked "How can I have a house made to suit my personal needs?" and you said: "You're imagining a structure that would fit your body the way a custom designed glove might slip over your hand, a house that, like the glove, would fit only you and no one else."

ARCH: I'm actually saying that this is what a custom house will do as well. Like the suit, it might be specific in some ways to your body and lifestyle, but like the suit, the final product will reflect very specific standards and will make it appear that your body fits those standards. The suit will make it appear that your body is symmetrical, which is a standard. As we said, no one has a perfectly symmetrical body. If the suit were really going reflect the specificity of your body, it would accentuate the fact that one shoulder is lower than the other. In fact, the suit itself is a standard. Why do you want a suit in the first place? Usually, the reason is to fit in, to look professional, or attractive, or powerful, etc. That is to meet some designed social *ideal* image above and beyond the physical body's particulars.

PHILO: With a house, then, it gets even more complicated, because barely anyone uses a house alone. People usually have guests visit.

ARCH: That's right. Even if it were for only a brief visit, guests would find it odd navigating a house that was designed solely for the needs, size, movements, cooking habits, or aesthetic preferences of the client.

PHILO: I agree. These are very important considerations in this discussion.

ARCH: Please note that the terms anthropometrics and ergonomics are distinct. The first refers to just average size; the second as I said before, ergonomics is an applied science, which is also called human engineering and aims at performance of tasks. If the kitchen is designed for the right handed, it may not function as well for the left handed.

My understanding comes from its use in architectural design, although its application extends to industrial design, interior design, and I imagine other design practices where the human body is concerned. It refers to measurements of the human body and more specifically to the variance in human measurements. Anthropometrics designates a set of measurements, for example, for arm length in the average human body, which would help designers determine the ideal height to design a desk or place a cabinet.

PHILO: So you've helped me make the point I was trying to establishing since the beginning of this discussion—that design has a particular way it imagines the human body, an ideal image of the human body.

ARCH: Ok, fine. What is the larger point you want to make? What's so significant about that fact?

PHILO: Obviously, I'm interested in the fact that even though no one's body fits into the ideal image presupposed by design, this doesn't stop designers from creating objects around that ideal.

ARCH: Ok, but before we go on. Clarify what you mean by "ideal." You don't mean "perfect," right?

PHILO: No, not exactly. I mean a model that always fails to line up with any particular body. Where's the average human body to be found? I'll tell you where—nowhere, that's where. Rather, the average human body exists only in the designer's renderings. And if that's the case, then that means that design is not something designed with the specifics of an individual human body in mind; rather, it's something the human body has to find a way to fit into.

ARCH: You're not wrong, but why is this so important to reflect upon? What are the implications of this ideal image of the body design assumes?

PHILO: We explored this in Chapter 3 on form and function.

ARCH: Yes, and there we discovered that it is very difficult to reduce all of architectural modernism to that one catch-phrase. We also realized how complex it is to define just the concept of function.

We have not yet spoken of the experience of space as a primary function of design. I often tell my students the following: Architecture is not just a walk through arcades, walls, and columns, although such movements are necessary in discovering architecture's most basic condition, that of interiority. Architectural experience, as a mode of knowing, originates and exists primarily in direct experience, the "being here" of bodily experience. It is the disembodied quality of many recent developments in architectural theory that I try to balance my teaching.

PHILO: What do you mean by experience? We're back to the same problem of assuming that everyone has the same body, or at least one that is similar to everyone else's, and that we all experience the same thing in comparable ways.

ARCH: You're right. That is a large assumption.

PHILO: OK. We should introduce here the truly important reevaluation of the body in motion as opposed to the static image of the body we have discussed so far. Let's start from the Vitruvian Man again.

The Static Body and the Dynamic Body:
From the Vitruvian Man to the *Promenade Architecturale*

ARCH: One of the earliest treatises on architecture, Vitruvius' *Ten Books on Architecture* (*De architectura* [ca. 25 BC]), promoted the notion that architecture should be designed to reflect the harmonious proportions of the human body. The art historian Rudolf Wittkower wrote, "As a proof of the harmony and perfection of the human body [Vitruvius] described how a well-built man [*hominis bene figurati*] fits with extended hands and feet exactly into the most perfect geometrical figures, circle, and square."[3]

PHILO: Hence the "Vitruvian Man," which many early modern/Renaissance artists and scholars, not only Leonardo da Vinci, drew countless times over.

ARCH: Yes, the early modern artists and scholars "rediscovered" Vitruvius and embraced his thinking about the harmonious proportionality of the human body because it validated their own belief that the human being reflected the harmony of the universe itself.

PHILO: Vitruvius thus served as a source of what is called "Renaissance humanism" and the idea that the human was the center of the universe.

ARCH: I have been taught that in high school and first year architecture school.

PHILO: Those are some pretty serious implications, even for architecture.

ARCH: Some of us handle the responsibility better than others, I have to admit.

PHILO: Still, it's a relatively static image of the body. The body fits into architecture, and architecture fits around the body.

ARCH: It's true. The idea of the "dynamic body" doesn't emerge until later, and it really takes hold in the later nineteenth early twentieth centuries.

PHILO: With the Industrial Revolution and modernism.

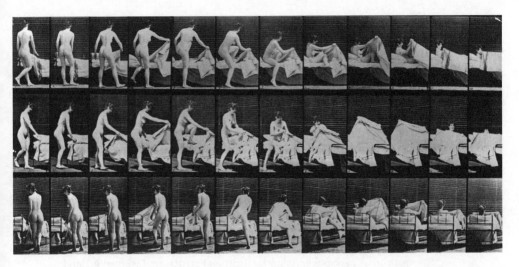

FIGURE 8.3
A nude woman climbs into bed in a series of photographs
depicting motion from a variety of angles. (Photo by Eadweard
Maybridge, "Woman Getting Into Bed," 1893.)

ARCH: Yes, because industrial construction allowed for the design of so-
called "kinetic art," particularly sculpture, which had parts and
moved.

PHILO: So this is one way movement first appears in terms of design.

ARCH: And an important precedent in theorizing the body's movement
through space can thus be found in one of the great figures of architectural modernism, Le Corbusier, who promoted this idea of the
"*promenade architecturale*," which I believe we talked a bit about in
our chapter on place.

PHILO: Yes, his idea, to summarize again, was that the body's movement
through architectural space would complete the "meaning" of that
space. It not only introduced the idea of movement in architecture,
but time as well.

ARCH: Exactly.

Designing and Disciplining the Body

PHILO: I think all this allows us to make two general claims about the body in design: (1) design relies on a certain measure of the body to be able to make its predictions about what the body 'will do' or what the user 'will experience' with a specific design; and (2) design also provides the means to further measure the body.

ARCH: To prove these claims, we'll need to go now to our critical reading passage, which has been taken from the French philosopher Michel Foucault's book *Discipline and Punish* (originally published in 1975).

PHILO: Yes, this is quite well-known among Foucault's works, especially in architecture schools. Many students read the book's section on "Panopticism," which refers to Jeremy Bentham's concept of the *panopticon*. A panopticon is an institutional structure designed around a central tower. From the tower one can see into each individual cell around it. Though commonly associated with the prison, its structure, as Bentham also conceived it, is applicable for the factory, the hospital, and the school, or anywhere that maximum efficiency is valued. It works on a basic principle: that people work hard and efficiently if they think someone is *always watching them.*

ARCH: Because most students read that part of Foucault's book, we thought we would present the section titled "Docile Bodies." A "docile body" is basically a body that has been put through various forms of discipline and that has been "educated" in "proper forms of training."

PHILO: Yes, and Foucault shows us that this proper training requires what he calls spaces of "enclosure" that isolate the body so that it can be worked on.

ARCH: The point, then, is that architecture doesn't just find bodies "in general" that will occupy its spaces. Those bodies have been identified already as ones belonging to architecture. Bodies are "subjected to" design is what you're saying.

PHILO: Exactly. After we read the excerpt from *Discipline and Punish,* it would be worth revisiting the whole idea of anthropometrics. The whole "science" of measuring the human body and coming up with a range of data for the body informs current design practices and attention to ergonomics of different designs, but I bet many will find it surprising that anthropometrics was first invented as means to measure the physical characteristics of criminals and support theories about racial supremacy.[3] What does that say for design?

ARCH: Oh my.

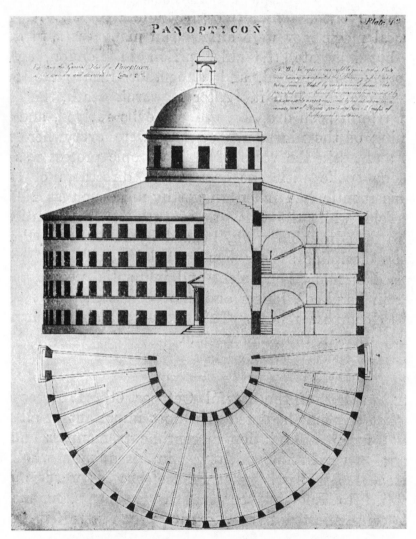

FIGURE 8.4 A drawing of a prison design called a panopticon, from the book *Management of the Poor* by philosopher Jeremy Bentham, 1796. Bentham's design shows a prison where each prisoner is housed in such a way as to prevent any of the prisoners from being aware of whether or not they are, at any given moment, under observation by the prison staff.

CRITICAL READING PASSAGE

Chapter 1, "Docile Bodies,"
from *Discipline and Punish: The Birth of the Prison*
Michel Foucault
1975

ABOUT THE AUTHOR

The work of French historian and philosopher Michel Foucault (1926–1984) has had far-reaching interdisciplinary influence over the last half-century, from history and philosophy, to anthropology, literary criticism, and art and design. Though he is associated most often with the intellectual movements of structuralism and post-structuralism, and even sometimes with the even more obscure notion of postmodernism, his work can be viewed as focused on the social and political implications of language. One of Foucault's most popular books, *Discipline and Punish* analyzes how the languages of such disciplines as psychology and medicine have contributed historically to Western society's conception of punishment. With the rise of modern psychology, Foucault argues, the criminal is transformed from a person who must be punished publicly via the spectacle of torture or execution into someone who possesses a "soul" or "mind" that can be rehabilitated. The following excerpt from *Discipline and Punish,* "Docile Bodies," contends that such "disciplinary discourses" work to shape social attitudes towards the human body and actually conceive the body as something that can be controlled and manipulated.

L et us take the ideal figure of the soldier as it was still seen in the early seventeenth century. To begin with, the soldier was someone who could be recognized from afar; he bore certain signs: the natural signs of his strength and his courage, the marks, too, of his pride; his body was the blazon of his strength and valour; and although it is true that he had to learn the profession of arms little by little—generally in actual fighting—movements like marching and attitudes like the bearing of the head belonged for the most part to a bodily rhetoric of honour; 'The signs for recognizing those most suited to this profession are a lively, alert manner, an erect head, a taut stomach, broad shoulders, long arms, strong fingers, a small belly, thick thighs, slender legs and dry feet, because a man of such a figure could not fail to be agile and strong'; when he becomes a pike-bearer, the soldier 'will have to march in step in order to have as much grace and gravity as possible, for the pike is an honourable weapon, worthy to be borne with gravity and boldness' (Montgommery, 6 and 7). By the late eighteenth century, the soldier has become something that can be made; out of a formless clay, an inapt body, the machine required can be constructed; posture is gradually corrected; a calculated constraint runs slowly through each part of the body, mastering it, making it pliable, ready at all times, turning silently into the automatism of habit; in short, one has 'got rid of the peasant' and given him 'the air of a soldier' (ordinance of 20 March 1764). Recruits become accustomed to 'holding their heads high and erect; to standing upright, without bending the back, to sticking out the belly, throwing out the chest and throwing back the shoulders; and, to help them acquire the habit, they are given this position while standing against a wall in such a way that the heels, the thighs, the waist and the shoulders touch it, as also do the backs of the hands, as one turns the arms outwards, without moving them away from the body . . . Likewise, they will be taught never to fix their eyes on the ground, but to look straight at those they pass . . . to remain motionless until the order is given, without moving the head, the hands or the feet . . . lastly to march with a bold step, with knee and ham taut, on the points of the feet, which should face outwards' (ordinance of 20 March 1764).

The classical age discovered the body as object and target of power. It is easy enough to find signs of the attention then paid to the body—to the body that is manipulated, shaped, trained, which obeys, responds, becomes skilful and increases its forces. The great book of Man-the-Machine was written simultaneously on two registers: the anatomico-metaphysical register, of which Descartes wrote the first pages and which the physicians and philosophers continued, and the technico-political register, which was constituted by a whole set of regulations and by empirical and calculated methods relating to the army, the school and the hospital, for controlling or correcting the operations of the body. These two registers are quite distinct, since it was a question, on the one hand, of submission and use and, on the other, of functioning and explanation: there was a useful body and an intelligible body. And yet there are points of overlap from one to the other. La Mettrie's *L'Homme-machine* is both a materialist reduction of the soul and a general theory of *dressage,* at the centre of which reigns the notion of 'docility', which joins the analysable body to the manipulable body. A body is docile that may be subjected, used, transformed and improved. The celebrated automata, on the other hand, were not only a way of illustrating an organism, they were also political puppets, small-scale models of power: Frederick II, the meticulous king of small machines, well-trained regiments and long exercises, was obsessed with them.

What was so new in these projects of docility that interested the eighteenth century so much? It was certainly not the first time that the body had become the object of such imperious and pressing investments; in every society, the body was in the grip *of* very strict powers, which imposed on it constraints, prohibitions or obligations. However, there were several new things in these techniques. To begin with, there was the scale of the control: it was a question not of treating the body, *en masse,* 'wholesale', as if it were an indissociable unity, but of working it 'retail', individually; of exercising upon it a subtle coercion, of obtaining holds upon it at the level of the mechanism itself—movements, gestures, attitudes, rapidity: an infinitesimal power over the active body. Then there was the object of the control: it was not or was no longer the signifying elements of behaviour or the language of the body, but the economy, the efficiency of movements, their internal organization; constraint bears upon the forces rather than upon the signs; the only truly important ceremony is that of exercise. Lastly, there is the modality: it implies an uninterrupted, constant coercion, supervising the processes of the activity rather than its result and it is exercised according to a codification that partitions as closely as possible time, space, movement. These methods, which made possible the meticulous control of the operations of the body, which assured the constant subjection of its forces and imposed upon them a relation of docility-utility, might be called 'disciplines.' Many disciplinary methods had long been in existence—in monasteries, armies, workshops. But in the course of the seventeenth and eighteenth centuries the disciplines became general formulas of domination. They were different from slavery because they were not based on a relation of appropriation of bodies; indeed, the elegance of the discipline lay in the fact that it could dispense with this costly and violent relation by obtaining effects of utility at least as great. They were different, too, from 'service', which was a constant, total, massive, non-analytical, unlimited relation of domination, established in the form of the individual will of the master, his 'caprice'. They were different from vassalage, which was a highly coded, but distant relation of submission, which bore less on the operations of the body than on the products of labour and the ritual marks of allegiance. Again, they were different from asceticism and from 'disciplines' of a monastic type, whose function was to obtain renunciations rather than increases of utility and which, although they involved obedience to others, had as their principal aim an increase of the mastery of each individual over his own body. The historical moment of the disciplines was the moment when an art of the human body was born, which was directed not only at the growth of its skills, nor at the intensification of its subjection, but at the formation of a relation that in the mechanism itself makes it more obedient as it becomes more useful, and conversely. What was then being formed was a policy of coercions that act upon the body, a calculated manipulation of its elements, its gestures, its behaviour. The human body was entering a machinery of power that explores it, breaks it down and rearranges it. A 'political anatomy', which was also a 'mechanics of power', was being born; it defined how one may have a hold over others' bodies, not only so that they may do what one wishes, but so that they may operate as one wishes, with the techniques, the speed and the efficiency that one determines. Thus discipline produces subjected and practised bodies, 'docile' bodies. Discipline increases the forces of the body (in economic terms of utility) and diminishes these same forces (in political terms of obedience). In short, it dissociates power from the body; on the one hand, it turns it into an 'aptitude', a 'capacity', which it seeks to increase; on the other hand, it reverses the course of the energy, the power that might result from it, and turns it into a relation of strict subjection. If economic exploitation separates the force and the product of labour, let us say that disciplinary coercion establishes in the body the constricting link between an increased aptitude and an increased domination.

The 'invention' of this new political anatomy must not be seen as a sudden discovery. It is rather a multiplicity of often minor processes, of different origin and scattered location, which overlap, repeat, or imitate one another, support one another, distinguish themselves from one another according to their domain of application, converge and gradually produce the blueprint of a general method. They were at work in secondary education at a very early date, later in primary schools; they slowly invested the space of the hospital; and, in a few decades, they restructured the military organization. They sometimes circulated very rapidly from one point to another (between the army and the technical schools or secondary schools), sometimes slowly and discreetly (the insidious militarization of the large workshops). On almost every occasion, they were adopted in response to particular needs: an industrial innovation, a renewed outbreak of certain epidemic diseases, the invention of the rifle or the victories of Prussia. This did not prevent them being totally inscribed in general and essential transformations, which we must now try to delineate.

There can be no question here of writing the history of the different disciplinary institutions, with all their individual differences. I simply intend to map on a series of examples some of the essential techniques that most easily spread from one to another. These were always meticulous, often minute, techniques, but they had their importance: because they defined a certain mode of detailed, political investment of the body, a 'new micro-physics' of power; and because, since the seventeenth century, they had constantly reached out to ever broader domains, as if they tended to cover the entire social body. Small acts of cunning endowed with a great power of diffusion, subtle arrangements, apparently innocent, but profoundly suspicious, mechanisms that obeyed economies too shameful to be acknowledged, or pursued petty forms of coercion—it was nevertheless they that brought about the mutation of the punitive system, at the threshold of the contemporary period. Describing them will require great attention to detail: beneath every set of figures, we must seek not a meaning, but a precaution; we must situate them not only in the inextricability of a functioning, but in the coherence of a tactic. They are the acts of cunning, not so much of the greater reason that works even in its sleep and gives meaning to the insignificant, as of the attentive 'malevolence' that turns everything to account. Discipline is a political anatomy of detail.

Before we lose patience we would do well to recall the words of Marshal de Saxe: 'Although those who concern themselves with details are regarded as folk of limited intelligence, it seems to me that this part is essential, because it is the foundation, and it is impossible to erect any building or establish any method without understanding its principles. It is not enough to have a liking for architecture. One must also know stone-cutting' (Saxe, 5). There is a whole history to be written about such 'stone-cutting'—a history of the utilitarian rationalization of detail in moral accountability and political control. The classical age did not initiate it; rather it accelerated it, changed its scale, gave it precise instruments, and perhaps found some echoes for it in the calculation of the infinitely small or in the description of the most detailed characteristics of natural beings. In any case, 'detail' had long been a category of theology and asceticism: every detail is important since, in the sight of God, no immensity is greater than a detail, nor is anything so small that it was not willed by one of his individual wishes. In this great tradition of the eminence of detail, all the minutiae of Christian education, of scholastic or military pedagogy, all forms of 'training' found their place easily enough. For the disciplined man, as for the true believer, no detail is unimportant, but not so much for the meaning that it conceals within it as for the hold it provides for the power that wishes to seize it. Characteristic is the great hymn to the 'little things' and to their eternal importance, sung by Jean-Baptiste de La Salle, in his *Traité sur les obligations des frères des Écoles chrétiennes*. The mystique of the everyday is joined here with the discipline of the minute. 'How dangerous it is to neglect little things. It is a very consoling reflection for a soul like mine, little disposed to great actions, to think that fidelity to little things may, by an imperceptible progress, raise us to the most eminent sanctity: because little things lead to greater ... Little things; it will be said, alas, my God, what can we do that is great for you, weak and mortal creatures that we are. Little things; if great things presented themselves would we perform them? Would we not think them beyond our strength? Little things; and if God accepts them and wishes to receive them as great things? Little things; has one ever felt this? Does one judge according to experience? Little things; one is certainly guilty, therefore, if seeing them as such, one refuses them? Little things; yet it is they that in the end have made great saints! Yes, little things; but great motives, great feelings, great fervour, great ardour, and consequently great merits, great treasures, great rewards' (La Salle, *Traité* ..., 238–9). The meticulousness of the regulations, the fussiness of the inspections, the supervision of the smallest fragment of life and of the body will soon provide, in the context of the school, the barracks, the hospital or the workshop, a laicized content, an economic or technical rationality for this mystical calculus of the infinitesimal and the infinite. And a History of Detail in the eighteenth century, presided over by Jean-Baptiste de La Salle, touching on Leibniz and Buffon, via Frederick II, covering pedagogy, medicine, military tactics and economics, should bring us, at the end of the century, to the man who dreamt of being another Newton, not the Newton of the immensities of the heavens and the planetary masses, but a Newton of 'small bodies', small movements, small actions; to the man who replied to Monge's remark, 'there was only one world to discover': 'What do I hear? But the world of details, who has never dreamt of that other world, what of that world? I have believed in it ever since I was fifteen. I was concerned with it then, and this memory lives within me, as an obsession never to be abandoned ... That other world is the most important of all that I flatter myself I have discovered: when I think of it, my heart aches' (these words are attributed to Bonaparte in the Introduction to Saint-Hilaire's *Notions synthétiques et historiques de philosophie naturelle*). Napoleon did not discover this world; but we know that he set out to organize it; and he wished to arrange around him a mechanism of power that would enable him to see the smallest event that occurred in the state he governed; he intended, by means of the rigorous discipline that he imposed, 'to embrace the whole of this vast machine without the slightest detail escaping his attention' (Treilhard, 14).

A meticulous observation of detail, and at the same time a political awareness of these small things, for the control and use of men, emerge through the classical age bearing with them a whole set of techniques, a whole corpus of methods and knowledge, descriptions, plans and data. And from such trifles, no doubt, the man of modern humanism was born.[1]

THE ART OF DISTRIBUTIONS

In the first instance, discipline proceeds from the distribution of individuals in space. To achieve this end, it employs several techniques.

1. Discipline sometimes requires *enclosure,* the specification of a place heterogeneous to all others and closed in upon itself. It is the protected place of disciplinary monotony. There was the great 'confinement' of vagabonds and paupers; there were other more discreet, but insidious and effective ones. There were the *collèges,* or secondary schools: the monastic model was gradually

---

[1] I shall choose examples from military, medical, educational and industrial institutions. Other examples might have been taken from colonization, slavery and child rearing.

imposed; boarding appeared as the most perfect, if not the most frequent, educational régime; it became obligatory at Louis-le-Grand when, after the departure of the Jesuits, it was turned into a model school (cf. Ariès, 308–13 and
Snyders, 35–41). There were the military barracks: the army, that vagabond
mass, has to be held in place; looting and violence must be prevented; the fears
of local inhabitants, who do not care for troops passing through their towns,
must be calmed; conflicts with the civil authorities must be avoided; desertion
must be stopped, expenditure controlled. The ordinance of 1719 envisaged the
construction of several hundred barracks, on the model of those already set up
in the south of the country; there would be strict confinements: 'The whole will
be enclosed by an outer wall ten feet high, which will surround the said houses,
at a distance of thirty feet from all the sides'; this will have the effect of maintaining the troops in 'order and discipline, so that an officer will be in a position
to answer for them' (*L'Ordonnance militaire*, IXL, 25 September 1719). In 1745,
there were barracks in about 320 towns; and it was estimated that the total
capacity of the barracks in 1775 was approximately 200,000 men (Daisy, 201–9;
an anonymous memoir of 1775, in Dépôt de la guerre, 3689, f. 156; Navereau,
132–5). Side by side with the spread of workshops, there also developed great
manufacturing spaces, both homogeneous and well defined: first, the combined
manufactories, then, in the second half of the eighteenth century, the works
or factories proper (the Chaussade ironworks occupied almost the whole of
the Médine peninsula, between Nièvre and Loire; in order to set up the Indret
factory in 1777, Wilkinson, by means of embankments and dikes, constructed an
island on the Loire; Toufait built Le Creusot in the valley of the Charbonnière,
which he transformed, and he had workers' accommodation built in the factory
itself); it was a change of scale, but it was also a new type of control. The factory was explicitly compared with the monastery, the fortress, a walled town;
the guardian 'will open the gates only on the return of the workers, and after
the bell that announces the resumption of work has been rung'; a quarter of an
hour later no one will be admitted; at the end of the day, the workshops' heads
will hand back the keys to the Swiss guard of the factory, who will then open the
gates (*Amboise*, f. 12, 1301). The aim is to derive the maximum advantages and
to neutralize the inconveniences (thefts, interruptions of work, disturbances
and 'cabals'), as the forces of production become more concentrated; to protect
materials and tools and to master the labour force: 'The order and inspection
that must be maintained require that all workers be assembled under the same
roof, so that the partner who is entrusted with the management of the manufactory may prevent and remedy abuses that may arise among the workers and
arrest their progress at the outset' (Dauphin, 199).

2. But the principle of 'enclosure' is neither constant, nor indispensable,
nor sufficient in disciplinary machinery. This machinery works space in a much
more flexible and detailed way. It does this first of all on the principle of elemen-

tary location or *partitioning*. Each individual has his own place; and each place its individual. Avoid distributions in groups; break up collective dispositions; analyse confused, massive or transient pluralities. Disciplinary space tends to be divided into as many sections as there are bodies or elements to be distributed. One must eliminate the effects of imprecise distributions, the uncontrolled disappearance of individuals, their diffuse circulation, their unusable and dangerous coagulation; it was a tactic of anti-desertion, anti-vagabondage, anti-concentration. Its aim was to establish presences and absences, to know where and how to locate individuals, to set up useful communications, to interrupt others, to be able at each moment to supervise the conduct of each individual, to assess it, to judge it, to calculate its qualities or merits. It was a procedure, therefore, aimed at knowing, mastering and using. Discipline organizes an analytical space.

And there, too, it encountered an old architectural and religious method: the monastic cell. Even if the compartments it assigns become purely ideal, the disciplinary space is always, basically, cellular. Solitude was necessary to both body and soul, according to a certain asceticism: they must, at certain moments at least, confront temptation and perhaps the severity of God alone. 'Sleep is the image of death, the dormitory is the image of the sepulchre ... although the dormitories are shared, the beds are nevertheless arranged in such a way and closed so exactly by means of curtains that the girls may rise and retire without being seen' (*Règlement pour la communauté des filles du Bon Pasteur*, in Delamare, 507). But this is still a very crude form.

3. The rule of *functional sites* would gradually, in the disciplinary institutions, code a space that architecture generally left at the disposal of several different uses. Particular places were defined to correspond not only to the need to supervise, to break dangerous communications, but also to create a useful space. The process appeared clearly in the hospitals, especially in the military and naval hospitals. In France, it seems that Rochefort served both as experiment and model. A port, and a military port is—with its circulation of goods, men signed up willingly or by force, sailors embarking and disembarking, diseases and epidemics—a place of desertion, smuggling, contagion: it is a crossroads for dangerous mixtures, a meeting-place for forbidden circulations. The naval hospital must therefore treat, but in order to do this it must be a filter, a mechanism that pins down and partitions; it must provide a hold over this whole mobile, swarming mass, by dissipating the confusion of illegality and evil. The medical supervision of diseases and contagions is inseparable from a whole series of other controls: the military control over deserters, fiscal control over commodities, administrative control over remedies, rations, disappearances, cures, deaths, simulations. Hence the need to distribute and partition off space in a rigorous manner. The first steps taken at Rochefort concerned things rather than men, precious commodities, rather than patients.

The arrangements of fiscal and economic supervision preceded the techniques of medical observation: placing of medicines under lock and key, recording their use; a little later, a system was worked out to verify the real number of patients, their identity, the units to which they belonged; then one began to regulate their comings and goings; they were forced to remain in their wards; to each bed was attached the name of its occupant; each individual treated was entered in a register that the doctor had to consult during the visit; later came the isolation of contagious patients and separate beds. Gradually, an administrative and political space was articulated upon a therapeutic space; it tended to individualize bodies, diseases, symptoms, lives and deaths; it constituted a real table of juxtaposed and carefully distinct singularities. Out of discipline, a medically useful space was born.

In the factories that appeared at the end of the eighteenth century, the principle of individualizing partitioning became more complicated. It was a question of distributing individuals in a space in which one might isolate them and map them; but also of articulating this distribution on a production machinery that had its own requirements. The distribution of bodies, the spatial arrangement of production machinery and the different forms of activity in the distribution of 'posts' had to be linked together. The Oberkampf manufactory at Jouy obeyed this principle. It was made up of a series of workshops specified according to each broad type of operation: for the printers, the handlers, the colourists, the women who touched up the design, the engravers, the dyers. The largest of the buildings, built in 1791, by Toussaint Barré, was 110 metres long and had three storeys. The ground floor was devoted mainly to block printing; it contained 132 tables arranged in two rows, the length of the workshop, which had eighty-eight windows; each printer worked at a table with his 'puller', who prepared and spread the colours. There were 264 persons in all. At the end of each table was a sort of rack on which the material that had just been printed was left to dry (Saint-Maur). By walking up and down the central aisle of the workshop, it was possible to carry out a supervision that was both general and individual: to observe the worker's presence and application, and the quality of his work; to compare workers with one another, to classify them according to skill and speed; to follow the successive stages of the production process. All these serializations formed a permanent grid: confusion was eliminated[2]: that is to say, production was divided up and the labour process was articulated, on the one hand, according to its stages or elementary operations, and, on the other hand, according to the individuals, the particular bodies, that carried it out: each variable of this force — strength, promptness, skill, constancy — would be observed, and therefore characterized, assessed, computed and related to the individual who was its particular agent. Thus, spread out in a perfectly legible way over the whole series of individual bodies, the work force may be analysed in individual units. At the emergence of

[2] Cf. what La Métherie wrote after a visit to Le Creusot: 'The buildings for so fine an establishment and so large a quantity of different work should cover a sufficient area, so that there will be no confusion among the workers during working time' (La Métherie, 66).

large-scale industry, one finds, beneath the division of the production process, the individualizing fragmentation of labour power; the distributions of the disciplinary space often assured both.

4. In discipline, the elements are interchangeable, since each is defined by the place it occupies in a series, and by the gap that separates it from the others. The unit is, therefore, neither the territory (unit of domination), nor the place (unit of residence), but the *rank:* the place one occupies in a classification, the point at which a line and a column intersect, the interval in a series of intervals that one may traverse one after the other. Discipline is an art of rank, a technique for the transformation of arrangements. It individualizes bodies by a location that does not give them a fixed position, but distributes them and circulates them in a network of relations.

Take the example of the 'class'. In the Jesuit colleges, one still found an organization that was at once binary and unified; the classes, which might comprise up to two or three hundred pupils, were subdivided into groups of ten; each of these groups, with its 'decurion', was placed in a camp, Roman or Carthaginian; each 'decury' had its counterpart in the opposing camp. The general form was that of war and rivalry; work, apprenticeship and classification were carried out in the form of the joust, through the confrontation of two armies; the contribution of each pupil was inscribed in this general duel; it contributed to the victory or the defeat of a whole camp; and the pupils were assigned a place that corresponded to the function of each individual and to his value as a combatant in the unitary group of his 'decury' (Rochemonteix, 51ff). It should be observed moreover that this Roman comedy made it possible to link, to the binary exercises of rivalry, a spatial disposition inspired by the legion, with rank, hierarchy, pyramidal supervision. One should not forget that, generally speaking, the Roman model, at the Enlightenment, played a dual role: in its republican aspect, it was the very embodiment of liberty; in its military aspect, it was the ideal schema of discipline. The Rome of the eighteenth century and of the Revolution was the Rome of the Senate, but it was also that of the legion; it was the Rome of the Forum, but it was also that of the camps. Up to the empire, the Roman reference transmitted, somewhat ambiguously, the juridical ideal of citizenship and the technique of disciplinary methods. In any case, the strictly disciplinary element in the ancient fable used by the Jesuit colleges came to dominate the element of joust and mock warfare. Gradually—but especially after 1762—the educational space unfolds; the class becomes homogeneous, it is no longer made up of individual elements arranged side by side under the master's eye. In the eighteenth century, 'rank' begins to define the great form of distribution of individuals in the educational order: rows or ranks of pupils in the class, corridors, courtyards; rank attributed to each pupil at the end of each task and each examination; the rank he obtains from week to week, month to month, year to year; an alignment of age groups, one after another; a succession of subjects taught and questions treated, according to an order of increasing difficulty. And, in this ensemble of compulsory alignments, each pupil, according to his age, his performance, his behaviour, occupies sometimes one rank, sometimes another; he moves constantly over a series of compartments—some of these are 'ideal' compartments, marking a hierarchy of knowledge or ability, others express the distribution of values or merits in material terms in the space of the college or classroom. It is a perpetual move-ment in which individuals replace one another in a space marked off by aligned intervals.

The organization of a serial space was one of the great technical muta-tions of elementary education. It made it possible to supersede the traditional system (a pupil working for a few minutes with the master, while the rest of the heterogeneous group remained idle and unattended). By assigning individual places it made possible the supervision of each individual and the simulta-neous work of all. It organized a new economy of the time of apprenticeship. It made the educational space function like a learning machine, but also as a machine for supervising, hierarchizing, rewarding. Jean-Baptiste de La Salle dreamt of a classroom in which the spatial distribution might provide a whole series of distinctions at once: according to the pupils' progress, worth, charac-ter, application, cleanliness and parents' fortune. Thus, the classroom would form a single great table, with many different entries, under the scrupulously 'classificatory' eye of the master: 'In every class there will be places assigned for all the pupils of all the lessons, so that all those attending the same lesson will always occupy the same place. Pupils attending the highest lessons will be placed in the benches closest to the wall, followed by the others according to the order of the lessons moving towards the middle of the classroom... Each of the pupils will have his place assigned to him and none of them will leave it or change it except on the order or with the consent of the school inspector.' Things must be so arranged that 'those whose parents are neglectful and ver-minous must be separated from those who are careful and clean; that an unruly and frivolous pupil should be placed between two who are well behaved and serious, a libertine either alone or between two pious pupils'.[3]

In organizing 'cells', 'places' and 'ranks', the disciplines create complex spaces that are at once architectural, functional and hierarchical. It is spaces that provide fixed positions and permit circulation; they carve out individual segments and establish operational links; they mark places and indicate values; they guarantee the obedience of individuals, but also a better economy of time and gesture. They are mixed spaces: real because they govern the disposition of buildings, rooms, furniture, but also ideal, because they are projected over this arrangement of characterizations, assessments, hierarchies. The first of

---

[3] J.-B. de la Salle, *Conduite des écoles chrétiennes*, B.N. Ms. 11759, 248–9. A little earlier Batencour proposed that classrooms should be divided into three parts: 'The most honourable for those who are learning Latin... It should be stressed that there are as many places at the tables as there will be writers, in order to avoid the confusion usually caused by the lazy.' In another, those who are learning to read: a bench for the rich and a bench for the poor 'so that vermin will not be passed on'. A third section for newcomers: 'When their ability has been recognized, they will be given a place' (M.I.D.B., 56–7).

the great operations of discipline is, therefore, the constitution of 'tableaux vivants', which transform the confused, useless or dangerous multitudes into ordered multiplicities. The drawing up of 'tables' was one of the great problems of the scientific, political and economic technology of the eighteenth century: how one was to arrange botanical and zoological gardens, and construct at the same time rational classifications of living beings; how one was to observe, supervise, regularize the circulation of commodities and money and thus build up an economic table that might serve as the principle of the increase of wealth; how one was to inspect men, observe their presence and absence and constitute a general and permanent register of the armed forces; how one was to distribute patients, separate them from one another, divide up the hospital space and make a systematic classification of diseases: these were all twin operations in which the two elements—distribution and analysis, supervision and intelligibility—are inextricably bound up. In the eighteenth century, the table was both a technique of power and a procedure of knowledge. It was a question of organizing the multiple, of providing oneself with an instrument to cover it and to master it; it was a question of imposing upon it an 'order'. Like the army general of whom Guibert spoke, the naturalist, the physician, the economist was 'blinded by the immensity, dazed by the multitude. . . the innumerable combinations that result from the multiplicity of objects, so many concerns together form a burden above his strength. In perfecting itself, in approaching true principles, the science of modern warfare might become simpler and less difficult'; armies 'with simple, similar tactics, capable of being adapted to every movement. . . would be easier to move and lead' (Guibert, xxxvi). Tactics, the spatial ordering of men; taxonomy, the disciplinary space of natural beings; the economic table, the regulated movement of wealth.

But the table does not have the same function in these different registers. In the order of the economy, it makes possible the measurement of quantities and the analysis of movements. In the form of taxonomy, it has the function of characterizing (and consequently reducing individual singularities) and constituting classes (and therefore of excluding considerations of number). But in the form of the disciplinary distribution, on the other hand, the table has the function of treating multiplicity itself, distributing it and deriving from it as many effects as possible. Whereas natural taxonomy is situated on the axis that links character and category, disciplinary tactics is situated on the axis that links the singular and the multiple. It allows both the characterization of the individual as individual and the ordering of a given multiplicity. It is the first condition for the control and use of an ensemble of distinct elements: the base for a micro-physics of what might be called a 'cellular' power.

QUESTIONS FOR REFLECTION

1. Review the description Foucault recounts of the soldier's body at the beginning of the Critical Reading Passage. List and explain three ways in which design functions similarly in determining the movements, posture, and capabilities of the body.

2. According to Foucault, the disciplined body is the result of a "'new micro-physics' of power." How does he come to make this claim?

3. How does the organization of space affect the body?

CRITICAL THINKING RESEARCH EXERCISES

1. What is the mind-body problem, and how does it affect design? Read and research the way Descartes defined the mind-body problem. Connect his definition to design and architectural issues.

2. Consider the issues of causality between design thought, or intention, purpose and designed objects, describe using your own experience in a design studio project. Follow your design process, and identify what decisions you have made based on three sources of influence on your design: (1) necessity or the demands of functional reality and the properties of material, (2) chance, such as the accidental aspects of a given site or the peculiarities of a client (such as budget or taste) and your own idiosyncratic, subjective attitudes towards the issue of "What is beauty?" and (3) the historical precedents and the construction rules and habits of a particular society at a certain time. Identify, describe, and explain moments of design decisions made by necessity, chance, or social code.

CRITICAL THINKING EXERCISE

Consider the following problem posed by an Irish philosopher engaged in teaching philosophy to 8- to 12-year-old students.

In the North Sea, marine archeologists found the broken remains of a Viking ship that had sunk 2,000 years earlier. Those boat parts would not survive being brought up and exposed to the air. They would quickly crumble. Instead they were reassembled in a large tub of sea water, where they were then photographed, measured, and otherwise documented. From those skeleton parts, the archeologists reconstructed the complete design and duplicated the Viking ship in its totality, but made out of new and similar wood. The replica was identical in design to the original ship. It could sail just as well.

The questions for the students are:

1. Is the reconstructed ship "old," or is it "new?"

2. Where does the essence of the ship's identity rest; is it in its design (mind) or in the actual original wood fibers of the old ship (the material body)?

 FOR FURTHER READING

Bordo, Susan. "The Body and the Reproduction of Femininity." *Writing on the Body: Female Embodiment and Feminist Theory,* ed. Katie Conboy, Nadia Medina, and Sarah Stanbury. New York: Columbia University Press, 1997.

Friedman, Alice T. "Architecture, Authority, and the Female Gaze: Planning and Representation in the Early Modern Country House." *Gender Space Architecture: An Interdisciplinary Introduction,* ed. Iain Borden; Barbara Penner and Jane Rendell (Routledge, 1999), 332–41.

Lock, Margaret, and Judith Farquhar, eds. *Beyond the Body Proper: Reading the Anthropology of Material Life.* Durham, NC. Duke University Press, 2007.

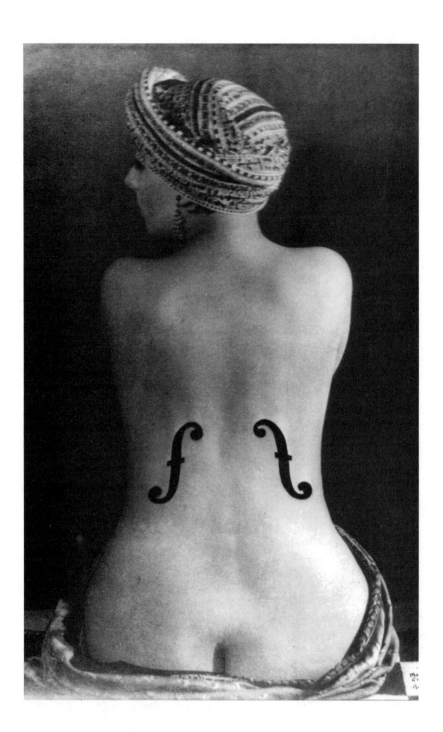

9

What Is Creativity?

FIGURE 9.1 A visual association of a violin and the shape
of woman's body by photographer Man Ray (1924).

ARCH: Because this book is aimed at design students, let's begin this chapter with common questions with which many students typically struggle:

- How do I begin?
- Do I start a design from my own imagination, or from the "given" or "found" facts in a situation?
- Do I start with the problem as given, or do I form an expression based on the construction materials and/or the physical attributes of a site?
- How do I find inspiration in historical precedents?
- What does it mean to be creative?
- Where is the beginning?
- What does it mean to be original?

Such questions are overwhelming at the beginning of any project.

PHILO: Of course, dear Arch, but it is important to keep in mind that these are universal questions, and therefore philosophical in nature.

Teaching Creativity

ARCH: The proposition is that we, as design teachers, begin with the teaching of creativity. Claiming to teach creativity seems to me somewhat arrogant and self-serving. How can creativity be taught? And if one can in fact teach creativity, what exactly is it?

PHILO: You got me! Creativity has always seemed like an illusive concept with many definitions.

ARCH: Well the term *creativity* is both powerful and necessary if we are to understand the nature of design. In the past I found the term *creativity* loaded with dated baggage from the 1960s (my own formative decade). There is a paradox in reviewing that time because, on one hand, it was a period of high creative energy and experimentation in all design fields (and in culture as a whole). On the other hand, the idea of creativity was linked with ways to achieve alternate consciousness with the help of biochemistry. And you know what I mean! I have grown uneasy with that method, yet one cannot fail to mention the role of drugs, legal and illegal, in the history of religion, science, and the arts.

We still see those same currents in today's mainstream culture (and its reactive subculture). Just consider the power of the pharmaceutical industry today!

PHILO: Well, that seems to fit the image of the 1960s with reference to creativity in my experience, although it was before my time. Of course, I have only *read* about mind-altering substances. But surely not everyone was altering their mind to be creative!

ARCH: What might be a more sophisticated criticism of the sixties is the notion that creativity was regarded as a moment of "rapture" (religious or sexual), and as a release of creative energy (sometimes compared to release of spiritual or sexual energy). However, I find that metaphor incomplete in the sense that there are other kinds of creativity borne through slow, patient, calm, and rigorous search for answers. Creativity happens through a process of critical thinking, as well as problem-solving and at the level of expressing a personal view of reality.

PHILO: So, what is the problem with attempting to teach how to be creative?

ARCH: That is the intriguing part of my own uneasiness with the word creativity—a word I live by and always hope for as a general quality of my life. Can it be taught? Is it really an ephemeral result of a private effort by singular creative genius? Or, as the current dominant model proposes, is all design a team effort with creative juices from many influencing the design of a project?

PHILO: This is a good question. Can a team be creative? We see this in science as normal activity. Most discoveries in science are signed by a long list of co-contributors. On the other hand works of art, books, films, pieces of music, a dress, a chair, and buildings are always attributed to typically only one author.

As far as receiving credit in the field of science, this has to do with the rules of the research game. In art, the protective shield is around the individual artist's process and that was the promise of an historical period called Romanticism, which began in Germany. Its influence spread to France and England as well. This movement coincided with the industrial revolution and the rise of the notion of an individual. With the concept of an individual becoming valued, the notion of a special creative individual with the ability to move history forward also developed. All of these historical ideas have been debated, but can be examined again today from a fresh perspective, given the latest crisis of capitalism we are living through.

ARCH: Although we are still within the topic of "creativity," we are straying a bit from the main issues of our book: the method and possibility of individual creative process. The issue of "team creativity" must wait for now—until we have finished defining the creative process itself. Can you describe more the collaborative "rules of the game" in science?

PHILO: Well, in science discoveries are a build-up or progression from one scientist's work to another's. Using each other's work is essential to moving science forward. In art, the work (we are told) is a lonely pursuit for subjective insight.[1] However, these are not necessarily at odds with each other, nevertheless they are different modes of looking into the unknown. Both methods are valid in their own terms, and can lead to *creativity*—that is the discovery of something new, not before known.

PHILO: OK, these may be distinct methodological and strategic approaches. But the idea of the lonely creative genius making a cultural breakthrough is still suspicious for the philosopher.

ARCH: I am not in a hurry to convince you for now. We might return to this notion later. In the meantime, there is a reading about psychological cognitive research carried out in the sixties. It investigated the creativity of famous architects: Le Corbousier, Frank Lloyd Wright, Mies van der Rohe, etc. This research is still unpublished, it was conducted at the beginning of identifying spatial abilities distinctly from verbal abilities. Designers and architects with high spatial abilities were viewed as exhibiting slight schizoid and anti-social tendencies, while of course, being very creative.

PHILO: Ha! I couldn't agree more. A single creative genius always seems alone.

ARCH: Well let's go on. As we suggested at the start of this dialogue, asking the question "What is creativity?" leads very important and large questions.

PHILO: OK. Can you list some of the other more important issues that flow from the question of creativity?

Creativity as the Prerogative of God Alone

PHILO: Creativity is a mysterious notion, praised by many, as central to human life and survival. However, this definition is rejected by others as an affront to God's singular right to be creative.

ARCH: Yes, of course. The first question that comes to mind is a religious one. Such a question cannot be settled here and is not really in our realm of concerns. But as critical thinkers, we can at least mention it as a question out there in the current cultural debate.

PHILO: Yes, you know, it is fact that some religious groups do argue that true creativity is the prerogative of God (and not of humans).

ARCH: Yes, and therefore, these groups rule against the teaching of creativity and of art in schools at any course level. Of course, this point of view is counter to anything we are attempting to do in this book or in the teaching design. However, I felt the need to mention it as it is a poignant point in current times. Creativity, however defined, must be part of all education.

Creation from Nothing

ARCH: The issue of creativity brings to mind another serious and old question that has preoccupied theologians for several millennia. The paradox of creation *ex-nihilo* (creation from nothing) is the major issue for early Hebrew and Greek thinkers, as well as the early Christian theologians.

PHILO: Yes, this question is perfect fodder for critical thinking. It harkens back to your favorite period, the sixties, when John Lennon put the *creatio ex nihilo* position rather succinctly when he said, "Before Elvis, there was nothing."

ARCH: Wow! You do know the sixties after all. Can we now tackle another huge topic? We must not exhaust it here, but a teacher and his students can expand on it in class if they find it stimulating.

Invention and Creation

ARCH: As we said earlier, the other interesting question that follows is the distinction between the notion of "invention" and "creation." In our common understanding of these words, we would say that scientists "invent," and artists, designers, or architects "create." [2]

PHILO: Yes, George Steiner said that. Scientists invent based on prior knowledge and research within a collaborative community for professional support. Artists, on the other hand, are individual rebels searching for singular and original discoveries (which is the standing common mythology on artistic creativity).

ARCH: Yes, and the very one I live my life around! There are other voices, but the central question is always about originality. It revolves around originality, even when it is denied. As you see in the following quotations, again from George Steiner:

> The Latin "*invenire*" would appear to presuppose that which is to be "*found*," to be "come upon." As is to invoke the question underlying this study, the universe has already been "there,"... Picasso use to say, "I do not search, I only find" just as Marcel Duchamp, the key figure of aesthetic of modernism ... objet trouvé. ... [3]

ARCH: Can we expand on this controversial topic? Can we speak of a major artist as a "creator," not as an "inventor"?

> Yet inventiveness may figure eminently among its virtues. However, that of the iconoclastic, prohibitions on "creation" can be cardinal. I have already cited the taboos on the "making of images" in Judaism and Islam. To create images is to "invent," it is to "fictionalize" in the cause of virtual reality, scenes, real presence beyond human perception. ... [4]

PHILO: That may be too much for our students. I can barely grasp it myself. I follow my gut feeling that this is important here, and we want our students at whatever level to at least think about it. Steiner's thoughts on creativity are insightful. They are at their best when he writes, "Invention is often thoroughly humorous. It surprises, whereas creation in the sense of the Greek term which generates all philosophy, *thaumazein,* amazes, astonishes us as does thunder or the blazes of the northern lights."

These thoughts on creativity have sources in *Genesis,* the *Timaeus,* Aristotelian physics of causation, and Neo Platonists. I would have a lot to comment on here.

ARCH: I would love to, but, before we wade too deeply into these philosophical waters, let's ask that the students first undertake the required reading from Edward de Bono. Then return to excerpts from "Grammers of Creation" by George Steiner, as a further suggested reading.

PHILO: I couldn't agree more. The Steiner reading, although important, is not meant for undergraduate students of design. I agree with you that it is relevant, but it may be a bit too esoteric. That does not mean we should not ask them to read it! Supplemented with class discussions it is a very helpful guide to a discussion about creativity.

ARCH: Let's look back at the image at the beginning of this chapter. Dear Philo, I think the famous work by the American artist Man Ray, a member of the modernist Dada art movement, is a good image to generate a concrete discussion on "What is Creativity?"

PHILO: For me, creativity in the arts, design, and architecture involves metaphoric operations, the kind of "poetic logic" that Giambaptista Vico defined a long time ago. Later, in the 1960s, Edward de Bono called poetic logic "lateral thinking." Lateral thinking is the ability to freely associate between discrete things and ideas to other things and ideas because they have something in common. What something is, is a complex set of possible relationships, sometimes purely visual, sometimes formal (geometry), and sometimes composed of cultural associations. In this case, the picture shows us the similarity of the shape of a women's body to that of an instrument (the violin). This takes us back to Chapter 6, "What Is Meaning?"

ARCH: Of course it does. But I don't want to be distracted here from the topic at hand, "What is Creativity?"

PHILO: I have always preferred the notion of *lateral thinking,* as defined by de Bono, over the more widely used term metaphoric thinking. Metaphoric thinking is normally used in linguistics, literary criticism and philosophy.

ARCH: So do I. So let's rediscover de Bono's ideas. He does, after all, title his book: "Lateral Thinking. Creativity Step by Step." With your agreement, I chose from his book as a required reading so that students can understand de Bono's discussion on "**Innovation**," "**Suspended Judgment**," and "**Design**."

PHILO: How appropriate and refreshing.

ARCH: Why refreshing?

PHILO: Because de Bono is practical and directive. He also freely uses innovation and creativity interchangeably. I would dare to say that his use of the words "suspended judgment" seem to be a perfect description of the role of a critical thinker in the design process. We touched on this in the first chapter.

ARCH: Hold on there! I happen to agree. But that does not mean that the preceding discussion on creativity, even if it was a bit philosophical, was not of practical value to our students.

PHILO: I said no such thing. In fact, I would like to return to it later. But in the meantime the advice that de Bono gives his readers (in the two-page introduction to his "Design" chapter) parallels the terms of critical thinking as we have established in this text book. It is actually provocative that he titles them (1) "Innovation," and (2) "Suspended Judgment." They literally coincide with the thinking procedures we suggest under critical thinking.

ARCH: Yes, I found them quite meaningful as steps towards creative critical thinking. Could you restate them here for our students?

PHILO: Well. For one, he advises that we, those involved in any design process, undertake the following: (1) generate alternative ways of looking at things, and (2) challenge assumptions.

ARCH: Well, we said that in Chapter 1 "What Is Critical Thinking," didn't we? I should also mention that both of these procedures de Bono describes are "Backward thinking, something that is there and working it over." We, in the design field, usually call this the site conditions and the given program, budget, and available construction material and technology.

PHILO: We sure did. De Bono goes farther to point out that: "These are for the purposes of description or analysis of a situation."[5]

ARCH: Yes, I know that. On the other hand all design, as I said, is future oriented. I was happy to see that de Bono also stresses this aspect by pointing out that: "Forward thinking involves moving forward. Forward thinking involves building something new rather than analyzing something old. Innovation and creation involve forward thinking."[6]

PHILO: Yes, of course, Arch. But, we should also immediately follow with de Bono's next cautionary note in which he writes that: "The distinction between backward and forward thinking is entirely arbitrary. There is no distinction because one may have to look backwards in a new way in order to move forward A creative description may be just as generative as a creative idea."[7]

ARCH: Now that is something I hear over and over again these days where I teach. Of course it is true, but it emphasizes process over end product. Students are all too happy to just describe and analyze existing conditions (sometimes referred to as site *forces*) and never commit themselves to making choices about a concrete solution. It is all process over end product. I find that avoidance of the task at hand.

PHILO: Arch, you seem so impatient. Hold off leaping forward before you have given time to critical thinking. De Bono is very clear on the topic. He writes, "Before going on to consider innovation it is necessary to consider an aspect of thinking that *applies much more* [emphasis added] to forward thinking than to backwards thinking. That is the matter *of evaluation and suspended judgment* [emphasis added]."

ARCH: Let's see how the Critical Thinking Exercise will stretch the student's imagination. After all, creativity and imagination have not been yet covered in full, except in a very tangential way, if at all.

CRITICAL READING PASSAGE

"Design,"

from *Lateral Thinking: Creativity Step by Step*
Edward de Bono

1973

ABOUT THE AUTHOR

Edward de Bono was born in Malta. He holds advanced degrees in medicine, psychology, and physiology. He was a Rhodes Scholar at Christ Church, Oxford, and holds a PhD from Cambridge. Dr. de Bono is the founder and director of the The Cognitive Research Trust in Cambridge and the Center for the Study of Thinking. He has written 25 books and produced two TV series for BBC on teaching thinking.

In so far as it is not just a matter of copying, design requires a good deal of innovation. Design is a convenient format for practising the lateral thinking principles that have been discussed up to this point. The design process itself is discussed at length in a later section; in this section design is used as practice for lateral thinking.

PRACTICE

The designs are to be visual and in black and white or colour. Verbal descriptions can be added to the pictures to explain certain features or to explain how they work.

The advantages of a visual format are many.

1. There has to be a definite commitment to a way of doing something rather than a vague generalized description.
2. The design is expressed in a manner that is visible to everyone.
3. Visual expression of a complicated structure is much easier than verbal expression. It would be a pity to limit design by the ability to describe it.

The designs could be worked out as a classroom exercise or they could be done as homework. It is easier if the students all work on the same design rather than on individual choices for then any comments apply to them all, there is more comparison and they are all more involved in the analysis.

It is convenient if all the designs are executed on standard sized sheets of paper. Once the design task has been set no additional information is given. No attempt is made to make the design project more specific. 'Do whatever you think is best' is the answer to any question.

Comment on results

Unless the group is small enough to actually cluster around the drawings these would have to be copied and shown on an overhead projector or epidiascope. Or they could just be pinned up. Adequate discussion could be carried out without showing the drawings at all but just redrawing the important features on the blackboard. In commenting on the results the teacher would want to bear the following points in mind:

1. Resist the temptation to judge. Resist the temptation to say, 'this would not work because . . . .'
2. Resist the temptation to choose one way of doing things as being much better than any other for fear of polarizing design in one direction.
3. Emphasize the variety of the different ways of carrying out a particular function. List the different suggestions and add others of one's own.
4. Try and look at the function underlying a particular design. Try to separate the intention of the designer from the actual way this was carried out.
5. Note the features that have been put there for a functional purpose and the ones that are there as ornaments to complete the picture.

6. Question certain points—not in order to destroy them but in order to find out if there was any special reason behind them which may not be manifest.

7. Note the borrowing of complete designs from what might have been seen on television, in the cinema or in comics.

Suggestions

Design projects can either ask for improvements on existing things or for the actual invention of something to carry out a task. It is easiest if the designs do involve something physical since this is easier to draw. They do not have to be mechanical in the strictest sense of the word, for instance the design of a new classroom or a new type of shoe would be very suitable. It is enough that they are concrete projects. In addition one can try organizational designs. Organizational designs would ask for ways of doing things such as building a house very quickly.

Design:
  An apple picking machine.
  A potato peeling machine.
  A cart to go over rough ground.
  A cup that cannot spill.
  A machine to dig tunnels.
  A device to help cars to park.

Redesign:
  The human body.
  A new milk bottle.
  A chair.
  A school.
  A new type of clothes.
  A better umbrella.

Organizational:
  How to build a house very quickly.
  How to arrange the checkout counters in a supermarket.
  How to organize garbage collection.
  How to organize shopping to take up the least time.
  How to put a drain across a busy road.

Variety

The purpose of the design session is to show that there can be different ways of doing something. It is not the individual designs that matter so much as the comparison between designs. In order to show this variety one could compare the complete designs but it is more effective to pick out some particular function and show how this was handled by the different designers.

For instance in the design of an apple picking machine one could choose the function of 'reaching the apples'. To reach the apples some students will have used extendable arms, others will have raised the whole vehicle on jacks, others will have tried to bring the apples to the ground, others might have planted the trees in trenches anyway. For each function the teacher lists the different methods used and asks for further suggestions, He can also add suggestions of his own or ones derived from previous experience with the design project.

Particular functions with the apple picking machine could include the following:

> Reaching the apples.
> Finding the apples.
> Picking the apples.
> Transporting the apples to the ground.
> Sorting out the apples.
> Putting the apples in containers.
> Moving onto the next tree.

It is not suggested that in carrying out the design the student will have tried to cover all these functions. Most of them would be covered quite unconsciously.

Nevertheless one can consciously analyse what has been done and show the different ways of doing it. In many cases no provision will have been made for carrying out a certain function (e.g. transporting the apples to the ground). In such cases one does not criticize the designs that do not show the function but commends those that do show it.

Evaluation

One could criticize designs for omissions, for errors of mechanics, for errors of efficiency, for errors of magnitude and for all sorts of other errors. It is difficult to resist the temptation to do this—but the temptation must be resisted.

If some designs have left things out then one shows this up by commenting on those designs which have put it in.

If some design shows an arrangement that is mechanically unsound then one comments on the function intended rather than the particular way of carrying it out.

If some designs show a very roundabout way of doing something one describes the design without criticism and then describes more efficient designs.

One of the most common faults with designs by students in the 10–13 age group is the tendency to lose sight of the design project and to go into great detail drawing some vehicle that is derived directly from another source such as television or space comics. Thus an apple picking machine will be shown bristling with guns, rockets, radar and jets. Details will be given about number of crew, speed, range, power, how much it would cost to build, how long it would take to build, how many nuts and bolts, the materials used in construction and so on. There is no point in criticizing the superfluity of all this. Instead one emphasizes the functional economy and effectiveness of other designs.

It is important not to criticize actual mechanics. One designer of an apple picking machine suggested putting bits of metal in each of the apples and then using powerful magnets buried in the ground under each tree to pull the apples down. It would be easy to criticize this as follows:

1. Just as much trouble to put bits of metal in each apple as to pick each one directly.
2. The magnet would have to be very powerful indeed to pull the apples down from such a distance.
3. The apples would he badly damaged on hitting the ground.
4. Buried magnets would only be able to collect apples from one tree.

These are all valid comments and one could make many more. But rather than criticizing in this manner one could say: 'Here is someone who instead of going up to pick the apples like everybody else wants to attract the apples to the ground. Instead of having to find the apples and then to pick them one by one he can get then all together and all at once.' Both these are very valid points. The actual method for carrying out the function is obviously inefficient but it is better to let that be than to appear to criticize the concept of function by criticizing the way it is carried out. When that particular designer learns more about magnets he will find that they would not be much good. At the moment however they represent the only method he knows for carrying out 'attraction from a distance'.

In another design for a cart that would go over rough ground the designer suggested some sort of 'smooth stuff,' that was sucked up by the cart from behind itself and then spread down in front of it. Thus the cart was always travelling over smooth stuff. There was even a reservoir for evening out the supply of the smooth stuff.

It would be easy to criticize the idea as follows:

1. What sort of 'smooth stuff' would fill in big hollows. One would need far too much.
2. One could never suck back all that had been laid down and so the supply would run out after a few feet.
3. The cart would have to move very slowly indeed.

Such criticisms are easy but instead one would appreciate that the designer had got away from the usual approach of providing special wheels or other devices for going over rough ground and instead was trying to alter the *ground itself.* From such a concept could come the notion of a tracked vehicle which does actually lay down smooth stuff and pick it up again. There are also those military vehicles which have a roll of steel mesh or glass fibre matting on their backs and this is laid down ahead of the vehicle to make a road on which the vehicle then runs.

Though an idea may seem silly in itself it can still lead to something useful. As shown in the diagram the smooth stuff idea though not a solution in itself might lead straight to the idea of a tracked vehicle. If one had rejected the smooth stuff idea then it might have been harder to get to the same point. The attitude is not, 'This won't work let's throw it out' but, 'This is not going to work but what does it lead us to.'

No one is silly for the sake of being silly no matter how it might appear to other people. There must be a reason why something made sense to the person who drew it at the moment when it was drawn. What it appears to other people is not so important if one is trying to encourage lateral thinking. In any case whatever the reason behind a design and however silly it may be it can still be a most useful stimulus to further ideas.

Assumptions

In the design process there is a tendency to use 'complete units'. This means that when one borrows a unit from somewhere else in order to carry out some special function that unit is used 'complete'. Thus a mechanical arm to pick apples will have five fingers because the human arm has that number. In an attempt to break up such complete units and isolate what is really required one can question the assumption behind them: 'Why does a hand need five fingers to pick apples?'

One may also question assumptions that seem to be basic to the design itself.

Why do we have to *pick* the apples off the trees?

Why do trees have to be that shape?

Why does the arm have to go up and down with every apple it picks?

Some of the points challenged could easily have been taken for granted. By challenging them one can open up new ideas. For instance one could shake apples from trees instead of picking them. In California, they are experimenting with growing trees in a special way which would make it possible to pick the fruit more easily. The arm does not need to go up and down with each apple, the apples could be dropped into a chute or container.

The 'why' technique can be applied to any part of the design project. To begin with the teacher would apply it after discussing the designs. The students could also apply it to their own designs or those of others. As usual the purpose of the 'why' technique is not to try and justify something but to see what happens when one challenges the uniqueness of a particular way of doing things.

SUMMARY

The design process is a convenient format for developing the idea of lateral thinking. The emphasis is on the *different* ways of doing things, the *different* ways of looking at things and the escape from cliché concepts, the challenging of assumptions. Critical evaluation is temporarily suspended in order to develop a generative frame of mind in which flexibility and variety can be used with confidence. For the design session to work it is essential that the person running it understands the purpose of the session. It is not practice in design but practice in lateral thinking.

QUESTIONS FOR REFLECTION

1. Select a decision-making moment in any of your design studio projects. Process and apply or interpret the notions of "innovation, suspended judgment, and design" as defined by de Bono. Be as precise and comprehensive as possible in describing your thoughts at that moment, and try to identify those thoughts that lead to your decision.

2. Draw, diagram, or otherwise express through drawings those design ideas that you excluded or ignored in choosing the final direction of your design.

VISUAL CRITICAL THINKING EXERCISE

Carefully read the following text and make one or more drawings on 11" × 17" paper illustrating the text. You can choose any medium or drawing technique (freehand, hard line, plans, or section to scale, perspective, etc.).

"The Funnel and Stamate" from *Urmuz* (*Weird Pages*) translated from Romanian

ABOUT THE AUTHOR: Urmuz is the pseudonym of Demetru Demetrescu-Buzau, the son of Dimitrie Ionescu Buzau, a physician and a scholar. Urmuz was born on March 17, 1883 in Curtea de Arges, and spent one year (1888) in Paris with his family. He finished high school in Bucharest, enrolled in medical school but graduated in law, saw action in World War I, suffered from recurrent malarial fever, and served as judge in various provincial towns of Romania and as Clerk of the Romanian Supreme Court. Tudor Arghezi, who thought up the Urmuz pseudonym, published "The Funnel and Stamate" in 1922.

A well-ventilated apartment consisting of three rooms, glass-enclosed terrace, and a doorbell.

Out front, a sumptuous living room its back wall taken up by a solid oak book-case perennially wrapped in soaking bed-sheets . . . A legless table right in the middle, based on probability calculus and supporting a vase containing eternal concentrate of the "thing in itself," a clove of garlic, the statuette a priest (from Ardeal) holding a book of syntax, . . . and twenty cents for tips, . . . the rest being without interest whatsoever. This room, it should be noted, which is ever engulfed in darkness, has no doors and no windows; it does not communicate with the outside world except through a tube, which sometimes gives off smoke, and down which, nights, one can have a glimpse of Ptolemy's seven hemispheres, and daytime, two human beings in the process of descending from the ape by the side of a finite string of dry okra right next to the infinite, and useless, Auto-Kosmos.

The second room is in Turkish style; is decorated in the grand manner, furnished with the most fantastic items of eastern luxury . . . Countless precious carpets, hundreds of old arms, the stains of heroic blood still on them, lining the colonnades; the walls, according to the oriental custom, are painted red every morning as they are measured, occasionally, with a pair of compasses for fear of random shrinkage.

From this area, and by the means of a trap door on the floor, one reaches an underground vault, and on the right, after traveling on a little handle-driven cart first, one enters a cool canal, one branch of which ends no one knows where, the other leading precisely in the opposite direction to a low enclosure with a dirt floor and a stake direction to a low enclosure with a dirt floor and a stake in its center to which the entire Stamate family is tethered.

FOR FURTHER READING

"Grammers of Creation" by George Steiner, Chapters 1 and 2.

IO

What Is Style?

FIGURE 10.1 Venus de Milo; technique:
marble; c. 130–100 BC; Louvre, Paris.

ARCH: Dear Philo, upon further reflection, I think this chapter's topic shows our age.

PHILO: Is that right?

ARCH: Yes, absolutely. We began with one of us believing we should devote this chapter to a discussion of beauty, and the other believing style is a more appropriate topic.

PHILO: That's right. You wanted to cover beauty whereas I thought style was more fitting.

Style versus Beauty

ARCH: Your argument was that students no longer refer to anything—much less designs—as being beautiful, and it's true that it's been a very long time since I ever heard anything being described as beautiful in a design studio.

PHILO: And if we did hear the word beauty used, it never carried much critical value. When it appears this day in the design context, it's more or less a throwaway term, something you say because you don't have anything else worth saying.

ARCH: Perhaps. Still, I always thought it took some courage and audacity, especially in our politically correct time, to declare, "This is beautiful!"

PHILO: How would political correctness affect whether one declared something beautiful or not?

ARCH: By declaring something beautiful, you isolate it from other things and imply that those other things are not beautiful. Judging something to be beautiful is an act of exclusion, and in today's world, everything is supposed to have value.

PHILO: Well, that indeed is unfortunate because clearly, not everything is the same.

ARCH: That doesn't prevent us from having the fantasy that everything is equally worthy of our praise. That's what I mean by today's politically correct climate. We might hurt someone's feelings if we say one thing is beautiful and don't include others in that judgment.

PHILO: Ok, so beauty may be outmoded. We still have to investigate why this may be the case. How does an emphasis on style show our age though?

ARCH: When was the last time you heard the word style used in the studio?

PHILO: Probably when I was last invited to participate in a studio crit.

ARCH: Why do you think that's the case?

PHILO: Well, in my experience, whenever I try to draw connections between a student's design and designs that have come before it historically, I usually get met with blank stares. It's not always the case, but I think it belongs to a general inattention to historical precedent and an unwillingness to entertain the idea that someone came up with a similar approach before the student did. Design is certainly not alone in this. I see this phenomenon all the time in the liberal arts as well. The name we use in the liberal arts is usually not style, but we do refer to earlier schools of thought, which I think works similarly to style in the arts.

ARCH: Indeed, perhaps the only time I hear the word style being used in architecture occurs when someone is speaking of the International Style.

PHILO: In other words, to refer to modernism.

ARCH: This confusion points out another hole in many design schools where the subject of aesthetics is absent from the curriculum. It is in such a course that notion of beauty and style should be discussed. You teach such a course, don't you?

PHILO: Yes. The required reading for this dialogue should be a good beginning.

ARCH: And what period of history are we living in now? I don't think it's even postmodernism anymore, when the whole idea of style was thoroughly debunked, most notably by Robert Venturi, Denise Scott Brown and Steven Izenour in *Learning from Las Vegas* (1972). They reversed at

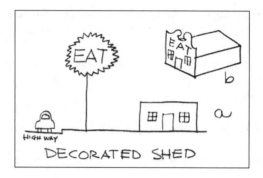

FIGURE 10.2 The "decorated shed" is the name
Robert Venturi gives to a building whose space
and structure reflect conventional methods
of organization, yet has ornament or symbols
"applied" to it.

least one version of modernism as subscribing to the "form follows
function" formula by declaring that all of architecture was just variations of a "decorated shed."

PHILO: I have to say I love that sequence in *Learning from Las Vegas*. It really
does give the lie to much of architectural ambition. But let's reflect
some more on our aims for this chapter, if not the book. Our goal is
not to advocate for any one theme or idea. So what if beauty and style
are outmoded? Don't we have a responsibility to students to go over
the history of these concepts, to show that they have a history? If
they are outmoded concepts, we should try to understand what they
meant and how they came to lose their meaning. In any case, you can't
master history. Who knows, maybe beauty and style will make their
comeback sometime in the future.

ARCH: I think that's a fine proposal. This is what we shall do. I'll start by
recounting my interest in beauty and my understanding of the use
of that term historically. Then you follow with a similar reflection on
style. Then, let's find out what our current historical circumstances
have to say about these concepts.

PHILO: Sounds good.

A Table of Definitions of Beauty

ARCH: I came across a book called *The Foundations of Aesthetics* by the philosophers C. K. Ogden, I. A. Richards, and James Wood at a sidewalk bookseller on the Upper West Side of Manhattan on a cold winter day about ten years ago. That slim old book that I got for a dollar opened, for me, a world I had either ignored or my education did not provide for. Here was a list of definitions of what beauty is. For me at that time, it was uncharted territory. The very question was taboo as it had been for modernist architects (and I regarded myself among them, deservingly or not).

Anything is beautiful—which . . .

I   possesses the simple quality of Beauty.

II   has a specified Form.

III   is an imitation of Nature.

IV   results from successful exploitation of a Medium.

V   is the work of Genius.

VI   reveals (1) Truth, (2) the Spirit of Nature, (3) the Ideal, (4) the Universal, (5) the Typical.

VII   produces Illusion.

VIII leads to desirable Social effects.

IX   is an Expression.

X   causes Pleasure.

XI   excites Emotions.

XII   promotes a Specific emotion.

XIII involves the processes of Empathy.

XIV   heightens Vitality.

XV   brings us into touch with exceptional Personalities.

XIV   conduces to Synaesthesis.

PHILO: This looks comprehensive and helpful.

ARCH: I thought of another definition the authors missed: "Anything is beautiful that sells the most." Of course I have to keep in mind they were writing in 1929. Although true for many, it is not what we hope for when we teach.

PHILO: Yes, but such discussion of branding and commercialism would bring our discussion up to date, although it is beyond the scope of this short dialogue.

ARCH: To state in a course a finite list of definitions seemed to me both courageous and dated. These days, we don't fix a table of definitions about any thing, including the table of elements, used by chemists. We moderns don't make tables of finite sets of items as they did in the classical times. We only draw drafts of open-ended lists of items we see in the world. The audacity to define beauty was refreshing at the time when I came across this book.

PHILO: I should say this remains a very common strategy in philosophy. By charting all the possible definitions of beauty, the philosopher of art can go through the various combinations and determine the cases in which each definition is "true" and the cases in which it is "false." It's very much like a truth table in logic, which charts out the truth and falsity of a proposition.

ARCH: I see. Well, I found it highly interesting that someone would even think it were possible to offer such a chart. In fact, recently I surveyed two of my colleagues on the matter of defining beauty in contrast to style. One of them, Donald, an architect, said, "Those are two hot potatoes." He also argued that the word "beauty," when used in popular language, implies universality, whereas the term "style" is always part of a limited experience a human group in time and space.

PHILO: That sounds like a good working distinction.

ARCH: Another friend of mine, Lex, a painter, had an even more visceral reaction to that distinction, as he is a painter. For him, as a "modern" painter (completely in tune with the spirit of modernist architecture) the word "style" invokes images of replication, conformity, as well as programmatic, industrial, and even fascist or socialist/communist forms of art making. For him, at the center of this ideology is the anonymity of the artist. I observed that cultural climate myself. In the world of architectural education, as I am familiar with the last 25 years, the question of beauty (or aesthetics) is always present but not spoken of as "beauty." The modernists rebelled against it and they also rebelled against the question of style. I was taught in the sixties to aim for a "no style" object of design. An example of an expressionist abstract painting, rooted in the painter's private memory of a landscape (i.e., a ridge from his birth place) would be an example of an object with "no style."

FIGURE 10.3 *Ridge*, painting (1998); oil on canvas; by Lex Braes.

PHILO: Let's go through Ogden's table of definitions and then move on to the problem of style. Let's just enumerate here a few of their definitions. Although we cannot fully discuss them, mentioning a few definitions could be a good trigger for class discussion.

ARCH: Good. Then what do we make of the old saying: "*Degustibus non se disputa*" (Latin for "In matters of taste there is no room for discussion")?

I like tea and you like coffee. That is not an answer for the design or architecture student. It sounds like Ogden's first definition of beauty. "Anything is beautiful which possesses the simple quality of beauty." Ogden then goes on to say, "Beauty as intrinsic supposes that things have the property of beauty as they have redness or temperature." Beauty has no connection with anything else and discussion is not possible, for example the beauty of a lion or an airplane. Beauty becomes an ultimate un-analyzable idea and not subject to criticism. I have heard this in design class often to my great irritation.

PHILO: This approach is the opposite of every notion of critical thinking. The possibility of discussion and criticism are fundamental to the method. That is, unless by just pointing to something one likes without words becomes the trigger to a conversation about the object or situation, etc.

ARCH: I agree. The term **style** seems to me best represented by the second definition in the Ogden's list of definitions. Of course there are others but for the moment let's focus on this: "Anything is beautiful which has a specified form." Some specified arrangement of physical features that has become in itself preferable to another similar arrangement. A well-established style of art and architecture belongs in this definition. These arrangements usually are based on a found, selected, or preferred system of order.

PHILO: We will pick up this topic in detail later.

ARCH: Can we now move to Ogden's next definition: "Anything is beautiful which is an imitation of Nature." The authors write, "This is the most popular view, that art is essentially Imitation. Aristotle combines this view with the pleasure doctrine urging that there is a special pleasure in recognition. With the advent of the camera, however, the unique function of the artist was challenged, and at the same time theological considerations no longer allowed a certain merit to every picture qua replica of God's handy work. The esteem felt for imitation is dwindling view in recent times."

PHILO: It has had a revival in the movement called **Organicism** and **Genetic Generative Design** based on a computer algorithm. That is a dominant model today.

ARCH: I know it well, and it is an important topic to dissect and understand. But here, for the sake of brevity, allow me to give you here another of Ogden's definitions: "Anything is beautiful which results from the successful exploitation of a Medium." This is Aristotle's second cause, the Material Cause. The artist, they say, must respect the character of his medium, which are material, tools of representation, and technology of construction, and exploit these components. Art is primarily the characteristic use of tools and materials.

One should recall here Louis Kahn's dictum: "What the brick wants to be."

PHILO: We have touched on this in earlier chapters. Let's go on and return to this issue later.

ARCH: Again, this opens up a rich topic about beauty. I feel obliged to name it here in order to create the opportunity of a wider class discussion by the professor and the students. Ogden's next definition number is "Anything is beautiful which reveals (1) Truth, (2) the Spirit of Nature, (3) the Ideal, (4) the Universal, (5) the Typical." Art reveals an invisible truth. The relevant definitions of truth are as varied as that of beauty. Aristotle suggests that the artist besides imitating should also preserve the type and at the same time ennoble it. By painting a "type" of object in a class, the artist is in one way interpreting the "universal." "The artist must imitate that which is within the thing, that which is active through form and figure, and discourses to us by symbols—the Naturegeist, or spirit of nature, elsewhere defining beauty."[2]

PHILO: That is a lot! I hope they take us on and dive into these topics one at the time. How many other definitions you plan to include here?

ARCH: "Anything is beautiful which leads to desirable social effects." The authors write: "Uplift doctrines which have emerged from the industrious homes of the late Victorian moralists. John Ruskin (Oxford lectures) maintained that Fine Arts have only three functions: (1) enforcing the religious sentiments of men, (2) perfecting their ethical state, and (3) doing them material service. The first two are stressed by Tolstoi in *What is Art?* Art is the expression of a certain attitude towards reality, an attitude of wander and value, a recognition of something greater than man; and where that recognition is not, art dies. The artist knows the impossible."[3]

PHILO: You are supported by the readings that elevate the artist as a prophet. We philosophers take a much more skeptical view of this, as you know.

ARCH: Yes I know. I realize that what we are doing here is not a dialogue any longer. But we both felt that stating these definitions here would draw the attention of the class to their precision and importance. Here are three more. We did not cover them all! The reading of the whole book at the library should supplement the missing items.

- "Anything is beautiful which has an expression."
- "Anything is beautiful which causes pleasure. Santayana says 'beauty is pleasure regarded as a quality of a thing.'"
- "Anything is beautiful which involves the processes of Empathy."[4]

Models of Critical Thinking on a Design Review

PHILO: I think that is enough for now about beauty and style. The students have the entire list of definitions. Can we now return for a moment other aspects of the way we judge a work of art, design, or architecture?

ARCH: Philo, may I ask you a question? Imagine a jury in a design school. You are one of the guest critics.

PHILO: Sure. I have been there. What do you have in mind?

ARCH: Can I offer a list of types of mindsets, or if you will, hats, you and other jurors may wear. These are just general inclinations, never so pure theoretical points of view, but I think they fit. Philo, here is a list of possible critical positions from which, you or others may approach the work:

1. Formalist/art for art's sake type (poet of words and images)
2. Engineer, functionalist, materialist, Marxist, etc.
3. Psychoanalyst of art, for whom art is reflecting the nature of a human's state of mind

These are three models of critical types of hats one can wear in a design jury. Or, maybe there is a fourth. That is, what I call the pedagogical pragmatic approach. It accepts the premise of the project, comments on the thought process of the students, yet focuses on the immediate design problems the student has and guides him/her. The aim is to help the development of a project to its own internal logic if even if it is wrong. It is then that the student learns something. The advice is concrete, specific and formal, and about the form's formal properties of the design, not about its meaning or functional response to the program. Those are placed on hold for a little while to see and scrutinize the object itself, and, for itself free for a moment from other contingent obligations.

PHILO: Do you really want me to choose one of those hats? I refuse. You wouldn't either. We all can wear one of those hats in a serial fashion and give the student a broad critical review. Such models of thinking are not mutually exclusive. On the contrary they are not only cooperative, but most of the time they coexist in anyone's mind.

ARCH: You are right. That would be my strategy. On the other hand, Philo, may I ask you another question? Are you a **formalist**? I am. These days calling someone a formalist is an insult. This requires, of course, a longer discussion. If we have the time we should take this up again. I just thought that under the present topic this question cannot be avoided.

PHILO: A formalist? Ha! Ha! You are provocative. Because we don't have the time to completely lay to rest that serious topic, we might go around it and address two other topics related to formalism and to beauty and style in general. The first is the question: What is order or ordering systems? Where do they originate in all design, and how are they determining form and, of course beauty and style?

There is a second question, somewhat indirect but crucial to the origins of form: What role does **intellect intuition** play in the design process? You can see how both of these questions belong in this chapter, although I can see them belonging under other topics we have discussed, too.

ARCH: Philo, you are, as the old saying goes, a gentleman and a scholar. That is that, although you seem to have a bias towards philosophical systems that exhibit non-hierarchical post-modern ways of thinking.

PHILO: What makes you say that?

ARCH: Well, you are quite patient in turning around a topic of discussion without rushing to one conclusion or another. These last questions, of "order" or "ordering systems" and the design process, are fertile for critical thinking, especially here at the end of the chapter on style.

PHILO: Could you explain what this topic means?

ARCH: You know what it means. In the end, in any design project, after we make allowances for all the contingent forces that contribute in shaping a design, such as material, site, technology, economics (budget), political (a client), history (precedents), the spirit of its own time (zeitgeist), the ultimate exact shape the design solution will take it still is in the hands of an individual designer, or an architect, or a team of them.

PHILO: Yes, but they could have a design process that is open to interdisciplinary technical information, to a client's desires and their budget, to environmental concerns and to cultural norms and meaning imbedded in the language and other social habits of any society. The personal wishes and biases of any individual and/or group must be tamed. Transparency and democracy in the design process is a desirable goal, wouldn't you say?

ARCH: Let's outline a definition of design that I subscribe to: a designer's task is still the *willful imposition of order*. We can discuss the multiple sources of order in a project, if you like.

PHILO: You know, you are out of step with the times we are living in. Could you list them before I agree or disagree with you?

ARCH: Sources of order and ordering systems.

PHILO: Again, tell me what are they.

ARCH: Here is the list of sources of order: I will number them.

1. **Nature**, material causation, automorphic genesis, morphology, site "forces" and all other material conditions in a design situation to which we have to pay attention. They all are sources of order (see Chapter 5 "What Is Natural? What Is Artificial?", Monod's term).

2. **Geometry as a tool of measurement** and more recently, any **computer algorithm** used to develop the material embodiment of a design or any method (step by step ritual) of production we employ.

3. **Social order, cultural historical body**—notions of the "ideal body" including **precedents** from **art and architecture**, history we consider, model after, or imitate because of habit or market demand.

PHILO: That is helpful. I can name a few more.

ARCH: I don't mind ending this dialogue by having opened up the question of "Where does order come from?" One could say that beauty or style always imply some form of order. Isn't that the challenge of all design?

CRITICAL READING PASSAGE

The Foundations of Aesthetics
C. K. Ogden, I. A. Richards, and James Wood
1922

ABOUT THE AUTHORS

Philosopher, linguist, and psychologist C. K. Ogden (1889–1957), literary critic I. A. Richards (1893–1979) and artist and art historian James Wood (1895–1975) published *The Foundations of Aesthetics* in 1922. Influenced to a great extent by the behavioral psychologist Ivan Pavlov (of Pavlov's dogs fame) and the linguistics of the American philosopher Charles Pierce, *The Foundations of Aesthetics,* produces a psychological theory of beauty.

Many intelligent people give up aesthetic, speculation and take no interest in discussions about the nature or object of Art, because they feel that there is little likelihood of arriving at any definite conclusion. Authorities appear to differ so widely in their judgments as to which things are beautiful, and when they do agree there is no means of knowing *what* they are agreeing about.

What in fact do they mean by Beauty? Prof. Bosanquet and Dr. Santayana, Signor Croce and Clive Bell, not to mention Ruskin and Tolstoi, each in his own way dogmatic, enthusiastic and voluminous, each leaves his conclusions equally uncorrelated with those of his predecessors. And the judgments of experts on one another are no less at variance.

But if there is no reason to suppose that people are talking about the same thing, a lack of correlation in their remarks need not cause surprise. We assume too readily that similar language involves similar thoughts and similar things thought of. Yet why should there be only one subject of investigation which has been called Aesthetics? Why not several fields to be separately investigated, whether they are found to be connected or not? Even a Man of Letters, given time, should see that if we say with the poet:

> "'Beauty is Truth, Truth Beauty'—that is
> all
> Ye know on earth, and all ye need to know."

We need not be talking about the same thing as the author who says:

> "The hide of the rhinoceros may be
> admired for its fitness; but as it scarcely
> indicates vitality, it is deemed less beautiful
> than a skin which exhibits mutable
> effects of muscular elasticity."

What reason is there to suppose that one aesthetic doctrine can be framed to include all the valuable kinds of what is called Literature:

> "All tongues speak of him, and the bleared
> sights
> Are spectacled to see him, your prattling nurse
> Into a rapture lets her baby cry
> While she chats him: the kitchen malkin pins
> Her richest lockram 'bout her reechy neck
> Clamb'ring the walls to eye him."

To this satire may be opposed the unsubstantial music of the following passage, yet both must take a high place in any account of literary values:—

> "Such a soft floating witchery of sound
> As twilight Elphins make, when they at eve
> Voyage on gentle gales from Fairyland,
> Where Melodies round honey-dropping flowers,
> Footless and wild, like birds of Paradise,
> Nor pause, nor perch, hovering on untam'd
> wing!"

No one explanation seems sufficient to cover such a wide difference. It is not surprising therefore that aesthetic theories are equally different. Let us nevertheless attempt to make a classification.

AESTHETIC EXPERIENCES

Whenever we have any experience which might be called 'aesthetic,' that is whenever we are enjoying, contemplating, admiring or appreciating an object, there are plainly different parts of the situation on which emphasis can be laid. As we select one or other of these so we shall develop one or other of the main aesthetic doctrines. In this choice we shall, in fact, be deciding which of the main Types of Definition[1] we are employing. Thus we may begin with the object itself; or with other things such as Nature, Genius, Perfection, The Ideal, or Truth, to which it is related; or with its effects upon us. We may begin where we please, the important thing being that we should know and make clear which of these approaches it is that we are taking, for the objects with which we come to deal, the referents to which we refer, if we enter one field will not as a rule be the same as those in another. Few persons will be equally interested in all, but some acquaintance with them will at least make the interests of other people more intelligible, and discussion more profitable. Differences of opinion and differences of interest in these matters are closely interconnected, but any attempt at a general synthesis, premature perhaps at present, must begin by disentangling them. A third quotation essentially unlike either of those already given above may help to make this quite clear:—

> "By the waters of Babylon
> We sat down and wept:
> When we remembered thee, O Sion.
> As for our harps, we hanged them up:
> Upon the trees that are therein.

---

[1] A full account of these will be found in Chapter V. of *The Meaning of Meaning* (Kegan Paul, 1922) by the same authors.

For they that led us away captive required
of us then a song,
And melody in our heaviness:
Sing us one of the songs of Sion.
How shall we sing the Lord's song:
In a strange land?
If I forget thee, O Jerusalem:
Let my right hand forget her cunning.
If I do not remember thee,
Let my tongue cleave to the roof of my
mouth:
Yea, if I prefer not Jerusalem in my mirth.
Remember the Children of Edom, O Lord,
In the day of Jerusalem:
How they said, Down with it, down with it,
Even to the ground.
O daughter of Babylon, wasted with misery:
Yea, happy shall he be that rewardeth thee,
As thou hast served us.
Blessed shall he be that taketh thy children:
and throweth them
Against the stones."

We have then to make plain the method of Definition which we are employ-ing. The range of useful methods is shown in the following table of definitions, most of which represent traditional doctrines, while others, not before empha-sized, render the treatment approximately complete. It should be borne in mind throughout this volume that anything judged to be beautiful is either a work of art or a natural object. A work of art may clearly *be regarded* in both ways, but not simultaneously. When we regard it as a work of art we take the attitude of the contemplator, our attitude, that is to say, is modified by the preceding activity of another mind; but when we look at it as a natural object (as we *may* do in painting a cathedral) we take the attitude of an artist, that is to say, we make our own selection.

THE SENSES OF BEAUTY

A
- I   *Anything is beautiful—which possesses the simple quality of Beauty.*
- II   *Anything is beautiful—which has a specified Form.*

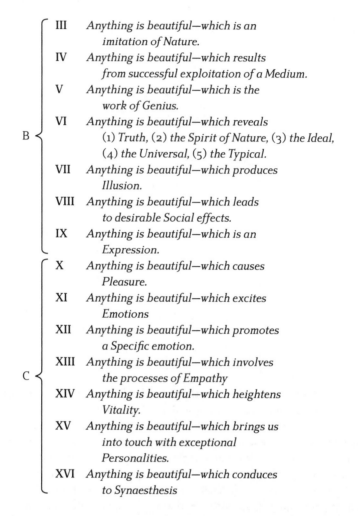

B

III   *Anything is beautiful—which is an*
       imitation of Nature.

IV   *Anything is beautiful—which results*
       from successful exploitation of a Medium.

V   *Anything is beautiful—which is the*
       work of Genius.

VI   *Anything is beautiful—which reveals*
       (1) Truth, (2) the Spirit of Nature, (3) the Ideal,
       (4) the Universal, (5) the Typical.

VII   *Anything is beautiful—which produces*
       Illusion.

VIII *Anything is beautiful—which leads*
       to desirable Social effects.

IX   *Anything is beautiful—which is an*
       Expression.

C

X   *Anything is beautiful—which causes*
       Pleasure.

XI   *Anything is beautiful—which excites*
       Emotions

XII   *Anything is beautiful—which promotes*
       a Specific emotion.

XIII *Anything is beautiful—which involves*
       the processes of Empathy

XIV   *Anything is beautiful—which heightens*
       Vitality.

XV   *Anything is beautiful—which brings us*
       into touch with exceptional
       Personalities.

XVI   *Anything is beautiful—which conduces*
       to Synaesthesis

The fields reached by these various approaches can all be cultivated and most of them are associated with well known names in the Philosophy of Art.[2]

Let us, however, suppose that we have selected one of these fields and cultivated it to the best of our ability; for what reasons was it selected rather than some other? For if we approach the subject in the spirit of a visitor to the Zoo, who, knowing that all the creatures in a certain enclosure are 'reptiles,' seeks for the common property which distinguishes them as a group from the fish in the Aquarium, mistakes may be made. We enter, for example, the Fitzwilliam Museum, and, assuming that all the objects there collected are beautiful, attempt similarly to establish some common property. A little consideration of how they came there might have raised serious doubts; but if, after the man-

---

[2] As this discussion is throughout concerned with the theory of Beauty, we are not called upon to examine the various senses in which the word Art has also been used. Thus when we refer to Art in connection with e.g., Imitation, we are referring to beauty in anything that has generally been called Art as opposed to Nature.

ner of many aestheticians, we persist, we may even make our discovery of some relevant common property appear plausible.

Anyone, however, who, after a study of these and similar objects, wished to know why he should prefer one to another would find himself confronted by the possibilities we have set forth in our list.

[. . .]

VI. TRUTH

The general method employed in this enquiry is nowhere more valuable than in the discussion of VI Revelation. By its aid we may free ourselves in part from the apparent conflicts which the phonetic and graphic overlaps of distinct vocabularies (*i.e.,* the use of the same terms to mean different things) occasion. In all revelatory doctrines, we are concerned in one sense or another with Truth. The relevant definitions of truth are at least as varied as those of Beauty. They cannot be adequately discussed here; one such set of opinions providing sufficient mental exercise for one occasion, but a few broad distinctions may be noted without overstraining the attention.

Thus when Aristotle suggests that the artist besides imitating should also preserve the type and at the same time ennoble it his suggestion may be taken in many ways. Eastlake, for instance, understands that, "The elephant with his objectionable legs and inexpressive hide, may still be supposed to be a very normal specimen and so worthy of imitation by the artist," which is one way of interpreting "the universal," namely as the typical. And Rymer in objecting to Shakespeare's Iago: "He would pass upon us a close, dissembling, false, insinuating rascal, instead of an open-hearted, frank, plain-dealing Souldier, a character constantly worn by them for some thousands of years in the World," provides another interpretation namely as the conventional. Thirdly, Croce remarks of the view that art is imitation: "Now truth has been maintained or at least shadowed with these words, now error. More frequently, nothing definite has been thought. One of the legitimate scientific meanings occurs when imitation is understood as representation or intuition of nature, a form of knowledge [*cf.* Plate VII]. And when this meaning has been understood, by placing in greater relief the spiritual character of the process, the other proposition becomes also legitimate; namely that art is the idealisation or idealising imitation of nature."

> "Hark, hark! the lark at heaven's gate sings,
>   And Phcebus 'gins arise,
> His steeds to water at those springs
>   On chaliced flowers that lies."

Yet other variants may be found in Matthew Arnold for whom commerce with certain forms of art seemed "to make those who constantly practiced it . . .

like persons who have had very weighty and impressive experience: more truly than others under the empire of facts, and more independent of the language current among those with whom they live"; and in Coleridge, "the artist must imitate that which is within the thing, that which is active through form and figure, and discourses to us by symbols,—the Naturegeist, or spirit of nature," elsewhere defining beauty as "the subjection of matter to spirit so as to be tansformed into a symbol, in and through which the spirit reveals itself."

MYSTICISM

It is plain that such different views as these require separate handling. Matthew Arnold's observation may be postponed until we discuss the doctrine of equilibrium within which it will find both a place and an explanation. Let us here consider the only other of the five views which requires attention, namely that of Coleridge. Having been stated as a mystical view, it can evidently only appeal in this form to those who adopt the special attitudes involved.

One natural statement of the mystical doctrine involved would be as follows. A certain emotion has occurred in the contemplation of a work of art or of nature, which represents or symbolizes either a special selection, or else in the supreme case the whole of, the past experience of the individual. It enables us to think of a complete range of experience, and this range is regarded as a datum upon a different level from any of the data provided by portions of that range, and capable of giving knowledge as to the nature of the universe which the partial data of everyday experience do not readily yield.

Those to whom such an idea appears extravagant will explain the peculiar character of the emotions in question by saying perhaps that they are associated with unrecalled events in past experience.

The view of the world of art as a better world into which we may escape from the drabness and dullness of the present has close affinities with some kinds of idealisation.

> "Then let the winds howl on! their harmony
> Shall henceforth be my music, and the night
> The sound shall temper with the owlets' cry,
>   As I now hear them in the fading light
>   Dim o'er the bird of darkness' native site,
>   Answer each other on the Palatine,
> With their large eyes, all glistening grey and
>   bright,
>   And sailing pinions. Upon such a shrine
> What are our petty griefs?—let me not number
>   mine."

QUESTIONS FOR REFLECTION

1. Review the various definitions of beauty Ogden, Richards, and Wood entertain. To what extent is each one applicable in the design context? Provide an argument for each of your answers.

2. Ogden, Richards, and Wood ultimately decide that synaesthesis is "the theory of Beauty *par excellence.*" Do you agree with their conclusion?

3. In their preface to the work, Ogden, Richards, and Wood suggest that the then recent discovery of non-European art has necessitated a reconsideration of the meaning of beauty. Why do you think that would be the case?

CRITICAL THINKING EXERCISE

Choose an object of art, design, or architecture that you think is beautiful.

Try to self-analyze the reasons why you find it so. Then show it to one or more of your fellow students and ask their opinions. Keep notes about the ensuing discussion and present your experience to the class.

FOR FURTHER READING

Beardsley, Monroe C. *Aesthetics from Classical Greece to the Present A Short History.*

Shapiro, Meyer. 1962. *Selected Papers: Theory and Philosophy of Art: Style, Artist, and Society.*

II

What Is Society? Or, What Is a Better Tomorrow?

TOPICS

- Utopia

- Sustainability and society

- Milton Keynes: town planning and designing the future

FIGURE 11.1
Constructivist painter and former director of the Bauhaus, László Moholy-Nagy, was commissioned to create effects sequences for the film *Things to Come*, 1936.

ARCH: Let's begin this chapter by discussing utopia.

PHILO: Utopia?

ARCH: Yes, utopia.

PHILO: I don't get it. Why utopia?

Utopia

ARCH: Because all design is directed at making things better. A better society, if you will.

PHILO: Really?

ARCH: Yes, really. You don't think so?

PHILO: I think *some* design is motivated by the desire to make things better. But I think *most* design, quite honestly, is motivated by the desire to make money. From tea kettles to window treatments to dresses to buildings, most design depends on the market and being able to sell one's designs in order to be successful.

ARCH: Well, that may be true in today's context, but you don't think that philosophy is necessarily different, do you?

PHILO: I beg your pardon?

ARCH: You work for a wage, correct?

PHILO: Yes.

ARCH: And if you offered classes that don't fill up with students, do you think you'd still get paid?

PHILO: Well—

ARCH: Do you think you would get paid just because you are a philosopher, or because you are able to provide a service that can be purchased?

PHILO: My classes are *opportunities* to engage in critical reflection through writing.

ARCH: And I suppose students are allowed to take advantage of these "opportunities" without having to pay anything?

PHILO: Of course not. Otherwise, how would I —

ARCH: Get paid?

PHILO: All right, I see your point. But getting paid for your labor is different from making a profit. Selling something isn't supposed to just reimburse someone for labor and costs. The aim is to make a profit.

ARCH: Fine, but my point is that the world in which we live does not allow us to separate *any* activity from market forces.

PHILO: OK.

ARCH: That does not mean our activities can be reduced to the market, however, and that is what I am saying about design.

PHILO: Go on.

ARCH: As I was beginning to say, then, all design has a utopian desire at its heart. The reason someone engages in design is to change the world, to make a task easier or more pleasurable, or to perform an action that someone was not able to do at any point beforehand.

PHILO: I'll grant you that point for the moment. If I were to respond to your claim more critically, I would point out that you are implicitly assuming that design responds to a need. However, when we sell things, we also invent needs. How many of the things we possess — all designed by someone, somewhere — fulfill an actual need rather than an imagined one?

ARCH: We could go round and round now.

PHILO: Yes, so I'll drop it.

ARCH: Let us just say for the moment that, ideally then, design is devoted to making things better.

PHILO: OK

ARCH: Well, then, we have a problem.

PHILO: We do?

ARCH: Yes, we do. You and I. See, our project is aimed at elaborating a practice of critical thinking in design, which I think we've demonstrated requires a certain degree of skepticism.

PHILO: Very true.

ARCH: Yet, as we discussed in Chapter 1, design requires us to close off the perpetual questioning that usually accompanies critical reflection. This is one reason I suggested that critical thinking is often opposed, maybe even "unnatural," to the design practice. Compared to design, which is directed towards the future, towards a solution, and which most of all harbors an optimism about the future, critical thinking can appear pessimistic.

PHILO: I recall our earlier discussion, and it explains why time is often such an issue in design. There is always a client waiting for the product. There's never enough time for pessimism, however pragmatic, or, as I would argue, necessary.

ARCH: You know I'm not saying you're pessimistic.

PHILO: But I am! That's what gives me my charm.

ARCH: No doubt. What I am saying, in any case, is that design and architecture require that we be optimists. I always tell students that we must assume that whatever we design will become an actual reality in the future. As such, we have to be aware of the consequences of our designs as well as believe in the ability of our designs to change the world, or at least our part of the world. In other words, we designers are utopians. We believe that our visions and designs at any scale will contribute to the betterment of human beings.

PHILO: As a teacher, and especially as someone who has had his designs realized in the real world with all its constraints and compromises, don't you think such an attitude is a bit naïve?

ARCH: Sure, when stated in an absolute sense, of course. It may be naïve. But to ask us to be skeptical towards our practice runs counter to that belief that design can change things. Perhaps it's a naïve determinism. Naïve or not, there is the *hope* that through better design we can change human beings and their behavior. How often do we hear a designer say, "By tilting the wall towards the entrance the space becomes more inviting and will cause more people to want to walk that way," etc.?

PHILO: Unfortunately, I have heard that many, many times in way too many crits than I care to remember. But what you are saying is different, if not in kind then certainly in degree. You are arguing that design harbors a belief that it *can* **change** the world, not that it necessarily *will*. Interestingly enough, we still need to discuss what we mean by change. Many designers, and even design critics, believe that change is an automatic result of design, which I don't believe is a claim that can be supported. It smacks of arrogance, to be sure.

ARCH: Oh, no doubt. I have myself experienced the utopian education and prevailing social engineering of the 1960s. In fact, having grown up in a communist country, I was the recipient of the notion that all art, design, and architecture are tools for the construction of the communist utopia. There is a parallel idea behind capitalism, but argued from different assumptions about the nature of human beings. And both communism and capitalism shared at a time a common belief in technology's power to bring about the utopian "Tomorrow." Mies van der Rohe was just one such figure. In fact, much of modern architecture had at its heart a utopian investment in technology.

PHILO: Contemporary architecture as well, no?

ARCH: Of course, don't get me started talking about this so-called new techno-utopia "computationalism" again. I think I made my objections clear during our discussion of form and function (in Chapter 3).

PHILO: Well, maybe we can review what you said at a later time. I'm struck by something you just said, though. When you declare that one of the great dilemmas of design is deciding whether "we" designers are poets or engineers, you mean that literally, at least in terms of being an engineer and design's dependence on technology?

ARCH: Yes, of course. How else could I mean it?

PHILO: Speaking of utopia and technology in design, I have to say I see this curious fetishization of technology going on in the current discourse on sustainability.

ARCH: I don't doubt it, but that really deserves its own focused discussion. Let's turn to that now.

Sustainability and Society

ARCH: What else are claims about sustainability if not claims about the future and, most of all, claims about humankind's ability to change the future, both negatively and positively? The turn to sustainable design harbors this deterministic assumption, which I think is strange because, philosophically speaking, can we really say anything about the future?

PHILO: Well, sure. We can always say whatever we want about the future. It does not mean it will happen the way we say it will.

ARCH: I mean, can we ever really say anything meaningful about the future? That events will result in this condition instead of another condition?

PHILO: Philosophically, all we can say about the future is that there will be a future.

ARCH: Ah, there you go.

PHILO: But, I don't know where that gets us.

ARCH: I suspect not very far. The uncertainty of the future's content does not invalidate claims about sustainability.

PHILO: Certainly not. I don't see the sense in arguing against sustainability based on the fact that we can't be sure about the future. While we deal with epistemological uncertainties, the world accelerates towards its end. To what degree we participate in environmental devastation seems to ignore the point that we have a profound share in it as the result of our attempts to master nature.

ARCH: Still, there's something odd about sustainability discourse, which I can't put my finger on. The way it's been embraced by the market should tell us something.

PHILO: Well, industries, as well as designers, have found ways to make money off of the trend. It's similar to organic foods, no? Sure, they're supposed to be healthier than conventionally farmed, corporate food, but more importantly, they're fashionable.

ARCH: There's all that, but there's also something else.

PHILO: Well, I would say that sustainability discourse relies on a specific image of what nature is on the one hand, an image of nature as pure and innocent. On the other hand, sustainability has a very one-sided view of society.

ARCH: How so?

PHILO: From the standpoint of sustainability, nature is passive and society is this active force, exploiting nature and ruining the possibility of future generations to live on the planet. What's missing in this picture?

ARCH: That human beings are part of nature as well.

PHILO: Almost. What's missing is the recognition that we can design as many sustainable technologies and objects as we'd like. It still won't change the fact that there are still other human beings we rely on to construct these technologies and make these objects. Behind these shiny, new sustainable objects are those human beings who very often cannot even afford the objects they make.

ARCH: Here we go. I was waiting for your Marxist argument.

PHILO: Well, I would love to take credit for it, but it's not mine. It's from Murray Bookchin, a scholar and activist of an area of research called "social ecology." In the introductory essay to his book *The Ecology of Freedom*, an excerpt of which we are including here as a critical reading passage, Bookchin recounts how he came upon his famous formulation that "the very notion of the domination of nature by man stems from the very real domination of human by human."[1] Thus, by having us consumers focus on the design and technological production of sustainable objects, sustainability discourse in its popular form distracts us from the very real conditions of human labor and the fact that as sustainable as the objects we make are, so-called sustainable practices do not address the need to find cheap labor to make sustainable products. That's why, I believe, sustainability is such a big business. We can make sustainable products cheaply, and that is not due primarily to the efficiency and availability of technology.

ARCH: Feel better, now that you've gotten that off your chest? I must interject that from an architect's perspective, sustainability is about planning responsible uses of resources for the immediate future as well as the long term. This does have direct involvement in the marketplace but it is a much more complex side to sustainability. It involves looking at how to best mesh the built world with the natural environment to decrease certain problems impacting human and wildlife health. It's much more than what you outlined above. Here you are only speaking to those who produce products, not buildings. I agree producing more materials for "sustainable" products isn't necessarily sustainable.

PHILO: Well, doesn't this make sense?

ARCH: It does. But I'm not sure how this connects to our present discussion.

PHILO: Well, for me our discussion is not really about utopia or whether we can decide finally what will happen in the future.

ARCH: What is it about, then?

PHILO: It's about what we mean when we say "society" and what we assume when we try to decide the proper role the designer has with respect to society. There are two assumptions: that society is some object *over there* and the designer is somehow separate from society. It may be true that human beings belong to nature, but I'm with Bookchin: designers are part of the very society for whom they design things. So they can't just decide how to make society better without carrying with them all the biases that they unavoidably inherit due to the simple fact that they are members of society as well.

ARCH: How then do we approach the problem correctly without getting caught up in distractions? I still think utopia and the desire to change the future are real problems we need to address, but I also see your point about the separation of the designer from society discussions about utopia usually assume.

PHILO: You mentioned an example earlier.

ARCH: Yes.

PHILO: Well, let's go there.

Milton Keynes: Town Planning and Designing the Future

ARCH: Here's a controversy I encountered when I was a student in England in the mid-seventies. This will bring together the concerns we elaborated in our previous discussion, while also giving a concrete example for students to practice their critical thinking skills.

In response to the housing situation in the years following World War II, the British government enacted what it named the New Towns Act of 1946. Although a number of "new towns" were built in the years immediately following, substandard housing and housing congestion persisted into the 1960s in Southeast England. In response, the new town of Milton Keynes was created. Planned for one million inhabitants, Milton Keynes offered a great laboratory of experiments for architects and planners. Two particular housing estates at Milton Keynes, Netherfield and Eaglestone, have been the subject of many evaluations and debates. The site plans of the two housing projects—one, Eaglestone, organized according to a "cluster scheme" and the other, Netherfield, following a linear organization—were considered by architects and critics as representative of two diametrically opposed philosophies of urban living. All debates linked the physical form (spatial organization) of each estate to certain social and political ideas. Echoing philosophical, sociological research, the architects and theoreticians link one's neighborhood to a sense of place and identity. These attempts by the architects to explain their thinking in the design process exploded into a total war of ideas about the role of architectural design in shaping a future society. The words attached to each design moved quickly to extremes: One was called fascist and elitist, but modern by its critics. That was the linear scheme. The other, the cluster scheme with social family grouping goals, was seen by its detractors as retrograde and claustrophobic in contrast.

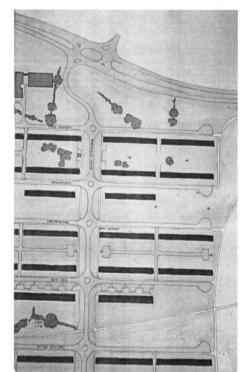

FIGURE 11.2
(Right) Milton Keynes'
Netherfield linear scheme plan.

FIGURE 11.3
(Below) Milton Keynes,
Netherfield Housing (photo by
Dan Bucsescu, 1974).

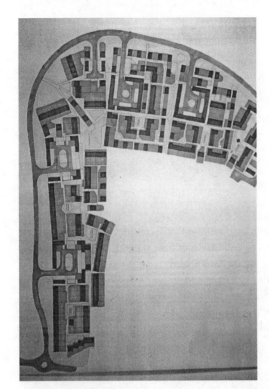

FIGURE 11.4
(Left) Milton Keynes'
Eaglestone cluster scheme
plan.

FIGURE 11.5
(Below) Milton Keynes,
Eaglestone Housing (photo
by Dan Bucsescu, 1974).

CRITICAL READING PASSAGE

"The Concept of Social Ecology,"
from *The Ecology of Freedom:*
The Emergence and Dissolution of Hierarchy
Murray Bookchin

2000

ABOUT THE AUTHOR

Murray Bookchin (1921-2006) was a social-political philosopher and American libertarian socialist committed to an anti-capitalist and anti-hierarchical organization of society. He wrote many books analyzing the relationship among the design and construction of urban space, citizenship, and democracy. His concept of social ecology, which this chapter's reading selection elucidates, locates the origin of the world's environmental maladies in social hierarchy and domination. In 1974, Bookchin co-founded and directed the Institute for Social Ecology.

The legends of the Norsemen tell of a time when all beings were apportioned their worldly domains: the gods occupied a celestial domain, Asgard, and men lived on the earth, Midgard, below which lay Niffleheim, the dark, icy domain of the giants, dwarfs, and the dead. These domains were linked together by an enormous ash, the World Tree. Its lofty branches reached into the sky, and its roots into the furthermost depths of the earth. Although the World Tree was constantly being gnawed by animals, it remained ever green, renewed by a magic fountain that infused it continually with life.

The gods, who had fashioned this world, presided over a precarious state of tranquility. They had banished their enemies, the giants, to the land of ice. Fenris the wolf was enchained, and the great serpent of the Midgard was held at bay. Despite the lurking dangers, a general peace prevailed, and plenty existed for the gods, men, and all living things. Odin, the god of wisdom, reigned over all the deities; the wisest and strongest, he watched over the battles of men and selected the most heroic of the fallen to feast with him in his great fortress, Valhalla. Thor, the son of Odin, was not only a powerful warrior, the defender of Asgard against the restive giants, but also a deity of order, who saw to the keeping of faith between men and obedience to the treaties. There were gods and goddesses of plenty, of fertility, of love, of law, of the sea and ships, and a multitude of animistic spirits who inhabited all things and beings of the earth.

But the world order began to break down when the gods, greedy for riches, tortured the witch Gullveig, the maker of gold, to compel her to reveal her secrets. Discord now became rampant among the gods and men. The gods began to break their oaths; corruption, treachery, rivalry, and greed began to dominate the world. With the breakdown of the primal unity, the days of the gods and men, of Asgard and Midgard, were numbered. Inexorably, the violation of the world order would lead to Ragnarok—the death of the gods in a great conflict before Valhalla. The gods would go down in a terrible battle with the giants, Fenris the wolf, and the serpent of the Midgard. With the mutual destruction of all the combatants, humanity too would perish, and nothing would remain but bare rock and overflowing oceans in a void of cold and darkness. Having thus disintegrated into its beginnings, however, the world would be renewed, purged of its earlier evils and the corruption that destroyed it. Nor would the new world emerging from the void suffer another catastrophic end, for the second generation of gods and goddesses would learn from the mistakes of their antecedents. The prophetess who recounts the story tells us that humanity thenceforth will "live in joy for as long as one can foresee."[1]

In this Norse cosmography, there seems to be more than the old theme of "eternal recurrence," of a time-sense that spins around perpetual cycles of birth, maturation, death, and rebirth. Rather, one is aware of prophecy infused with historical trauma; the legend belongs to a little-explored area of mythology

---

[1] Norse account and quotations drawn from P. Grappin, "German Lands: The Mortal Gods," in *Larousse World Mythology* (New York: Hamlyn Publishing Group, Ltd., 1965), pp. 363–83.

that might be called "myths of disintegration." Although the Ragnarok legend is known to be quite old, we know very little about when it appeared in the evolution of the Norse sagas. We do know that Christianity, with its bargain of eternal reward, came later to the Norsemen than to any other large ethnic group in western Europe, and its roots were shallow for generations afterward. The heathenism of the north had long made contact with the commerce of the south. During the Viking raids on Europe, the sacred places of the north had become polluted by gold, and the pursuit of riches was dividing kinsman from kinsman. Hierarchies erected by valor were being eroded by systems of privilege based on wealth. The clans and tribes were breaking down; the oaths between men, from which stemmed the unity of their primordial world, were being dishonored, and the magic fountain that kept the World Tree alive was being clogged by the debris of commerce. "Brothers fight and slay one another," laments the prophetess, "children deny their own ancestry . . . this is the age of wind, of wolf, until the very day when the world shall be no more."

What haunts us in such myths of disintegration are not their histories, but their prophecies. Like the Norsemen, and perhaps even more, like the people at the close of the Middle Ages, we sense that our world, too, is breaking down—institutionally, culturally, and physically. Whether we are faced with a new, paradisical era or a catastrophe like the Norse Ragnarok is still unclear, but there can be no lengthy period of compromise between past and future in an ambiguous present. The reconstructive and destructive tendencies in our time are too much at odds with each other to admit of reconciliation. The social horizon presents the starkly conflicting prospects of a harmonized world with an ecological sensibility based on a rich commitment to community, mutual aid, and new technologies, on the one hand, and the terrifying prospect of some sort of thermonuclear disaster on the other. Our world, it would appear, will either undergo revolutionary changes, so far-reaching in character that humanity will totally transform its social relations and its very conception of life, or it will suffer an apocalypse that may well end humanity's tenure on the planet.

The tension between these two prospects has already subverted the morale of the traditional social order. We have entered an era that consists no longer of institutional stabilization but of institutional decay. A widespread alienation is developing toward the forms, the aspirations, the demands, and above all, the institutions of the established order. The most exuberant, theatrical evidence of this alienation occurred in the 1960s, when the "youth revolt" in the early half of the decade exploded into what seemed to be a counterculture. Considerably more than protest and adolescent nihilism marked the period. Almost intuitively, new values of sensuousness, new forms of communal lifestyle, changes in dress, language, music, all borne on the wave of a deep sense of impending social change, infused a sizable section of an entire generation. We still do not know in what sense this wave began to ebb: whether as a historic retreat or as a transformation into a serious project for inner and social development. That the symbols of this movement eventually became the artifacts for a new culture industry does not alter its far-reaching effects. Western society will never be the same again—all the sneers of its academics and its critics of "narcissism" notwithstanding.

What makes this ceaseless movement of deinstitutionalization and delegitimation so significant is that it has found its bedrock in a vast stratum of western society. Alienation permeates not only the poor but also the relatively affluent, not only the young but also their elders, not only the visibly denied but also the seemingly privileged. The prevailing order is beginning to lose the loyalty of social strata that traditionally rallied to its support and in which its roots were firmly planted in past periods.

Crucial as this decay of institutions and values may be, it by no means exhausts the problems that confront the existing society. Intertwined with the social crisis is a crisis that has emerged directly from man's exploitation of the planet.* Established society is faced with a breakdown not only of its values and institutions, but also of its natural environment. This problem is not unique to our times. The desiccated wastelands of the Near East, where the arts of agriculture and urbanism had their beginnings, are evidence of ancient human despoilation, but this example pales before the massive destruction of the environment that has occurred since the days of the Industrial Revolution, and especially since the end of the Second World War. The damage inflicted on the environment by contemporary society' encompasses the entire earth. Volumes have been written on the immense losses of productive soil that occur annually on almost every continent of the earth; on the extensive destruction of tree cover in areas vulnerable to erosion; on lethal air-pollution episodes in major urban areas; on the worldwide diffusion of toxic agents from agriculture, industry, and power-producing installations; on the chemicalization of humanity's immediate environment with industrial wastes, pesticide residues, and food additives. The exploitation and pollution of the earth has damaged not only the integrity of the atmosphere, climate, water resources, soil, flora and fauna of specific regions, but also the basic natural cycles on which all living things depend.

Yet modern man's capacity for destruction is quixotic evidence of humanity's capacity for reconstruction. The powerful technological agents we have unleashed against the environment include many of the very agents we require for its reconstruction. The knowledge and physical instruments for promoting a harmonization of humanity with nature and of human with human are largely at hand or could easily be devised. Many of the physical principles used to construct such patently harmful facilities as conventional power plants, energy-consuming vehicles, surface-mining equipment and the like could be directed

---

*I use the word "man," here, advisedly. The split between humanity and nature has been precisely the work of the male, who, in the memorable lines of Theodor Adorno and Max Horkheimer, "dreamed of acquiring absolute mastery over nature, of converting the cosmos into one immense hunting-ground." (*Dialectic of Enlightenment,* New York: Seabury Press, 1972, p. 248). For the words "one immense hunting-ground," I would be disposed to substitute "one immense killing-ground" to describe the male-oriented "civilization" of our era.

to the construction of small-scale solar and wind energy devices, efficient means of transportation, and energy-saving shelters. What we crucially lack is the consciousness and sensibility that will help us achieve such eminently desirable goals—a consciousness and sensibility far broader than customarily meant by these terms. Our definitions must include not only the ability to reason logically and respond emotionally in a humanistic fashion; they must also include a fresh awareness of the relatedness between things and an imaginative insight into the possible. On this score, Marx was entirely correct to emphasize that the revolution required by our time must draw its poetry not from the past but from the future, from the humanistic potentialities that lie on the horizons of social life.

The new consciousness and sensibility cannot be poetic alone; they must also be scientific. Indeed, there is a level at which our consciousness must be neither poetry nor science, but a transcendence of both into a new realm of theory and practice, an artfulness that combines fancy with reason, imagination with logic, vision with technique. We cannot shed our scientific heritage without returning to a rudimentary technology, with its shackles of material insecurity, toil, and renunciation. And we cannot allow ourselves to be imprisoned within a mechanistic outlook and a dehumanizing technology—with its shackles of alienation, competition, and a brute denial of humanity's potentialities. Poetry and imagination must be integrated with science and technology, for we have evolved beyond an innocence that can be nourished exclusively by myths and dreams.

Is there a scientific discipline that allows for the indiscipline of fancy, imagination, and artfulness? Can it encompass problems created by the social and environmental crises of our time? Can it integrate critique with reconstruction, theory with practice, vision with technique?

In almost every period since the Renaissance, a very close link has existed between radical advances in the natural sciences and upheavals in social thought. In the sixteenth and seventeenth centuries, the emerging sciences of astronomy and mechanics, with their liberating visions of a heliocentric world and the unity of local and cosmic motion, found their social counterparts in equally critical and rational social ideologies that challenged religious bigotry and political absolutism. The Enlightenment brought a new appreciation of sensory perception and the claims of human reason to divine a world that had been the ideological monopoly of the clergy. Later, anthropology and evolutionary biology demolished traditional static notions of the human enterprise along with its myths of original creation and history as a theological calling. By enlarging the map and revealing the earthly dynamics of social history, these sciences reinforced the new doctrines of socialism, with its ideal of human progress, that followed the French Revolution.

In view of the enormous dislocations that now confront us, our own era needs a more sweeping and insightful body of knowledge — scientific as well as social — to deal with our problems. Without renouncing the gains of earlier scientific and social theories, we must develop a more rounded critical analysis of our relationship with the natural world. We must seek the foundations for a more reconstructive approach to the grave problems posed by the apparent "contradictions" between nature and society. We can no longer afford to remain captives to the tendency of the more traditional sciences to dissect phenomena and examine their fragments. We must combine them, relate them, and see them in their totality as well as their specificity.

In response to these needs, we have formulated a discipline unique to our age: *social ecology*. The more well-known term "ecology" was coined by Ernst Haeckel a century ago to denote the investigation of the interrelationships between animals, plants, and their inorganic environment. Since Haeckel's day, the term has been expanded to include ecologies of cities, of health, and of the mind. This proliferation of a word into widely disparate areas may seem particularly desirable to an age that fervently seeks some kind of intellectual coherence and unity of perception. But it can also prove to be extremely treacherous. Like such newly arrived words as holism, decentralization, and dialectics, the term ecology runs the peril of merely hanging in the air without any roots, context, or texture. Often it is used as a metaphor, an alluring catchword, that loses the potentially compelling internal logic of its premises.

Accordingly, the radical thrust of these words is easily neutralized. "Holism" evaporates into a mystical sigh, a rhetorical expression for ecological fellowship and community that ends with such in-group greetings and salutations as "holistically yours." What was once a serious philosophical stance has been reduced to environmentalist kitsch. Decentralization commonly means logistical alternatives to gigantism, not the human scale that would make an intimate and direct democracy possible. Ecology fares even worse. All too often it becomes a metaphor, like the word dialectics, for any kind of integration and development.

Perhaps even more troubling, the word in recent years has been identified with a very crude form of natural engineering that might well be called *environmentalism.*

I am mindful that many ecologically oriented individuals use "ecology" and "environmentalism" interchangeably. Here, I would like to draw a semantically convenient distinction. By "environmentalism" I propose to designate a mechanistic, instrumental outlook that sees nature as a passive habitat composed of "objects" such as animals, plants, minerals, and the like that must merely be rendered more serviceable for human use. Given my use of the term, environmentalism tends to reduce nature to a storage bin of "natural resources" or "raw materials." Within this context, very little of a social nature is spared from the environmentalist's vocabulary: cities become "urban resources" and their inhabitants "human resources." If the word *resources* leaps out so frequently from environmentalistic discussions of nature, cities, and people, an issue more important than mere word play is at stake. Environmentalism, as I use this term, tends to view the ecological project for attaining a harmonious relationship between humanity and nature as a truce rather than a lasting equilibrium. The "harmony" of the environmentalist centers around the development of new techniques for plundering the natural world with minimal disruption of the human "habitat." Environmentalism does not question the most basic premise of the present society, notably, that humanity must dominate nature; rather, it seeks to *facilitate* that notion by developing techniques for diminishing the hazards caused by the reckless despoliation of the environment.

To distinguish ecology from environmentalism and from abstract, often obfuscatory definitions of the term, I must return to its original usage and explore its direct relevance to society. Put quite simply, ecology deals with the dynamic balance of nature, with the interdependence of living and nonliving things. Since nature also includes human beings, the science must include humanity's role in the natural world—specifically, the character, form, and structure of humanity's relationship with other species and with the inorganic substrate of the biotic environment. From a critical viewpoint, ecology opens to wide purview the vast disequilibrium that has emerged from humanity's split with the natural world. One of nature's very unique species, *homo sapiens,* has slowly and painstakingly developed from the natural world into a unique social world of its own. As both worlds interact with each other through highly complex phases of evolution, it has become as important to speak of a social ecology as to speak of a natural ecology.

Let me emphasize that the failure to explore these phases of human evolution—which have yielded a succession of hierarchies, classes, cities, and finally states—is to make a mockery of the term social ecology. Unfortunately, the discipline has been beleaguered by self-professed adherents who continually try to collapse all the phases of natural and human development into a universal "oneness" (not wholeness), a yawning [2] "night in which all cows are black," to borrow one of Hegel's caustic phrases. If nothing else, our common use of the word *species* to denote the wealth of life around us should alert us to the fact of *specificity,* of *particularity*—the rich abundance of *differentiated* beings and things that enter into the very subject-matter of natural ecology. To explore these differentia, to examine the phases and interfaces that enter into their making and into humanity's long development from animality to society—a development latent with problems and possibilities—is to make social ecology one of the most powerful disciplines from which to draw our critique of the present social order.

---

[2] G. W. F. Hegel, *Phenomenology of Mind* (New York: Humanities Press, 1931 edition), p. 79.

But social ecology provides more than a critique of the split between humanity and nature; it also poses the need to heal them. Indeed, it poses the need to radically transcend them. As E. A. Gutkind pointed out, "the goal of Social Ecology is wholeness, and not mere adding together of innumerable details collected at random and interpreted subjectively and insufficiently."[3] The science deals with social and natural relationships in communities or "ecosystems."* In conceiving them holistically, that is to say, in terms of their mutual interdependence, social ecology seeks to unravel the forms and patterns of interrelationships that give intelligibility to a community, be it natural or social. Holism, here, is the result of a conscious effort to discern how the particulars of a community are arranged, how its "geometry" (as the Greeks might have put it) makes the "whole more than the sum of its parts." Hence, the "wholeness" to which Gutkind refers is not to be mistaken for a spectral "oneness" that yields cosmic dissolution in a structureless nirvana; it is a richly articulated structure with a history and internal logic of its own.

History, in fact, is as important as form or structure. To a large extent, the history of a phenomenon is the phenomenon itself. We are, in a real sense, everything that existed before us and, in turn, we can eventually become vastly more than we are. Surprisingly, very little in the evolution of life-forms has been lost in natural and social evolution, indeed in our very bodies as our embryonic development attests. Evolution lies within us (as well as around us) as parts of the very nature of our beings.

For the present, it suffices to say that wholeness is not a bleak undifferentiated "universality" that involves the reduction of a phenomenon to what it has in common with everything else. Nor is it a celestial, omnipresent "energy" that replaces the vast material differentia of which the natural and social realms are composed. To the contrary, wholeness comprises the variegated structures, the articulations, and the mediations that impart to the whole a rich variety of forms and thereby add unique qualitative properties to what a strictly analytic mind often reduces to "innumerable" and "random" details.

Terms like wholeness, totality, and even community have perilous nuances for a generation that has known fascism and other totalitarian ideologies. The words evoke images of a "wholeness" achieved through homogenization, standardization, and a repressive coordination of human beings. These fears are reinforced by a "wholeness" that seems to provide an inexorable finality to the course of human history—one that implies a suprahuman, narrowly teleological concept of social law and denies the ability of human will and individual choice to shape the course of social events. Such notions of social law and teleology have been used to achieve a ruthless subjugation of the individual to

---

[3] E. A. Gutkind, *Community and Environment* (New York: Philosophical Library, 1954), p. 9.

*The term ecosystem—or ecological system—is often used loosely in many ecological works. Here, I employ it, as in natural ecology, to mean a fairly demarcatable animal-plant community and the abiotic, or nonliving, factors needed to sustain it. I also use it in social ecology to mean a distinct human and natural community, the social as well as organic factors that interrelate to provide the basis for an ecologically rounded and balanced community.

suprahuman forces beyond human control. Our century has been afflicted by a plethora of totalitarian ideologies that, placing human beings in the service of history, have denied them a place in the service of their own humanity.

Actually, such a totalitarian concept of "wholeness" stands sharply at odds with what ecologists denote by the term. In addition to comprehending its heightened awareness of form and structure, we now come to a very important tenet of ecology: ecological wholeness is not an immutable homogeneity but rather the very opposite—a dynamic *unity of diversity*. In nature, balance and harmony are achieved by ever-changing differentiation, by ever-expanding diversity. Ecological stability, in effect, is a function not of simplicity and homogeneity but of complexity and variety. The capacity of an ecosystem to retain its integrity depends not on the uniformity of the environment but on its diversity.

A striking example of this tenet can be drawn from experiences with ecological strategies for cultivating food. Farmers have repeatedly met with disastrous results because of the conventional emphasis on single-crop approaches to agriculture or *monoculture,* to use a widely accepted term for those endless wheat and corn fields that extend to the horizon in many parts of the world. Without the mixed crops that normally provide both the countervailing forces and mutualistic support that come with mixed populations of plants and animals, the entire agricultural situation in an area has been known to collapse. Benign insects become pests because their natural controls, including birds and small mammals, have been removed. The soil, lacking earthworms, nitrogen-fixing bacteria, and green manure in sufficient quantities, is reduced to mere sand—a mineral medium for absorbing enormous quantities of inorganic nitrogen salts, which were originally supplied more cyclically and timed more appropriately for crop growth in the ecosystem. In reckless disregard for the complexity of nature and for the subtle requirements of plant and animal life, the agricultural situation is crudely simplified; its needs must now be satisfied by highly soluble synthetic fertilizers that percolate into drinking water and by dangerous pesticides that remain as residues in food. A high standard of food cultivation that was once achieved by diversity of crops and animals, one that was free of lasting toxic agents and probably more healthful nutritionally, is now barely approximated by single crops whose main supports are toxic chemicals and highly simple nutrients.

If we assume that the thrust of natural evolution has been toward increasing complexity, that the colonization of the planet by life has been possible only as a result of biotic variety, a prudent rescaling of man's hubris should call for caution in disturbing natural processes. That living things, emerging ages ago from their primal aquatic habitat to colonize the most inhospitable areas of the earth, have created the rich biosphere that now covers it has been possible only because of life's incredible mutability and the enormous legacy of life-forms inherited from its long development. Many of these life-forms, even the most primal and simplest, have never disappeared—however much they have been modified by evolution. The simple algal forms that marked the beginnings of plant life and the simple invertebrates that marked the beginnings of animal life still exist in large numbers. They comprise the preconditions for the existence of more complex organic beings to which they provide sustenance, the sources of decomposition, and even atmospheric oxygen and carbon dioxide. Although they may antedate the "higher" plants and mammals by over a billion years, they interrelate with their more complex descendants in often unravelable ecosystems.

To assume that science commands this vast nexus of organic and inorganic interrelationships in all its details is worse than arrogance: it is sheer stupidity. If unity in diversity forms one of the cardinal tenets of ecology, the wealth of biota that exists in a single acre of soil leads us to still another basic ecological tenet: the need to allow for a high degree of natural spontaneity. The compelling dictum, "respect for nature," has concrete implications. To assume that our knowledge of this complex, richly textured, and perpetually changing natural kaleidoscope of life-forms lends itself to a degree of "mastery" that allows us free rein in manipulating the biosphere is sheer foolishness.

Thus, a considerable amount of leeway must be permitted for natural spontaneity—for the diverse biological forces that yield a variegated ecological situation. "Working with nature" requires that we foster the biotic variety that emerges from a spontaneous development of natural phenomena. I hardly mean that we must surrender ourselves to a mythical "Nature" that is beyond all human comprehension and intervention, a Nature that demands human awe and subservience. Perhaps the most obvious conclusion we can draw from these ecological tenets is Charles Elton's sensitive observation: "The world's future has to be managed, but this management would not be just like a game of chess— [but] more like steering a boat."[4] What ecology, both natural and social, can hope to teach us is the way to find the current and understand the direction of the stream.

What ultimately distinguishes an ecological outlook as uniquely liberatory is the challenge it raises to conventional notions of hierarchy. Let me emphasize, however, that this challenge is implicit: it must be painstakingly elicited from the discipline of ecology, which is permeated by conventional scientistic biases. Ecologists are rarely aware that their science provides strong philosophical underpinnings for a nonhierarchical view of reality, like many natural scientists, they resist philosophical generalizations as alien to their research and conclusions—a prejudice that is itself a philosophy rooted in the Anglo-American empirical tradition. Moreover, they follow their colleagues in other disciplines and model their notions of science on physics. This prejudice, which goes back to Galileo's day, has led to a widespread acceptance of

---

[4] Charles Elton, *The Ecology of Invasions by Plants and Animals* (New York: John W. Wiley, 1953), p. 101.

systems theory in ecological circles. While systems theory has its place in the repertoire of science, it can easily become an all-encompassing, quantitative, reductionist theory of energetics if it acquires preeminence over *qualitative* descriptions of ecosystems, that is, descriptions rooted in organic evolution, variety, and holism. Whatever the merits of systems theory as an account of energy flow through an ecosystem, the primacy it gives to this quantitative aspect of ecosystem analysis fails to recognize life-forms as more man consumers and producers of calories.

Having presented these caveats, I must emphasize that ecosystems cannot be meaningfully described in hierarchical terms. Whether plant-animal communities actually contain "dominant" and "submissive" individuals *within* a species can be argued at great length. But to rank species within an ecosystem, that is to say, *between* species, is anthropomorphism at its crudest. As Allison Jolly has observed:

> The notion of animal hierarchies has a checkered history. Schjelderup-Ebbe, who discovered the pecking-order of hens, enlarged his findings to a Teutonic theory of despotism in the universe. For instance, water eroding a stone was "dominant" . . . Schjelderup-Ebbe called animals' ranking "dominance," and many [research] workers, with an "aha," recognized dominance hierarchies in many vertebrate groups.[5]

If we recognize that every ecosystem can also be viewed as a food web, we can think of it as a circular, interlacing nexus of plant-animal relationships (rather than a stratified pyramid with man at the apex) that includes such widely varying creatures as microorganisms and large mammals. What ordinarily puzzles anyone who sees food web diagrams for the first time is the impossibility of discerning a point of entry into the nexus. The web can be entered at any point and leads back to its point of departure without any apparent exit. Aside from the energy provided by sunlight (and dissipated by radiation), the system to all appearances is closed. Each species, be it a form of bacteria or deer, is knitted together in a network of interdependence, however indirect the links may be. A predator in the web is also prey, even if the "lowliest" of organisms merely makes it ill or helps to consume it after death.

Nor is predation the sole link that unites one species with another. A resplendent literature now exists that reveals the enormous extent to which symbiotic mutualism is a major factor in fostering ecological stability and organic evolution. That plants and animals continually adapt to unwittingly aid each other (be it by an exchange of biochemical functions that are mutually beneficial or even dramatic instances of physical assistance and succor) has opened an entirely new perspective on the nature of ecosystem stability and development.

[5] Allison Jolly, *The Evolution of Primate Behavior* (New York: MacMillan Co., 1992), p. 172.

The more complex the food-web, the less unstable it will be if one or several species are removed. Hence, enormous significance must be given to interspecific diversity and complexity within the system as a whole. Striking breakdowns will occur in simple ecosystems, such as arctic and desert ones, say, if wolves that control foraging animal populations are exterminated or if a sizable number of reptiles that control rodent populations in arid ecosystems are removed. By contrast, the great variety of biota that populate temperate and tropical ecosystems can afford losses of carnivores or herbivores without suffering major dislocations.

Why do terms borrowed from human social hierarchies acquire such remarkable weight when plant-animal relations are described? Do ecosystems really have a "king of the beasts" and "lowly serfs"? Do certain insects "enslave" others? Does one species "exploit" another?

The promiscuous use of these terms in ecology raises many farreaching issues. That the terms are laden with socially charged values is almost too obvious to warrant extensive discussion. Many individuals exhibit a pathetic gullibility in the way they deal with nature as a dimension of society. A snarling animal is neither "vicious" nor "savage," nor does it "misbehave" or "earn" punishment because it reacts appropriately to certain stimuli. By making such anthropomorphic judgements about natural phenomena, we deny the integrity of nature. Even more sinister is the widespread use of hierarchical terms to provide natural phenomena with "intelligibility" or "order." What this procedure does accomplish is reinforce human social hierarchies by justifying the command of men and women as innate features of the "natural order." Human domination is thereby transcribed into the genetic code as biologically immutable — together with the subordination of the young by the old, women by men, and man by man.

The very promiscuity with which hierarchical terms are used to organize all differentia in nature is inconsistent. A "queen" bee does not know she is a queen. The primary activity of a beehive is reproductive, and its "division of labor," to use a grossly abused phrase, lacks any meaning in a large sexual organ that performs no authentic economic functions. The purpose of the hive is to create more bees. The honey that animals and people acquire from it is a natural largesse; within the ecosystem, bees are adapted more to meeting plant reproductive needs by spreading pollen than to meeting important animal needs. The analogy between a beehive and a society, an analogy social theorists have often found too irresistible to avoid, is a striking commentary on the extent to which our visions of nature are shaped by self-serving social interests.

To deal with so-called insect hierarchies the way we deal with so-called animal hierarchies, or worse, to grossly ignore the very different functions animal communities perform, is analogic reasoning carried to the point or the preposterous. Primates relate to each other in ways that seem to involve "dominance" and "submission" for widely disparate reasons. Yet, terminologically and conceptually, they are placed under the same "hierarchical" rubric as insect "societies"— despite the different forms they assume and their precarious stability. Baboons on the African savannas have been singled out as the most rigid hierarchical troops in the primate world, but this rigidity evaporates once we examine their "ranking order" in a forest habitat. Even on the savannas, it is questionable whether "alpha" males "rule," "control," or "coordinate" relationships within the troop. Arguments can be presented for choosing any one of these words, each of which has a clearly different meaning when it is used in a human social context. Seemingly "patriarchal" primate "harems" can be as loose sexually as brothels, depending on whether a female is in estrus, changes have occurred in the habitat, or the "patriarch" is simply diffident about the whole situation.

Baboons, it is worth noting, are monkeys, despite the presumed similarity of their savanna habitat to that of early hominids. They branched off from the hominoid evolutionary tree more than 20 million years ago. Our closest evolutionary cousins, the great apes, tend to demolish these prejudices about hierarchy completely. Of the four great apes, gibbons have no apparent "ranking" system at all. Chimpanzees, regarded by many primatologists as the most human-like of all apes, form such fluid kinds of "stratification" and (depending upon the ecology of an area, which may be significantly affected by research workers) establish such unstable types of association that the word hierarchy becomes an obstacle to understanding their behavioral characteristics. Orangutans seem to have little of what could be called dominance and submission relations. The mountain gorilla, despite its formidable reputation, exhibits very little "stratification" except for predator challenges and internal aggression.

All these examples help to justify Elise Boulding's complaint that the "primate behavior model" favored by overly hierarchical and patriarchal writers on animal-human parallels "is based more on the baboon, not the gibbon." In contrast to the baboon, observes Boulding, the gibbon is closer to us physically and, one might add, on the primate evolutionary scale. "Our choice of a primate role model is clearly culturally determined," she concludes:

> Who wants to be like the unaggressive, vegetarian, food-sharing gibbons, where father is as much involved in child-rearing as mother is, and where everyone lives in small family groups, with little aggregation beyond that?' Much better to match the baboons, who live in large, tightly-knit groups carefully closed against outsider baboons, where everyone knows who is in charge, and where mother looks after the babies while father is out hunting and fishing.[6]

---

[6] Elise Boulding, *The Underside of History* (Boulder, Colorado: Westview Press, 1976), p. 39.

In fact, Boulding concedes too much about the savanna-dwelling primates. Even if the term dominance were stretched to include "queen" bees and "alpha" baboons, *specific* acts of coercion by *individual* animals can hardly be called domination. Acts do not constitute institutions; episodes do not make a history. And highly structured insect behavioral patterns, rooted in instinctual drives, are too inflexible to be regarded as social. Unless hierarchy is to be used in Schjelderup-Ebbe's cosmic sense, dominance and submission must be viewed as *institutionalized* relationships, relationships that living things literally institute or create but which are neither ruthlessly fixed by instinct on the one hand nor idiosyncratic on the other. By this, I mean that they must comprise a clearly *social* structure of coercive and privileged ranks that exist apart from the idiosyncratic individuals who seem to be dominant within a given community, a hierarchy that is guided by a social logic that goes beyond individual interactions or inborn patterns of behavior.[*]

Such traits are evident enough in human society when we speak of "self-perpetuating" bureaucracies and explore them without considering the individual bureaucrats who compose them. Yet, when we turn to nonhuman primates, what people commonly recognize as hierarchy, status, and domination are precisely the idiosyncratic behaviorisms of individual animals. Mike, Jane van Lawick-Goodall's "alpha" chimpanzee, acquired his "status" by rambunctiously charging upon a group of males while noisily hitting two empty kerosene cans. At which point in her narrative, van Lawick-Goodall wonders, would Mike have become an "alpha" male without the kerosene cans? She replies that the animal's use of "manmade objects is probably an indication of superior intelligence."[7] Whether such shadowy distinctions in intelligence rather than aggressiveness, willfulness, or arrogance produce an "alpha" male or not is evidence more of the subtle projection of historically conditioned human values on a primate group than the scientific objectivity that ethology likes to claim for itself.

The seemingly hierarchical traits of many animals are more like variations in the links of a chain than organized stratifications of the kind we find in human societies and institutions. Even the so-called class societies of the

---

[*]An important distinction must be made here between the words *community* and *society*. Animals and even plants certainly form communities; ecosystems would be meaningless without conceiving animals, plants, and their abiotic substrate as a nexus of relationships that range from the intraspecific to the interspecific level. In their interactions, life-forms thus behave "communally" in the sense that they are interdependent in one way or another. Among certain species, particularly primates, this nexus of interdependent relationships may be so closely knit that it approximates a society or, at least, a rudimentary form of sociality. But a society, however deeply it may be rooted in nature, is nevertheless *more* than a community. What makes human societies unique communities is the fact that they are *institutionalized* communities that are highly, often rigidly, structured around clearly manifest forms of responsibility, association and personal relationship in maintaining the material means of life. Although all societies are necessarily communities, many communities are not societies. One may find nascent social elements in animal communities, but only human beings form societies—that is, institutionalized communities. The failure to draw this distinction between animal or plant communities and human societies has produced considerable ideological mischief. Thus, predation within animal communities has been speciously identified with war; individual linkages between animals with hierarchy and domination; even animal foraging and metabolism with labor and economics. All the latter are strictly *social* phenomena. My remarks are not intended to oppose the notion of society to community but to take note of the distinctions between the two that emerge when human society develops beyond the levels of animal and plant communities.

[7] Jane van Lawick-Goodall, *In the Shadow of Man* (New York: Delta Publishing Co., 1971), p. 123.

Northwest Indians, as we shall see, are chain-like links between individuals rather than the class-like links between strata that early Euro-American invaders so naively projected on Indians from their own social world. If acts do not constitute institutions and episodes do not constitute history, individual behavioral traits do not form strata or classes. Social strata are made of sterner stuff. They have a life of their own apart from the personalities who give them substance.

How is ecology to avoid the analogic reasoning that has made so much of ethology and sociobiology seem like specious projections of human society into nature? Are there any terms that provide a common meaning to unity in diversity, natural spontaneity; and nonhierarchical relations in nature *and* society? In view of the many tenets that appear in natural ecology, why stop with these alone? Why not introduce other, perhaps less savory, ecological notions like predation and aggression into society?

In fact, nearly all of these questions became major issues in social theory in the early part of the century when the so-called Chicago School of urban sociology zealously tried to apply almost every known concept of natural ecology to the development and "physiology" of the city. Robert Park, Ernest Burgess, and Roderick McKenzie, enamored of the new science, actually imposed a stringently biological model on their studies of Chicago with a forcefulness and inspiration that dominated American urban sociology for two generations. Their tenets included ecological succession, spatial distribution, zonal distribution, anaboliccatabolic balances, and even competition and natural selection that could easily have pushed the school toward an insidious form of social Darwinism had it not been for the liberal biases of its founders.

Despite its admirable empirical results, the school was to founder on its metaphoric reductionism. Applied indiscriminately, the categories ceased to be meaningful. When Park compared the emergence of certain specialized municipal utilities to "successional dominance" by "other plant species" that climaxes in a "beech or pine forest," the analogy was patently forced and absurdly contorted. His comparison of ethnic, cultural, occupational, and economic groups to "plant invasions" revealed a lack of theoretical discrimination that reduced human social features to plant ecological features.[8] What Park and his associates lacked was the philosophical equipment for singling out the phases that both unite and separate natural and social phenomena in a developmental continuum. Thus, merely superficial similarity became outright identity—with the unfortunate result that social ecology was repeatedly reduced to natural ecology. The richly mediated evolution of the natural into the social that could have been used to yield a meaningful selection of ecological categories was not part of the school's theoretical equipment.

---

[8] See Robert E. Park, *Human Communities* (Glencoe, Illinois: The Free Press, 1952) for the classical statement of the Chicago School's viewpoint.

Whenever we ignore the way human social relationships transcend plant-animal relationships, our views tend to bifurcate in two erroneous directions. Either we succumb to a heavy-handed dualism that harshly separates the natural from the social, or we fall into a crude reductionism that dissolves the one into the other. In either case, we really cease to think out the issues involved. We merely grasp for the least uncomfortable "solution" to a highly complex problem, namely, the need to analyze the phases through which "mute" biological nature increasingly becomes conscious human nature.

What makes unity in diversity in nature more than a suggestive ecological metaphor for unity in diversity in society is the underlying philosophical concept of wholeness. By wholeness, I mean varying levels of actualization, an unfolding of the wealth of particularities, that are latent in an as-yet-undeveloped potentiality. This potentiality may be a newly planted seed, a newly born infant, a newly born community, or a newly born society. When Hegel describes in a famous passage the "unfolding" of human knowledge in biological terms, the fit is almost exact:

> The bud disappears in the bursting-forth of the blossom, and one might say that the former is refuted by the latter, similarly, when the fruit appears, the blossom is shown up in its turn as a false manifestation of the plant, and the fruit now emerges as the truth of it instead. These forms are not just distinguished from one another, they also supplant one another as mutually incompatible. Yet at the same time their fluid nature makes them moments of an organic unity—in which they not only do not conflict, but in which each is as necessary as the other, and this mutual necessity—alone constitutes the life of the whole.[9]

I have turned to this remarkable passage because Hegel does not mean it to be merely metaphoric. His biological example and his social subject matter converge in ways that transcend both, notably, as similar aspects of a *larger* process. Life itself, as distinguished from the nonliving, emerges from the inorganic latent with all the particularities it has immanently produced from the logic of its most nascent forms of self-organization. So do society as distinguished from biology, humanity as distinguished from animality, and individuality as distinguished from humanity. It is no spiteful manipulation of Hegel's famous maxim, "The True is the whole," to declare that the "whole is the True."[10] One can take this reversal of terms to mean that the true lies in the self-consummation of a *process* through its development, in the flowering of its latent particularities into their fullness or wholeness, just as the potentialities of a child achieve expression in the wealth of experiences and the physical growth that enter into adulthood.

---

[9] Hegel, *The Phenomenology of the Mind*, p. 81.

[10] *Ibid.*, p. 68. The translation by Baille inaccurately renders this famous Hegelian maxim as "The truth is the whole."

We must not get caught up in direct comparisons between plants, animals, and human beings or between plant-animal ecosystems and human communities. None of these is completely congruent with another. We would be regressing in our views to those of Park, Burgess, and McKenzie, not to mention our current bouquet of sociobiologists, were we lax enough to make this equation. It is not in the particulars of differentiation that plant-animal communities are ecologically united with human communities but rather in their *logic of differentiation.* Wholeness, in fact, is completeness. The dynamic stability of the whole derives from a visible level of completeness in human communities as in climax ecosystems. What unites these modes of wholeness and completeness, however different they are in their specificity and their qualitative distinctness, is the logic of development itself. A climax forest is whole and complete as a result of the same unifying process—the same *dialectic*—that a particular social form is whole and complete.

When wholeness and completeness are viewed as the result of an immanent dialectic within phenomena, we do no more violence to the uniqueness of these phenomena than the principle of gravity does violence to the uniqueness of objects that fall within its "lawfulness." In this sense, the ideal of human roundedness, a product of the rounded community, is the legitimate heir to the ideal of a stabilized nature, a product of the rounded natural environment. Marx tried to root humanity's identity and self-discovery in its productive interaction with nature. But I must add that not only does humanity place its imprint on the natural world and transform it, but also nature places its imprint on the human world and transforms it. To use the language of hierarchy against itself: it is not only we who "tame" nature but also nature that "tames" us.

These turns of phrase should be taken as more than metaphors. Lest it seem that I have rarefied the concept of wholeness into an abstract dialectical principle, let me note that natural ecosystems and human communities interact with each other in very existential ways. Our animal nature is never so distant from our social nature that we can remove ourselves from the organic world outside us and the one within us. From our embryonic development to our layered brain, we partly recapitulate our own natural evolution. We are not so remote from our primate ancestry that we can ignore its physical legacy in our stereoscopic vision, acuity of intelligence, and grasping fingers. We phase into society as individuals in the same way that society, phasing out of nature, comes into itself.

These continuities, to be sure, are obvious enough. What is often less obvious is the extent to which nature itself is a realm of potentiality for the emergence of *social* differentia. Nature is as much a precondition for the *development* of society—not merely its emergence—as technics, labor, language, and mind. And it is a precondition not merely in William Petty's sense—that if labor is the "Father" of wealth, nature is its "Mother." This formula, so dear to Marx, actually slights nature by imparting to it the patriarchal notion of feminine "passivity."[11] The affinities between nature and society are more active than we care to admit. Very specific forms of nature—very specific *ecosystems*—constitute the ground for very specific forms of society. At the risk of using a highly embattled phrase, I might say that a "historical materialism" of natural development could be written that would transform "passive nature"—the "object" of human labor—into "active nature," the creator of human labor. Labor's "metabolism" with nature cuts both ways, so that nature interacts *with* humanity to yield the actualization of their common potentialities in the natural and social worlds.

An interaction of this kind, in which terms like "Father" and "Mother" strike a false note, can be stated very concretely. The recent emphasis on bioregions as frameworks for various human communities provides a strong case for the need to readapt technics and work styles to accord with the requirements and possibilities of particular ecological areas. Bioregional requirements and possibilities place a heavy burden on humanity's claims of sovereignty over nature and autonomy from its needs. If it is true that "men make history" but not under conditions of their own choosing (Marx), it is no less true that history makes society but not under conditions of its own choosing. The hidden dimension that lurks in this word play with Marx's famous formula is the natural history that enters into the making of social history—but as active, concrete, existential nature that emerges from stage to stage of its own evermore complex development in the form of equally complex and dynamic ecosystems. Our ecosystems, in turn, are interlinked in highly dynamic and complex bioregions. How concrete the hidden dimension of social development is—and how much humanity's claims to sovereignty must defer to it—has only recently become evident from our need to design an alternative technology that is as adaptive to a bioregion as it is productive to society. Hence, our concept of wholeness is not a finished tapestry of natural and social relations that we can exhibit to the hungry eyes of sociologists. It is a fecund natural history, ever active and ever changing—the way childhood presses toward and is absorbed into youth, and youth into adulthood.

The need to bring a sense of history into nature is as compelling as the need to bring a sense of history into society. An ecosystem is never a random community of plants and animals that occurs merely by chance. It has potentiality, direction, meaning, and self-realization in its own right. To view an ecosystem as given (a bad habit, which scientism inculcates in its theoretically neutral observer) is as ahistorical and superficial as to view a human community as given. Both have a history that gives intelligibility and order to their internal relationships and directions to their development.

At its inception, human history is largely natural history as well as social—as traditional kinship structures and the sexual division of labor clearly indicate. Whether or not natural history is the "slime," to use Sartre's maladroit

---

[11] Marx's observation on "man" and the conditions for historical change appears in "The Eighteenth Brumaire of Louis Napoleon," in *Selected Works*, Vol. 1 (Moscow: Progress Publishers, 1969), p. 398.

term, that clings to humanity and prevents its rational fulfillment will be considered later. For the present, one fact should be made clear: human history can never disengage itself or disembed itself from nature. It will always be embedded in nature, as we shall see— whether we are inclined to call that nature a "slime" or a fecund "mother." What may prove to be the most demanding test of our human genius is the *kind* of nature we will foster—one that is richly organic and complex or one that is inorganic and disastrously simplified.

Humanity's involvement with nature not only runs deep but takes on forms more increasingly subtle than even the most sophisticated theorists could have anticipated. Our knowledge of this involvement is still, as it were, in its "prehistory." To Ernst Bloch, we not only share a common history with nature, all the differences between nature and society aside, but also a common destiny. As he observes:

> *Nature in its final manifestation, like history in its final manifestation, lies at the horizon of the future. The more a common technique* [Allianztecbnik] *is attainable instead of one that is external—one that is mediated with the co-productivity* [Mitproduktivitat] *of nature—the more we can be sure that the frozen powers of a frozen nature will again be emancipated. Nature is not something that can be consigned to the past. Rather it is the construction-site that has not yet been cleared, the building tools that have not yet been attained in an adequate form for the human house that itself does not yet exist in an adequate form. The ability of problem-laden natural subjectivity to participate in the construction of this house is the objective-utopian correlate of the human-utopian fantasy conceived in concrete terms. Therefore it is certain that the human house stands not only in history and on the ground of human activity; it stands primarily on the ground of a mediated natural subjectivity on the construction site of nature. Nature's conceptual frontier* [Grenzbegriff] *is not the beginning of human history, where nature (which is always present in history and always surrounds it) turns into the site of the human sovereign realm* [regnum bominis], *but rather where it turns into the adequate site [for the adequate human house] as an unalienated mediated good* [und sie unentfremdet aufgebt, als vermitteltes Gut].[12]

One can take issue with the emphasis Bloch gives to human sovereignty in the interaction with nature and the structural phraseology that infiltrates his brilliant grasp of the organic nature of that interaction. *Das Prinzip Hoffnung (The Principle of Hope)* was written in the early 1940s, a grim and embattled period, when such a conceptual framework was totally alien to the antinaturalistic, indeed, militaristic spirit of the times. His insight beggars our hindsight, redolent with its "pop" ecological terminology and its queasy mysticism. In any

---

[12] Ernst Bloch, *Das Prinzip Hoffnung,* Band II (Frankfurt am Main: Suhrkamp Verlag, 1967), pp. 806–7.

case, enough has been written about the differences between nature and society. Today, together with Bloch, it would be valuable to shift our emphasis to the commonalities of nature and society, provided we are wary enough to avoid those mindless leaps from the one to the other as though they were not related by the rich phases of development that authentically unite them.

Spontaneity enters into social ecology in much the same way as it enters into natural ecology—as a function of diversity and complexity, Ecosystems are much too variegated to be delivered over completely to what Ernst Bloch called the *regnum bominis* or, at least, to humanity's claim of sovereignty over nature. But we may justly ask if this is any less true of social complexity and history's claims of sovereignty over humanity. Do the self-appointed scientists or "guardians" of society know enough (their normally self-serving views aside) about the complex factors that make for social development to presume to control them? And even after the "adequate form for the human house" has been discovered and given substantiality, how sure can we be of their disinterested sense of service? History is replete with accounts of miscalculation by leaders, parties, factions, "guardians," and "vanguards." If nature is "blind," society is equally "blind" when it presumes to know itself completely, whether as social science, social theory, systems analysis, or even social ecology. Indeed, "World Spirits" from Alexander to Lenin have not always served humanity well. They have exhibited a willful arrogance that has damaged the social environment as disastrously as the arrogance of ordinary men has damaged the natural environment.

Great historical eras of transition reveal that the rising flood of social change must be permitted to find its own level spontaneously. Vanguard organizations have produced repeated catastrophes when they sought to force changes that people and the conditions of their time could not sustain materially, ideologically, or morally. Where forced social changes were not nourished by an educated and informed popular consciousness, they were eventually enforced by terror—and the movements themselves have turned savagely upon and devoured their most cherished humanistic and liberatory ideals. Our own century is closing under the shadow of an event that has totally beclouded the future of humanity, notably the Russian Revolution and its terrifying sequelae. Where the revolution, unforced and easily achieved by the popular movement, ended and Lenin's *coup d'etat* of October, 1917, replaced it can be easily fixed and dated. But how the will of a small cadre, abetted by the demoralization and stupidity of its opponents, turned success into failure in the very name of "success" is more difficult to explain. That the movement would have come to rest had it been left to its own spontaneous popular momentum and self-determination—possibly with gains that might have reinforced more advanced social developments abroad—is perhaps the safest judgment we can make with the hindsight time has given us. Social change, particularly social revolution, tends to find its worst enemies in leaders whose wills supplant the spontaneous movements of the people. Hubris in social evolution is as dangerous as it is in natural evolution and for the same reasons. In both cases, the complexity of a situation, the limitations of time and place, and the prejudices that filter into what often merely *appear* as foresight conceal the multitude of particulars that are truer to reality than any ideological preconceptions and needs.

I do not mean to deny the superadded significance of will, insight, and knowledge that must inform human spontaneity in the social world. In nature, by contrast, spontaneity operates within a more restrictive set of conditions. A natural ecosystem finds its climax in the greatest degree of stability it can attain within its given level of possibilities. We know, of course, that this is not a passive process. But beyond the level and stability an ecosystem can achieve and the apparent striving it exhibits, it reveals no motivation and choice. Its stability, given its potentialities and what Aristotle called its "entelechy," is an end in itself, just as the function of a beehive is to produce bees.[13] A climax ecosystem brings to rest for a time the interrelationships that comprise it. By contrast, the social realm raises the objective possibility of freedom and self-consciousness as the superadded function of stability. The human community, at whatever level it comes to rest, remains incomplete until it achieves uninhibited volition and self-consciousness, or what we call *freedom*—a complete state, I should add, that is actually the point of departure for a new beginning. How much human freedom rests on the stability of the natural ecosystem in which it is always embedded, what it means in a larger philosophical sense beyond mere survival, and what standards it evolves from its shared history with the entire world of life and its own social history are subjects for the rest of this book.

Within this highly complex context of ideas we must now try to transpose the nonhierarchical character of natural ecosystems to society. What renders social ecology so important is that it offers no case whatsoever for hierarchy in nature and society; it decisively challenges the very function of hierarchy as a stabilizing or ordering principle in *both* realms. The association of order as such with hierarchy is ruptured. And this association is ruptured without rupturing the association of nature with society—as sociology, in its well-meaning opposition to sociobiology, has been wont to do. In contrast to sociologists, we do not have to render the social world so supremely autonomous from nature that we are obliged to dissolve the continuum that phases nature into society. In short, we do not have to accept the brute tenets of sociobiology that link us crudely to nature at one extreme or the naïve tenets of sociology that cleave us sharply from nature at the other extreme. Although hierarchy does exist in present-day society, it need not continue—irrespective of its lack of mean-

---

[13] Aristotle, *Metaphysics* (Richard Hope Translation) (Ann Arbor: The University of Michigan Press, 1960), 1036b5–6. "... or they are materials to be given actualization." which Aristotle describes as *entelechia* or "fulfillment."

ing or reality for nature. But the case against hierarchy is not contingent on its uniqueness as a social phenomenon. Because hierarchy threatens the existence of social life today, it *cannot* remain a social fact. Because it threatens the integrity of organic nature, it will not continue to do so, given the harsh verdict of "mute" and "blind" nature.

Our continuity with nonhierarchical nature suggests that a nonhierarchical society is no less random than an ecosystem. That freedom is more than the absence of constraint, that the Anglo-American tradition of mere pluralism and institutional heterogeneity yields substantially less than a social ecosystem—such concepts have been argued with telling effect. In fact, democracy as the apotheosis of social freedom has been sufficiently denatured, as Benjamin R. Barber has emphasized, to yield

> the gradual displacement of participation by representation. Where democracy in its classical form meant quite literally rule by the demos, by the plebes, by the people themselves, it now often seems to mean little more than elite rule sanctioned (through the device of representation) by the people. Competing elites vie for the support of a public, whose popular sovereignty is reduced to the pathetic right to participate in choosing the tyrant who will rule it.[14]

Perhaps more significantly, the concept of a public sphere, of a body politic, has been literally dematerialized by a seeming heterogeneity—more precisely, an atomization that reaches from the institutional to the personal—that has replaced political coherence with chaos. The displacement of public virtue by personal rights has yielded the subversion not only of a unifying ethical principle that once gave substance to the very notion of a public, but of the very personhood that gave substance to the notion of right.

A broad, frequently raised question remains to be answered: To what extent does nature have a reality of its own that we can legitimately invoke? Assuming that nature really exists, how much do we know about the natural world that is not exclusively social or, to be even more restrictive, the product of our own subjectivity? That nature is all that is nonhuman or, more broadly, nonsocial is a presumption rooted in more than rational discourse. It lies at the heart of an entire theory of knowledge—an epistemology that sharply bifurcates into objectivity and subjectivity. Since the Renaissance, the idea that knowledge lies locked within a mind closeted by its own supranatural limitations and insights has been the foundation for all our doubts about the very existence of a coherent constellation that can even be called nature. This idea is the foundation for an antinaturalistic body of epistemological theories.

The claim of epistemology to adjudicate the validity of knowledge as a formal and abstract inquiry has always been opposed by the claim of history to treat knowledge as a problem of genesis, not merely of knowing in a formal and

[14] Benjamin R. Barber, *The Death of Communal Liberty* (Princeton: Princeton University Press, 1974), p. 5.

abstract sense. From this historical standpoint, mental processes do not live a life of their own. Their seemingly autonomous construction of the world is actually inseparable from the way they are constructed *by* the world—a world that is richly historical not only in a social sense but in a natural one as well. I do not mean that nature "knows" things that we do not know, but rather that we are the very "knowingness" of nature, the embodiment of nature's evolution into intellect, mind and self-reflexivity." *

In the abstract world of Cartesian, Lockean, and Kantian epistemology, this proposition is difficult to demonstrate. Renaissance and post-Renaissance epistemology lacks all sense of historicity. If it looks back at all to the history of mind, it does so within a context so overwhelmingly social and from historical levels so far-removed from the biological genesis of mind that it can never make contact with nature. Its very claim to "modernity" has been a systematic unravelling of the interface between nature and mind that Hellenic thought tried to establish. This interface has been replaced by an unbridgeable dualism between mentality and the external world. In Descartes, dualism occurs between soul and body; in Locke, between the perceiving senses and a perceived world; in Kant, between mind and external reality. Thus, the problem of nature's knowingness has traditionally been seen from the knowing end of a long social history rather than from its beginnings. When this history is instead viewed from its origins, mentality and its continuity with nature acquires a decisively different aspect. An authentic epistemology is the physical anthropology of the mind, of the human brain, not the cultural clutter of history that obstructs our view of the brain's genesis in nature and its evolution in society conceived as a unique elaboration of natural phenomena.

In the same vein, I do not wish to accord mind a "sovereignty" over nature that it patently lacks. Nature is a perpetual kaleidoscope of changes and fecundity that resists hard-and-fast categorization. Mind can grasp the *essence* of this change but *never all of its details.* Yet it is precisely in matters of detail that human hubris proves to be most vulnerable. To return to Charles Elton's sensitive metaphors: we have learned to navigate our way through the deeper waters of this natural world, but not through the countless and changing reefs that always render our debarkment precarious. It is here, where the details of the shoreline count so tellingly, that we do well not to ignore the currents that experience assures us are safe and that will spare us from the dangers of foundering.

Ultimately, organic knowledge is mobilized insight that seeks to know nature within nature, not to abandon analysis for mysticism or dialectic for intuition. Our own thinking is itself a natural process, albeit deeply condi-

---

*In fact, natural hierarchy is meaningless in the literal sense of the term because it presupposes a knowingness—an *intellectuality*—that has yet to emerge until the evolution or humanity and society. This knowingness or intellectuality does not suddenly explode in ecosystems with the appearance of humankind. What is antecedent to what exists may contain the potentialities of what will emerge, but those antecedents do not acquire the actualization of these potentialities after they have emerged. That we now exist to give the word hierarchy meaning hardly imparts any hierarchical reality to plants and animals that are locked into their own antecedent historical confines. If there is hierarchy in nature, it consists of our vain attempt to establish a sovereignty over nature that we can never really achieve. It also presupposes that we are sufficiently part of nature to render the nonhuman world hierarchical, a notion that dualism is inclined to resist.

tioned by society and richly textured by social evolution. Our capacity to bring thought into resonance with its organic history (its evolution from the highly reactive organic molecules that form the fundament for the sensitivity of more complex ones, the extravagant cloudburst of life-forms that follows, and the evolution of the nervous system) is part of the knowledge of "knowing" that provides thought with an organic integument as real as the intellectual tools we acquire from society. More than intuition and faith, thought is literally as real as birth and death, when we first begin to know and when we finally cease to know. Hence nature abides in epistemology as surely as a parent abides in its child. What often is mistakenly dismissed as the intuitive phase of knowledge is the truth that our animality gives to our humanity and our embryo stage of development to our adulthood. When we finally divorce these depth phases of our being and thinking from our bodies and our minds, we have done worse than narrow our epistemological claims to Kantian judgements based on a harsh dualism between thought and nature; we have divided our intellects from ourselves, our state of mind from the development of our bodies, our insight from our hindsight, and our understanding from its ancient memories.

In more concrete terms, what tantalizing issues does social ecology raise for our time and our future? In establishing a more advanced interface with nature, will it be possible to achieve a new balance between humanity and nature by sensitively tailoring our agricultural practices, urban areas, and technologies to the natural requirements of a region and its ecosystems? Can we hope to "manage" the natural environment by a drastic decentralization of agriculture, which will make it possible to cultivate land as though it were a garden balanced by diversified fauna and flora? Will these changes require the decentralization of our cities into moderate-sized communities, creating a new balance between town and country? What technology will be required to achieve these goals and avoid the further pollution of the earth? What institutions will be required to create a new public sphere, what social relations to foster a new ecological sensibility, what forms of work to render human practice playful and creative, what sizes and populations of communities to scale life to human dimensions controllable by all? What kind of poetry? Concrete questions—ecological, social, political, and behavioral—rush in like a flood heretofore dammed up by the constraints of traditional ideologies and habits of thought.

The answers we provide to these questions have a direct bearing on whether humanity can survive on the planet. The trends in our time are visibly directed against ecological diversity; in fact, they point toward brute simplification of the entire biosphere. Complex food chains in the soil and on the earth's surface are being ruthlessly undermined by the fatuous application of industrial techniques to agriculture; consequently, soil has been reduced in many areas to a mere sponge for absorbing simple chemical "nutrients." The cultivation of single crops over vast stretches of land is effacing natural, agricultural, and even physiographic variety. Immense urban belts are encroaching unrelentingly on the countryside, replacing flora and fauna with concrete, metal and glass, and enveloping large regions in a haze of atmospheric pollutants. In this mass urban world, human experience itself becomes crude and elemental, subject to brute noisy stimuli and crass bureaucratic manipulation. A national division of labor, standardized along industrial lines, is replacing regional and local variety, reducing entire continents to immense, smoking factories and cities to garish, plastic supermarkets.

Modern society, in effect, is disassembling the biotic complexity achieved by aeons of organic evolution. The great movement of life from fairly simple to increasingly complex forms and relations is being ruthlessly reversed in the direction of an environment that will be able to support only simpler living things. To continue this reversal of biological evolution, to undermine the biotic food-webs on which humanity depends for its means of life, places in question the very survival of the human species. If the reversal of the evolutionary process continues, there is good reason to believe—all control of other toxic agents aside—that the preconditions for complex forms of life will be irreparably destroyed and the earth will be incapable of supporting us as a viable species.

In this confluence of social and ecological crises, we can no longer afford to be unimaginative; we can no longer afford to do without utopian thinking. The crises are too serious and the possibilities too sweeping to be resolved by customary modes of thought—the very sensibilities that produced these crises in the first place. Years ago, the French students in the May–June uprising of 1968 expressed this sharp contrast of alternatives magnificently in their slogan: "Be practical! Do the impossible!" To this demand, the generation that faces the next century can add the more solemn injunction: "If we don't do the impossible, we shall be faced with the unthinkable!"

In the Norse legends, Odin, to obtain wisdom, drinks of the magic fountain that nourishes the World Tree. In return, the god must forfeit one of his eyes. The symbolism, here, is clear: Odin must pay a penalty for acquiring the insight that gives him a measure of control over the natural world and breaches its pristine harmony. But his "wisdom" is that of a one-eyed man. Although he sees the world more acutely, his vision is one-sided. The "wisdom" of Odin involves a renunciation not only of what Josef Weber has called the "primordial bond with nature," but also of the honesty of perception that accords with nature's early unity.[15] Truth achieves exactness, predictability, and above all, manipulability; it becomes science in the customary sense of the term. But science as we know it today is the fragmented one-sided vision of a one-eyed god, whose vantage-

---

[15] The quotation from Josef Weber appears in "The Ring of the Nibelung." (Wilhelm Lunen, pseud.), in *Contemporary Issues*, Vol. 5, No. 19, pp. 156–99.

point entails domination and antagonism, not coequality and harmony. In the Norse legends, this "wisdom" leads to Ragnarok, the downfall of the gods and the destruction of the tribal world. In our day, this one-sided "wisdom" is laden with the prospects of nuclear immolation and ecological catastrophe.

Humanity has passed through a long history of one-sidedness and of a social condition that has always contained the potential of destruction, despite its creative achievements in technology. The great project of our time must be to open the other eye: to see all-sidedly and wholly, to heal and transcend the cleavage between humanity and nature that came with early wisdom. Nor can we deceive ourselves that the reopened eye will be focused on the visions and myths of primordial peoples, for history has labored over thousands of years to produce entirely new domains of reality that enter into our very humanness. Our capacity for freedom—which includes our capacity for individuality, experience, and desire—runs deeper than that of our distant progenitors. We have established a broader material basis for free time, play, security, perception, and sensuousness—a material potentiality for broader domains of freedom and humanness—than humanity in a primordial bond with nature could possibly achieve.

But we cannot remove our bonds unless we know them. However unconscious its influence may be, a legacy of domination permeates our thinking, values, emotions, indeed our very musculature. History dominates us all the more when we are ignorant of it. The historic unconscious must be made conscious. Cutting across the very legacy of domination is another: the legacy of freedom that lives in the daydreams of humanity, in the great ideals and movements—rebellious, anarchic, and Dionysian—that have welled up in all great eras of social transition. In our own time, these legacies are intertwined like strands and subvert the clear patterns that existed in the past, until the language of freedom becomes interchangeable with that of domination. This confusion has been the tragic fate of modern socialism, a doctrine that has been bled of all its generous ideals. Thus, the past must be dissected in order to exorcise it and to acquire a new integrity of vision. We must reexamine the cleavages that separated humanity from nature, and the splits within the human community that originally produced this cleavage, if the concept of wholeness is to become intelligible and the reopened eye to glimpse a fresh image of freedom.

QUESTIONS FOR REFLECTION

1. Explain how Bookchin connects "man's exploitation of the planet" to the destabilization of institutions, which he says characterizes contemporary Western society, and the experience of alienation.

2. In what ways does environmentalism perpetuate the human domination of nature?

3. How is social ecology an "indiscipline" that combines Bookchin's call for a creative reconstruction of humankind's relationship to nature?

4. Explain how social ecology works against hierarchical structures in both human and natural relationships.

CRITICAL THINKING EXERCISES

1. Judging from the site plans on pages 252 and 253, which spatial organization would you say promotes a "fascist and elitist" mode of living? Which is "retrograde and claustrophobic?" Why? Define what you understand by the terms "fascist," "elitist," "retrograde," and "claustrophobic," and justify how you believe the respective plans and use of materials implies those meanings. Describe what sort of living community each plan promotes.

2. Research the history and design of Netherfield and Eaglestone, and compare the reflections you conducted for Question 1 with the descriptions the architects offered of their designs. Is there any evidence that the plans worked according to their designers' original intentions? Is there any evidence to the contrary? Present your findings. These two housing schemes were fully presented and discussed in "The Architects' Journal" (December 10, 1975) a British publication and in the full issue of "Architectural Design" (AD Volume XLV, December 1975) dedicated to New Town Milton Keynes.

FOR FURTHER READING

Ihde, Don. "Technology, Utopia and Dystopia." *Consequences of Phenomenology.* SUNY Press 1986.

Tafuri, Manfredo. 1979. *Architecture and Utopia: Design and Capitalist Development.* Cambridge, MA: MIT Press.

White, Frederic R. *Famous Utopias of the Renaissance.* Chicago, IL: Packard & Co, 1946.

ENDNOTES

CHAPTER 1

[1] John Dewey, *How We Think* (Boston: D.C. & Heath, 1910), 6.
[2] http://www.npr.org/templates/story/story.php?storyId=4531474
[3] Susan Braudy, "The Architectural Metaphysic of Louis Kahn; 'Is the center of a column filled with hope?' 'What is a wall?' 'What does this space want to be?'" *New York Times Magazine,* November 15, 1970).
[4] Wallace Stevens, "Theory" in *The Collected Poems of Wallace Stevens* (1990).
[5] Charles Altieri, *The Art of Twentieth-Century American Poetry: Modernism and After* (Wiley-Blackwell, 2006), 129.

CHAPTER 3

[1] Leslie Topp, *Architecture and Truth in Fin-de-Siècle Vienna* (Cambridge: Cambridge University Press), 148.
[2] Louis Sullivan, *Kindergarten Chats* (1901–02), cited in Hugh Morrison, Louis Sullivan: *Prophet of Modern Architecture* (New York: W.W. Norton & Co., 2001), 216.
[3] *Ibid.* pp. 217–218.

CHAPTER 4

[1] Christian Norberg-Schultz in "Concept of Dwelling, On the way to figurative architecture" 1985 New York. Rizzoli.
[2] Richard Sorabji, *Matter, Space, & Motion: Theories in Antiquity and Their Sequel* (Ithaca: Cornell University Press, 1988), 187.

[3] Benjamin Morison, *On Location: Aristotle's Concept of Place* (Oxford, UK: Oxford University Press), 139.
[4] Heidegger definition of "place" King, 1964.

CHAPTER 5

[1] Jacques Monod, *Chance and Necessity: An Essay on the Natural Philosophy of Modern Biology,* Austryn Wainhouse (trans.), Vintage Books, 1972.
[2] *Ibid.*
[3] Karl R. Popper and John C. Eccles, *The Self and its Brain,* RKP 1977, p.16.
[4] *Ibid.*
[5] *Ibid.*
[6] Richard Dawkins, *The Selfish Gene,* Chapter 5.
[7] *Ibid.*
[8] *Ibid.*
[9] *Ibid.*
[10] Labce Hosey, "Why the Future of Architecture Does Not Need Us," http://archrecord.com/InTheCause/0602ArchiFuture/archiFuture.asp ("Why the Future of Architecture does not need us" by Labce Hosey, AIA.)
[11] *Ibid.*

CHAPTER 6

[1] G. M. Cantacuzino, 1945.
[2] Nelson Goodman, "How Buildings Mean"
[3] *Ibid.*
[4] Roman Jakobson, "Linguistics and Poetics," in T. Sebeok, ed., *Style in Language* (Cambridge, MA: MIT Press, 1960), pp. 350–377.
[5] From "Semiology" by Pierre Guiraud

CHAPTER 7

[1] Glenn Adamson, ed. *Industrial Strength Design: How Brooks Stevens Shaped Your World* (Cambridge: MIT Press, 2003), 129.
[2] Guy Debord, *Society of the Spectacle,* trans. Ken Knabb (Rebel Press, 2006).

CHAPTER 8

[1] G. S. Kirk and J. E. Raven, eds. "Fragment15," in *The Presocratic Philosophers* (Cambridge, UK: Cambridge University Press, 1957), 169.
[2] *Architectural Principles in the Age of Humanism* (London: Academy Editions/ New York: St. Martin's Press, 1988), 22, 24 n. 58.
[3] Alphonse Bertillon, *Alphonse Bertillon's Instructions for Taking Descriptions for the Identification of Criminals, and Others, by the Means of Anthropometric*

Indications (American Bertillon Prison Bureau, 1889) and Francis Galton, Hereditary Genius, 2nd ed. (Macmillan, 1891).

CHAPTER 9

[1] Henri Bergson, "Perception of Change," required reading for Chapter 7, "What Is Time?" George Steiner, *The Grammars of Creation*
[3] *Ibid.*
[4] *Ibid.*
[5] Edward de Bono, *Lateral Thinking: Creativity Step by Step,* Chapter 9 (New York: Harper Perennial, 1970).
[6] *Ibid.*
[7] *Ibid.*

CHAPTER 10

[1] Henri Bergson, *An Introduction to Metaphysics,* "Perception of Change" (trans. Mabelle L. Andison), New York: Kensington Publishing Corp., pp. 130–157.
[2] C. K. Ogden, I. A. Richards, and James Wood, *The Foundations of Aesthetics* (1922).
[3] *Ibid.*
[4] *Ibid.*

CHAPTER 11

[1] Murray Bookchin, "The Concept of Social Ecology," *The Ecology of Freedom: The Emergence and Dissolution of Hierarchy* (Oakland, CA: AK Press, 2005) 80–108.

CREDITS

4.3 Recreated from "The City and Its Elements" by Kevin Lynch, MIT Press, 1970.

CHAPTER 5

5.2 Dan Bucsescu
5.3 Dan Bucsescu
5.4 *The Scribe,* an automaton by Pierre Jaquet-Droz (1721–90), 1770. Musee d'Art et d'Histoire, Neuchatel, Switzerland/The Bridgeman Art Library

CHAPTER 6

6.1 Gall/General Photographic Agency/Hulton Archive/Getty Images
6.2 © Art Resource, NY/Art Resource
6.3 Bildarchiv Steffens/Henri Stierlin

CHAPTER 7

7.1 © 2009 Artists Rights Society (ARS), New York/ADAGP, Paris/ Succession Marcel Duchamp/*Nude Descending a Staircase, No. 2,* 1912 (oil on canvas) by Marcel Duchamp (1887–1968) Philadelphia Museum of Art, Pennsylvania, PA, USA/The Bridgeman Art Library
7.2 Recreated from *The Elegant Universe,* by Brian Greene, First Vintage Books Edition, March 2000.

CHAPTER 8

8.1 © Alinari/Art Resource
8.2 © Photograph by Barbara Morgan
8.3 © Hulton-Deutsch Collection/Corbis
8.4 Time & Life Pictures/Getty Images

CHAPTER 9

9.1 © 2009 Artists Rights Society (ARS), New York/ADAGP, Paris/*Le Violon d'Ingres,* 1924 (b/w photo) by Man Ray (1890–1976) Private Collection/The Bridgeman Art Library

CHAPTER 10

10.1 © Erich Lessing/Art Resource
10.2 © Robert Venturi, Denise Scott Brown and Steven Izenour, *Learning from Las Vegas: The Forgotten Symbolism of Architectural Form* (Cambridge, MA: MIT Press, 1977), 89.

CHAPTER 11

INDEX